Schools, Markets and Choice Policies

Stephen Gorard, Chris Taylor
and John Fitz

RoutledgeFalmer
Taylor & Francis Group

First published 2003
by RoutledgeFalmer
11 New Fetter Lane, London EC4P 4EE

Simultaneously published in the USA and Canada
by RoutledgeFalmer
29 West 35th Street, New York, NY 10001

RoutledgeFalmer is an imprint of the Taylor & Francis Group

© 2003 Stephen Gorard, Chris Taylor and John Fitz

Typeset in Palatino by Exe Valley Dataset Ltd, Exeter
Printed and bound in Great Britain by TJ International Ltd, Padstow, Cornwall

British Library Cataloguing in Publication Data
A catalogue record for this book is available
from the British Library

Library of Congress Cataloging in Publication Data
A catalog record for this book has been requested

ISBN 0–415–30422–9 (hbk)
ISBN 0–415–30423–7 (pbk) ✓

Contents

Figures

Tables

Abbreviations

AEN	Additional educational need
CRE	Commission for Racial Equality
CSE	Certificate of Secondary Education
CTC	City Technology College
D	Dissimilarity index
DES	Department of Education and Science
DfE	Department for Education
DfEE	Department for Education and Employment
DfES	Department for Education and Skills
ED	Enumeration district
ERA88	The Education Reform Act 1988
FAS	Funding Agency for Schools
FSM	Free school meals
GCE	General Certificate of Education
GCSE	General Certificate of Secondary Education
GIS	Geographical Information System
GM	Grant-maintained school
GP	General practitioner
I*	Isolation index
LEA	Local Education Authority
MP	Member of Parliament
NAfW	National Assembly for Wales
NHS	National Health Service
OFSTED	Office for Standards in Education
PAN	Planned admission number
PANDA	Performance and assessment score
PISA	Programme for International Student Assessment
QCA	Qualifications and Curriculum Authority
S	Segregation index
SEN	Special educational need
SR	Segregation ratio
SSFA	School Standards and Framework Act 1998
TES	The Times Educational Supplement
TIMSS	Third International Mathematics and Science Study
VA	Voluntary-aided school
VC	Voluntary-controlled school

Preface

The introduction of market principles into the provision of United Kingdom (UK) public services in the 1980s was accompanied by promises that more competition and choice in the public sector could bring about better standards of service and greater consumer satisfaction. In the case of education it was argued that increasing parental choice between schools, and creating conditions where schools had to compete for students, would provide a situation where schools would have to increase the levels of student attainment in order to survive. It was also argued that these policies implied the closure of schools that failed to attract students, and that schools would be increasingly under pressure to recruit only the most able students. As popular schools used their market advantage to achieve that end a danger was envisaged that market policies would give rise to poorly resourced 'sink' schools composed of low achieving and economically disadvantaged student populations. The UK Education Reform Act 1988 (ERA88) provided one policy framework where these ideas were applied, and the study reported here investigates the impact of market policies in British education over a 13-year period.

This book emerges from an Economic and Social Research Council-funded study of the secondary school system of England and Wales undertaken since 1996. On the basis of our findings we present an account of the impact of markets in public policy – one which is based on history, geography and sociology, as much as the theories of classical economics. The project represents the largest and most sustained study of the impact of policies of school choice in the world, and its results have already drawn interest from academics, policy-makers and administrators in the USA, Pacific rim and Europe, as well as in the UK. The findings have been the subject of numerous television, radio and press accounts and, as a consequence, the authors have become political advisers and keynote speakers in this area.

Why the interest? First, the scale of the project, which uses data from approximately 24,000 schools in England and Wales, is unique in the field of school choice research. It is also unique in that it surveys the application and consequences of educational markets across a national system of education. The great majority of studies of markets and choice policies in education focus on smaller units of analysis – local education authorities, states or regions and then scale up their findings. In this study, no scaling up is necessary. Our national study also captures the regional and local variations in market effects, and consequently considers in detail the factors which give rise to local variations in a way few other studies have hitherto attempted. Second, the longitudinal character of the data has enabled the examination of an education system as it operated, prior to and after the introduction of market-driven educational policies. The techniques used in this book to measure markets have proved sufficiently delicate to record their effects on the social composition of schools. For that reason this study has been able to report on the impact of market policies as they progressively unrolled over a period of 13 years. Third, the combination of secondary data analysis along with documentary analysis and in-depth fieldwork yields a very new picture of educational markets in operation in the UK. The book is organised in four parts.

Part I   Introduction to the debates

Chapter 1 outlines policies introduced in England and Wales since 1944, aimed at improving the school system by altering the way in which children are allocated to schools. Chapter 2 introduces two debates about increased parental choice of schools – the impacts on equity and standards – and illustrates these debates by presenting arguments and prior evidence. The questions raised in these two main debates form the basis for the rest of the book.

Part II   School choice and equity

Chapter 3 shows how to measure social segregation in a school system, using a range of socio-economic indicators, and at various levels of aggregation. It uses a number of indices to compare changes in these indicators over time and place. In doing so it builds on a debate that has been important in the measurement of social inequality since at least the 1930s. Chapter 4 uses official secondary statistics for all schools in England and Wales to measure segregation – the tendency for students with similar socio-economic characteristics to attend the same schools. It describes the main changes in segregation between schools as assessed by a variety of indicators from 1989 to 2001. Together Chapters 3 and 4 investigate the first main claim for market forces in education – that they will increase equity.

Part III   School choice and standards

Chapter 5 is based on the growing literature about school effects and comparative education, and on our own work in this area. It explains the difficulties in attempting to judge educational standards across place and time, and presents some of the research tools available for doing so. Chapter 6 uses a variety of official secondary datasets to examine the claim that educational standards have improved over time, especially since 1988. Chapters 5 and 6 thereby introduce our investigation of the second main claim for market forces in education – that they will drive up standards.

Part IV   Explanation and case studies

Chapters 7 to 10 present a cumulative explanation for the patterns observed in the first three parts of the book. All are based on a variety of sources, most notable of which are regression models created from the official datasets, supplemented by contextual information, a documentary analysis of local education authority (LEA) and school admission policies, interviews with LEA officers, school managers and parents, and our previous large-scale surveys of children and parents in the process of changing school. Chapter 7 focuses on the most important set of explanations of local school segregation – geographical factors such as the nature of local housing, levels of poverty and ethnic diversity, and the quality of transport facilities. Consecutive chapters examine factors that successively decrease in importance in our regression model. Chapter 8 illustrates the importance of the nature and organisation of local schools. Chapter 9 describes how LEAs, their admissions policies, and their political control, retain a role in determining school segregation. Chapter 10 considers the role played by individual schools and families, especially in terms of the growing number of appeals against school placements.

Chapter 11 summarises the key findings of the book which have surprised many commentators by presenting neither an endorsement of the power of markets in education nor an empirical assessment of their damaging effects on the social stratification of schools. We may well have disappointed ideologues on both sides of the public choice debate. Instead we emphasise the role of the specific and the local, of the history and geography, in determining the impact of national policy changes. We emerge with a 'new' economic sociology of markets, with important implications for policy and the conduct of research in this area.

The appendix continues the theme of Chapter 3 in considering alternative approaches to measuring socio-economic between schools. It also briefly rehearses our consideration of the question why our findings are different from those of some other smaller studies.

In addition to the ESRC, we would like to thank Patrick White, Emma Smith, the DfES, the National Assembly for Wales, and all of the informants in LEAs and schools. We do not name individual informants or schools here, unless their stories are already in the public domain (as in the case of national politicians).

Part I

Introduction to the debates

Chapter 1

Markets in public policy

The case of school compositions

Introduction

This book is an investigation of the long-term impact of market forces in public policy provision. Market elements – such as increased consumer choice, published performance indicators and financial reward for success – have been introduced in many areas of public policy in the UK and elsewhere. For scholars interested in the restructuring effects of market forms of public services provision generally, and education particularly, the UK has become something of a 'social laboratory' by virtue of the extent to which policies promoting 'competition' and 'choice' have been developed. So-called post-welfare policies have had the broadest and deepest effects in the health services and in education, and of these the market in education is the most complete and comprehensive. Education is, therefore, the focus for the extensive new research described in this book.

In the UK, a national programme of parental choice of schools was established, particularly by the Education Reform Act 1988, and through subsequent case law and amending legislation. Consequently, all publicly funded or state-maintained schools in England and Wales are 'choice schools', and all published raw-score outcome figures termed 'performance' tables from 1990 to 2001. Previously, most local authorities assigned children to schools almost entirely on the basis of where they lived. The Education Reform Act of 1988 gave all families the right to express a preference for any school (even one outside their local education authority), and denied schools the right to refuse anyone entry until a standard or planned admission number (PAN) was reached. Most of the funding to schools then followed students *per capita*, making this effectively a national 'voucher' scheme. After 1988 the number of families selecting schools other than the local catchment (neighbourhood) school increased substantially. Where families are denied access to their selected schools (due to over-subscription for example), they now had the right to appeal against their assigned schools. The number of parents exercising this right to appeal has also risen greatly.

Increased parental choice of schools linked to a policy of publishing student performance data and school inspection reports and allowing funds to follow students was intended to mean that good schools thrived and poor schools either changed or perished. An intrinsically monopolistic state provision was supposedly replaced by choice and diversity. This market is a limited one since, among other things, schools do not operate to maximise their profit nor does money change hands between client and provider (Le Grand and Bartlett, 1993). That being said, the UK alone among developed nations has gone furthest to replace a residence-based system of school allocation with a system of national choice. Thirteen or so years later, now that two complete generations of school children have passed through the system, we have sufficient evidence to assess the impact of the policy. This has important implications for policy-makers in the UK and overseas. For US readers, this book is, in part, an answer to the question posed by Goldhaber (2000) – 'School choice: Do we know enough?'. It provides evidence for the first time concerning the long-term impact of markets in education of the type that some commentators have rightly complained did not exist (Archbald 1996, Jeynes 2000). This is because, elsewhere, school choice 'has rarely been put into practice in any but the most restricted form, so little has accrued about its consequences' (Weiss, 1996: vii). Another commentator noted that 'The debate over school choice is rich in rhetoric but dismally poor when it comes to hard evidence' (Fuller *et al.*, 1996: 11). Therefore 'research comparing the distribution of students by social class in a system of choice to the social class distribution that would have existed based solely on neighbourhood school assignment is clearly needed' (Goldring and Hausman, 1999: 497). This book presents the results of just such research.

Summary of the relevant legislation

While mention is made throughout this book of other countries, age groups and sectors of education, the focus throughout is on publicly-maintained secondary schools (for students from age 11 onwards) in England and Wales. Of the other home countries of the UK, Scotland and Northern Ireland have separate education systems. They share many of the same elements of the education system as England and Wales (whose systems only devolved after this research had started), but it is important to realise that, even where legislation affected the UK, schools in Scotland and Northern Ireland do not feature in our study.

School allocation 1944–1979

Problems in allocating the available school places to students are not new, and have faced legislators since the introduction of universal secondary education in the UK in 1944. The relative emphasis placed on the role of parents, for example, in allocating school places for their children has varied considerably since 1944, both over time and between local authorities. Viewed in this longer-term perspective, recent changes in school admissions appear less radical and less significant than originally supposed in this study and by other commentators.

The 1944 Education Act underlined a general principle that children were to be educated in accordance with the wishes of their parents, and allowed parents to appeal against the decisions of their local education authority (LEA) if they wished (Stillman, 1990). This principle and its associated rights for parents were extended by the 1946 *Circular 83: Choice of Schools* (operational until 1980), which clearly allowed school choices and appeals against allocation to be made on a wide range of criteria, and not merely on religious 'denominational grounds'. The regular use of choice procedures among more privileged families coupled with selection by ability is believed to have limited the role of education in promoting social mobility at that time (Pohlmann, 1956).

In principle, the process of allocating places at school had two components. First, the 11+ examination (taken around the age of 11) was used to determine a 'suitable' type of school within a tripartite system of grammar, secondary-modern and technical schools. This selection was made largely on the basis of ability. Second, a specific school was selected within that type where 'allocation here is achieved largely through consultation between parents and primary school and secondary school, under the guidance of general principles laid down by LEAs' (NFER, 1969: 1). In fact, in two authorities taking part in one study, *all* parents were interviewed by schools, and the LEA left 'the choice of school to the parents with no limitations with regard to type of school' (p. 18). However, the head of each secondary school still had the power to refuse admission. Similarly, places in Berkshire schools were allocated on 'directly expressed parental preference' before 1977 (CRE, 1983: iii). These two aspects of practice were later embodied in the 1980 Education Act, and more fully in the 1988 Education Reform Act (ERA). As the above evidence demonstrates, the 1988 legislation was not solely responsible for initiating choice policies; they had been in existence at a local level for at least 20 years.

By 1969 the selective tripartite system and the notion of selection at 11+ were beginning to disappear. Most LEAs moved towards a system of comprehensive secondary schools which were of one type only, and catered for students across the ability range. The variation among the allocation procedures in the authorities in England and Wales in 1969 more generally can be glimpsed from the following. Of the 161 LEAs, 26 did not operate an allocation procedure at all (a practice especially prevalent in Wales) and 42 operated one in only part of the area. In areas with no other system of allocation, an automatic system of linked or feeder schools operated. Dore and Flowerdew (1981) describe significant variation between the admissions arrangements of LEAs in this comprehensive era, identifying eight general varieties. There was also considerable variation over time in the relative popularity of these different methods, leading to the increasing use, from 1968 to 1977, of catchment area systems for secondary schools (51 per cent) replacing the use of examination results and other methods (3 per cent). Feeder or matched primary schools (19 per cent) and parental choice (27 per cent) remained fairly constant over the same period.

In Berkshire, in 1978 for example, the system of allocation was replaced by a zoning scheme, in which students at each primary school were automatically allocated a place at a specified comprehensive secondary (an arrangement of matched feeder primary schools). This scheme was supposed to be fairer, and to reduce the existing disparities between the standard of education obtained by different families. In practice, evidence arose that such a procedure was unintentionally racially discriminatory because of the racially segregated nature of local housing. The report of the Commission for Racial Equality suggested that the desire to use neighbourhood schools must be set against the need for a balanced social and academic intake in all schools (CRE, 1983). The conclusion was that while the prior scheme of parental preferences was itself flawed, the policy of link/feeder schools exacerbated the already existing divisions of residential segregation (intriguingly, the opposite argument to that used by many present commentators in the UK, see Chapter 2).

The age of transfer from primary to secondary schools, the allocation of students to places, the proportions of schools based on academic selection, and the existence of bilateral admission or all-ability intakes were matters for the LEAs. What tended to emerge reflected the arrangements that had existed in the past, and local beliefs about what counted as a 'good education'. But this also gave rise to differing structures of opportunity. The chances of going to a grammar school were higher in Wales than in most of England. More grammar school places were made available for boys than girls. All-ability comprehensive schools emerged unevenly, with Leicester, Coventry and London being foremost in their introduction. LEAs' admissions policies mattered because they set the framework for who got what, and as LEAs pursued their own agendas a mosaic of admissions policies emerged, with a consequent variation in the patterns of secondary education opportunities available to students.

One reason why LEAs exercised so much independence in the decades after the 1944 Act was central government's overriding concern to fund and provide schools and teachers in sufficient numbers to meet both the demographic boom and the increased numbers staying in full-time education (Maclure, 2000). One of the earliest central initiatives intended to shape the local provision of secondary schooling in the direction of comprehensivisation was the then Labour government's Circular 10/65 which called for LEAs to submit development plans setting out proposals for comprehensive schools. Typical of the way centre–local relations worked, the policy was not embedded in primary legislation, but in guidance to LEAs that only developments in line with central government policy would be supported financially.

Before we consider the series of legislative steps leading to a more explicit market in secondary schooling, it is important to consider also the considerable diversity of schooling at this point. Around 92 per cent of all secondary students in England, and approximately 99 per cent in Scotland and Wales, attended state-funded schools (Benn and Chitty 1996). Among the 130 authorities in the midst of change to a comprehensive system, at least nine different types of 'comprehensive' school were identified (NFER, 1969), including tiered, 11–16 age range, and 13–16 middle schools, as well as the most common 11–18 age range. In many cases, each LEA contained more than one of these types of school. Some LEAs retained selection (as they do today) and a bipartite system of school provision. Some of the schools in most LEAs had a religious basis, including Anglican, Roman Catholic and Jewish. While nominally comprehensive, these routinely selected children on the basis of their family religion and observance (and therefore, of course, sometimes on the basis of ethnicity). Some schools were single-sex and 'selected' their intake accordingly. In addition, there was a nationwide system of private, fee-paying or independent schools. These 'selected' their intake by ability-to-pay, and sometimes more directly by aptitude as well.

1980–present

The construction of education markets in the UK involved the creation of interlocking policy instruments aimed at forcing competition between schools and increasing parental choice (Whitty et al., 1998; Finkelstein and Grubb, 2000). A 'limited market' at the school level in England and Wales was created and advanced by the legislation outlined below (Taylor, 2001). The prior nationwide system of allocation of students to places by local education authorities, largely based on locally defined neighbourhood or catchment areas with a minimum of selection, was intended to be replaced by parents exercising 'choice' in a 'market' featuring a 'diversity' of schools.

The Education Act 1980 formally legislated, at a national level, the parental right to a voice in the allocation of school places (CRE, 1983), and also created the Assisted Places Scheme allowing able children from poor families to attend fee-paying schools at public expense (Edwards et al., 1989). This legislative trend towards explicit parental preference continued with the Education Reform Act 1988, the Parents' Charter 1991 and the subsequent White Paper in 1992 (Jowett, 1995). All of these steps represented a shift away from the period before the 1980s when the practices were set by individual LEAs, and parental preference was, at least according to national legislation, only relevant to selective or single-sex schools, voluntary-aided schools, or opting out to the fee-paying sector.

The introduction of the 1988 Education Reform Act (ERA88), and associated legislation and court judgements, increased the right of families to choose schools for their children. The common catchment-area system, in which children were routinely placed in the 'nearest' school, was abolished for secondary schools. Parents could express a preference for any school, even one in another local authority, and that school was unable to refuse their child entry until a standard enrolment number had been reached. Unsuccessful applicants had the right to appeal against an unwanted school placement. These changes were underpinned by a *per capita* funding regime combined with an expansion of choice for parents in their selection of schools. Considerable powers for self-management were devolved to schools, who could, after a ballot of parents, also opt out of local education authority control to become 'grant-maintained' (GM) institutions (now termed foundation schools).

In the early 1990s, despite this transfer of power to schools and parents, it was still the LEAs which generally determined the rules for admissions where demand exceeded capacity in a particular school. Whatever the legislation in force at any one time, schools and authorities have always had considerable leeway in terms of the interpretation and application of that legislation. In the late 1980s, for example, city technology colleges operated with explicitly laid down criteria for the allocation of their limited places, such as the intake being 'representative of the community they serve'. In practice, researchers found considerable variation between colleges in how these criteria were applied (Murphy *et al.*, 1990). Voluntary-aided schools had a majority of their governors appointed by a (religious) foundation and, since it was the governing body of these schools that determined admissions, the differences between them in terms of admissions policy were substantial. Add to these the GM schools, which were able to apply their own selection procedures for a significant proportion of their intake, and the picture of school allocation, despite relatively prescriptive national legislation, remained a complex one.

There continued to exist considerable diversity in admission arrangements for secondary schools. In a study of 10 LEAs in the early 1990s, four different models of practice for allocating places were identified (Jowett, 1995). This was despite the existence of a supposedly national framework of parental choice within an essentially comprehensive system. Some LEAs still used the 11+ examination; others encouraged individual applications to schools (especially in areas with high proportions of GM schools or cross-border transfers). A different strategy involved the LEAs asking parents to state a preference, but most authorities merely published their intended allocation of schools and waited for objections. A null response was treated as approval, and objections had to be accompanied by reasons. In each model the actual allocation, in the case of over-subscription, was made using only four discriminatory criteria – catchment areas, distance between school and home, the attendance of siblings, and medical or personal circumstances. These are all considered valid under the law, unlike random allocation by computer for example, since they provide a basis for appeal, whereas there are no grounds for appeal against placement by chance alone. The role of the LEA was to ensure that all students get a place and to 'balance parental preference with common sense' (Jowett, 1995: 17).

Several interlocking policies within ERA88 diminished the LEAs' traditional role as planners and providers of education. First, local management of schools (LMS) effectively devolved funding directly to schools; LEAs were left with a decreasing proportion of the general schools budget with which to run their operations. Second, LEA representation on governing bodies was reduced in favour of greater community and parental membership. Third, open enrolment meant parents could express a preference for any school in an LEA (and, after the Greenwich judgement, any school in any area) and, moreover, their children had a right to *attend* any school with surplus places. Finally, the grant-maintained (GM) schools policy enabled schools, after a ballot of parents, to 'opt out' of LEAs and receive funding directly from central government. The cumulative effects of these policies transferred many LEA functions to schools and parents. Previous plans to amalgamate, redesignate or close schools in order to reduce surplus places were disrupted by schools opting out from LEA control, or threatening to do so. Most striking is the fact that the very great majority of the grammar schools, which comprised 4 per cent of all secondary school in England, became grant-maintained. They preserved their selective admissions policies in the face of LEAs, such as Gloucestershire, that had progressively attempted to become fully comprehensive. Subsequent to the 1988 Act LEAs lost further ground through funding arrangements that progressively reduced their share of the aggregated school budget from 15 per cent to 5 per cent and the so-called 'double-funding' of GM schools. There was downward pressure for LEAs to become service agencies for schools, providing advice on teaching and school effectiveness measures, at a cost.

The School Standards and Framework Act 1998

Following the 1997 change of administration in the UK, the incoming Labour government introduced new legislation affecting the allocation of school places. There were three related issues the Act sought to address. The first concerned increasing selection of students by self-governing schools, by academic ability or aptitude and, in the case of over-subscribed schools, pre-admission interviews relating to student interests, ambitions and family commitment to the school. The second related to 'cream skimming' by schools which had independence in the admissions policies, thereby leading to advantaged intakes and the exclusion of less able and financially poor students. Third, and related to the previous point, was the inability of some children to obtain places in nearby schools who were therefore required to travel an unreasonable distance to an alternative. Part 1 of the 1998 School Standards and Frameworks Act was devoted to the standards-driven reforms that characterised the Labour Party's pre- and post-1997 education policy. Parts 2 and 3 related to the planning and organisation of schools, and created a renewed role for LEAs in education provision. Specifically, they addressed inequities in school admissions policies, arising in the main from the actions of the former GM and voluntary schools (West and Ingram, 2001).

Part 2 created three new kinds of schools: community (former county/ LMS schools), foundation (with a few exceptions, former GM schools) and voluntary (former GM and faith-based) schools, each with a different degree of independence from their LEAs. It gave LEAs greater representation on governing bodies again, and it also terminated some of the funding advantages previously enjoyed by GM schools. In that sense it attempted to level the playing field between all maintained schools. Part 3 set out measures for a coherent system of admissions. Primarily, the Act placed a duty on the Secretary of State to issue a Code of Practice on School Admissions. The subsequent codes published in England and Wales contained measures designed to ease any admissions confusion.

The guidance contained in the code set out the duties and responsibilities of LEAs, the governing bodies of grant-maintained schools and the appeals panels. It made similar prescriptions for all admissions authorities (whether these were individual schools or LEAs), which must publish their admissions arrangements for the benefit of parents. In addition to the code, the legislation introduced three new elements into the schools admissions framework. *Appeals panels* replaced appeals committees, LEAs were required to establish *Admissions forums* to oversee and advise on local admission arrangements, and the legislation also introduced ministerially appointed *Adjudicators* with powers to consider and resolve admissions disputes between parents and admission authorities.

Appeal panels, which replace appeal committees, are bodies established to arbitrate between admissions authorities and parents when a child has been denied a place at the school preferred by its parents. They are composed of three to five members, and they must include at least one member with experience in educational administration and one 'lay' member. They are supervised by the Council on Tribunals.

Admissions forums are designed to play a key part in the process of consultation and resolution. They are intended to 'be the vehicle for consultation and discussion of issues arising proposed admission arrangements' (paragraph 4.5) and should contain representatives from LEAs, school governors, headteachers, parents and other special interest groups in the area. They form an arena for discussion of issues related to the formulation of admissions arrangements and are also responsible for dealing with proposals aimed at the introduction of partial academic selection, and objections to existing systems based on selective education.

Adjudicators are responsible for the determination of disputes between admissions authorities in cases where arrangements cannot be agreed in admissions forums. In effect, any admissions authority can object to the admissions arrangements of any other admissions authority or to any proposed variation in admissions policy. Thus, it enables LEAs to challenge either the existing admission policies of 'foundation' or voluntary schools, or any proposed changes to these.

This legislation was ambiguous in a number of key areas. There remains a delicate balance between the sovereignty of admissions authorities and the right for parents to express a preference, laid down in the 1944 Act. Admission authorities can still exercise a good deal of control over their admissions criteria, always provided these are published and available to parents and that they do not overtly infringe equal opportunities legislation. In addition, measures to end the remaining fully selective systems of education are very muted. While parents may ballot for an end to grammar schools, the code at the same time promotes admissions criteria that include partial selection, based on specific aptitudes or abilities. In addition, the expansion of the specialist schools initiative takes that trend further. This is in line with an agenda of modernising the comprehensive ideal, but may well go against the grain of other desirable outcomes such as balanced intakes.

The School Standards and Framework Act 1998 also prompted the creation of a School Admission Appeals Code of Practice 1999 designed to ensure that 'the appeal system is as open, fair and effective as possible' (Foreword by the Secretary of State, DfEE, 1999a). One aim of this code of practice is to ensure that 'parents find appeal arrangements easy to understand' (DfEE, 1999a: 2), thereby actively promoting the appeals process. The principle behind this appeals process has remained the same since it was first introduced (see Chapter 10). However, the Labour government sought to produce greater transparency in this process by providing guidelines for the membership of the appeals panel and outlining how an appeal should operate. Another significant feature of this code of practice was to allow parents to make a separate appeal for each school place they were refused. Before this modification to the appeals process parents would appeal in one 'sitting' irrespective of the number of different schools in which they did not get places. Importantly for any analysis of appeals in England and Wales this means that, by definition, the number of appeals may rise without the number of parents who go through this process going up. As this change was only effective from the 2000/2001 admissions year onwards this will not have impacted upon the analysis and results presented here. However, future analysts will need to bear this in mind.

Objectives of the study

ERA88 was justified by its advocates on the grounds that it would improve the social mix in schools and the standard of education provided in them (as well as to make changes in the curriculum and the nature of statutory assessment). This was to be achieved by downgrading the notion of catchment areas, based all too often on residentially segregated areas, allowing children from the most disadvantaged areas the choice of attending schools in the most advantaged areas. The policies of *per capita* funding, open enrolment, and publicised performance indicators (benchmarks, or league tables of results) would supposedly drive up standards since poor schools would be unpopular. Poor schools would lose students until they either closed or improved. Good schools would be popular and would grow. The remainder of this book considers what happened to the social mix in schools, and the standard of education provided in them, in the light of these intentions.

In one sense, the purpose of this book is very simple. In 1997, we were present at a conference dispute concerning the findings of a group of researchers at Kings College, London (represented by Gewirtz *et al.*, 1995). Their finding was that the process of choosing a new school was undertaken differently by different social classes in England and Wales, and their conclusion was that, therefore, schools would have become more polarised by class after the Education Reform Act 1988 than they were before. This finding was disputed by a researcher from Manchester (represented by Tooley, 1997), who presented evidence of inconsistency and inaccuracy in the Kings' research – claiming that they classified the same families differently in different papers, that the vast majority of their sample was middle-class anyway, and ignored the difference between choosing a school for the first child and for all subsequent children (see Gorard, 1997a). While there was an ideological gulf between the researchers which we believe no amount of evidence would have bridged, there was the further difficulty that the debate was focused on interview narratives in a couple of London LEAs in one snapshot year. It involved no data on actual school compositions, and no before and after figures. We believed what was required was a broader-based study, that included data about school compositions both before and after the introduction of market-driven policies, and with a more national character. This, we believed, was the preferred way to test whether schools in England and Wales had in fact become more socially stratified after 1988.

In another sense, even this rather simple test proved unpredictably complex in implementation, especially as we decided to consider also the relationship between the changing composition of schools and their examination outcomes. The project led us into consideration of issues that we had not foreseen, such as, what exactly is 'social polarisation' and how can we measure it most efficiently?

The research in this book is distinctive in four respects. First, the scale of the investigation contrasts with the local, case study and qualitatively-based studies which have dominated British studies of educational markets. Second, its development of a robust comparator, of the kind which would enable us to track the stratifying effects of markets in comparison with the situation pre-1988. Third, the combination of different forms of data in a complex set, using multidisciplinary techniques. Fourth, the focus of the study was on the outcomes of a choice programme and not the process of choice itself. It relates schools to the changes in wider social structure in ways which have not been attempted before. Our research was guided by the following research questions:

- To what extent are schools more or less stratified in terms of social class composition (and related indicators) since the Education Reform Act 1988? What are the differences in the social composition of schools in different sectors such as grant-maintained (Foundation) schools, and voluntary schools?
- To what extent do national, regional and district variations in the implementation of local markets relate to patterns of between-school segregation? Specifically, to what extent does the LEA have an impact on the formation of local markets and their subsequent effects on the social composition of schools?
- Is it possible to decide whether schools have generally become more or less effective in terms of examination performance since the Education Reform Act 1988? What is the relationship between school effects and changes in social composition? Do schools enter 'spirals of decline'?

These questions are answered in the remainder of this book. In the process we also present areas of enquiry not anticipated at the outset of the research. The results are surprising, and of considerable importance for policy-makers, academics and concerned citizens alike.

Chapter 2

Introducing two debates about markets in education

The two debates

In considering the longer-term impact of school choice it is useful to recall the possible objectives of the legislation. As was shown in Chapter 1, school choice is purported to have three main advantages over a system of strict areal assignment to school (Witte, 1990), and the loose alliance of politicians who pushed through the mixture of measures in ERA88 probably represent each of these constituencies (Gorard, 1997b). First, there is the libertarian notion of choice for its own sake (Erickson, 1989). We all appreciate choice as consumers in some areas, so why not others? This approach is apparently justified by the popularity of school choice programmes in opinion polls, and the increasing participation of many sections of society after such policies have been introduced. This is so much so that at the time of writing it is probably politically unacceptable to take away the right of parents to choose (MacLeod, 2001). In turn, because school performance information is officially seen as an important basis on which parents make their choice of schools, it is unlikely that league tables of examination results will cease to be published in England (West and Pennell, 2000), even though they have been abolished in Wales. Many headteachers in our study agreed with the sentiment of one who said 'What I would like to see is local people and people from further afield saying that this school is the best one for my child'. Many would also recognise this description of the LEA officer for a rural county school, 'I certainly know that the lead officer [LEA] is very passionate about parental choice and he is right'. In fact it is not clear that opposition to the notion of choice can be sustained logically (Brighouse, 2000), and there are relatively few critics of increased choice in practice (Willms, 1996). In the US, for example, the supporters of choice include the Catholic church and African-American representatives, and they cross presidential administrations. We do not examine this libertarian claim any further here.

Second, there is the argument for equity (Cookson, 1994). Choice of school extends a privilege to all that was previously available only to those able to afford houses in desirable suburban catchment areas, or to send their child to a fee-paying school (equivalent to private schools in the US). School policies enable children from poor families and those from ethnic minority families, in principle, to 'break the iron cage of zoning' (as it was expressed in New Zealand by Waslander and Thrupp, 1995). The third argument, which is perhaps the most important for choice advocates, is that market forces will drive up educational standards (Chubb and Moe, 1990). Successful schools will be popular. Weaker schools will be unpopular, progressively losing their *per capita* funding until they either improve or close. Over time, therefore, the general standard of schools will be higher. These last two arguments provide the structure for the remainder of this book. While many commentators have made claims about the impact of market forces, both for and against, these have not until now been definitively tested in a national education system.

Choice and equity

One key debate about markets in public policy concerns changes in equity. One side of this argument is that market policies undermine welfare states. Welfare policies came into existence on the premise that state action was necessary in order to achieve any kind of social justice within capitalist economies. This was to be achieved through the redistribution of wealth, and the provision of health, education and social welfare services which were free at the point of delivery, and ensured that those who could not afford to pay could benefit from them. The introduction of markets may have the effect of dismantling the machinery through which equity is achieved. Moreover, it can be argued that the nature of the market as such is that it increases the rewards for the already privileged strata of societies, and reduces them for everyone else.

The counter-argument is that allowing people choice in public services may actually increase equity rather than reducing it, thus leading to less socially segregated institutions. Markets, by reducing bureaucratic rules and procedures (such as catchment areas) enable families and individuals to make choices previously not open to them, including seeking a better quality of service elsewhere. In practical terms the eradication of catchment areas, for example, may open up schools to families who were previously denied admission to what are locally thought to be 'good schools' and/or well-resourced schools. Whether markets have worked this way is an empirical question which can be explored by examining the social composition of schools to determine the extent to which they became socio-economically polarised.

Different writers have used different terms in which to express this phenomenon. Some refer to 'polarisation' and others to 'stratification', 'white-flight', 'ghettoisation' or simply increasing inequality of access or opportunity (Ball, 1993; Ambler, 1997). Whatever the terms used, the condition is characterised by an increasing separation of identifiable socio-economic groups, with the more disadvantaged sections of the society becoming concentrated in some schools, and the more advantaged sections concentrated in others. The root cause of this change is deemed to be the different time, money, and taste available to different sections of society. The logic of argument is as follows. Those families with knowledge of the system, confidence, and, above all, the ability to transport children to non-adjacent schools have an advantage in looking for places in popular schools. Those families who are already advantaged in educational terms are therefore even more likely to gain places at desirable schools. Schools would tend to become socially segregated, reinforcing their existing polarisation in terms of raw-score results, leading to further loss of students in less successful schools, and so on. Popular schools would be over-subscribed and in the allocation of their contested places may, at least inadvertently, show preference to students likely to boost their raw-scores.

Theoretical models have, therefore, predicted a growth in social stratification between schools as a result of increased market forces in school placements (Bourdieu and Passeron, 1992; Bowe *et al.*, 1994; Bourdieu, 1997), and much academic writing is based on the social science 'fact' that markets in education have an increasingly stratifying impact on the makeup of schools (Conway, 1997). It has been suggested that the market will inevitably lead to selection by ability and social class (Glennerster 1991). Waslander and Thrupp (1995: 21) state that 'those endowed with material and cultural capital will simply add to their existing advantages through choice policies'. Reay (1998: 1) claims that the 'market system of education provides the middle-classes with a competitive edge, of which they will increasingly take advantage'. Gipps (1993: 35) states that 'the concept of market choice allows the articulate middle and educated classes to exert their privilege whilst not appearing to'.

However, this view of the segregating effect of choice in education does have dissenters who point to the lack of evidence that other systems of school allocation are any better (Friedman and Friedman, 1980; Tooley, 1994). In another light, markets can be seen as extending a privilege that some members of society already have (Coons and Sugarman, 1978). 'Choice' programmes in the US usually involve measures intended to enable socially disadvantaged and low income parents to choose private fee-paying schools through some form of fees waiver. Increased 'choice' and 'participation' is therefore justified by some as an antidote to social stratification, which it was argued, routinely takes place in schools systems where the allocation of students to places is based on a catchment or neighbourhood system (Maynard, 1975; Spring, 1982). Compulsory state education schemes in the USA (as in the UK and elsewhere) have up to now appeared powerless to do anything about this (Cookson, 1994).

Coleman (1992) suggests that changing the basis for allocating school places from one based on fixed attendance zones to one based on choice will simply alter the basis for segregation, rather than increase it. He continues that 'stratification by merit' is the basis of US colleges for example, and that this would be unlikely to be improved by fixed local attendance zones (and, of course, no one has suggested it for this reason). Why do some commentators want a different system for compulsory-age education? 'A second consequence of the absence of choice in education is that there is extensive stratification of schools' (Coleman, 1992: 260) by income and race. Choice could instead lead to a school system stratified by performance and behaviour (and therefore to improvement). In another context, and staking out a claim for the ameliorating effects of choice policies, the current US president claimed 'our nation will not accept one education system for those who can afford to send their children to the school of their choice and one for those who can't' (Bush in Phillips, 2002: 18). This was a commentary on the Supreme Court decision to allow a scheme in one state for poor children to be paid by the state to go to private (religious) schools. All states can now follow suit. Some in the US argue therefore that choice, largely in relation to private sector or vouchers, will disproportionately favour disadvantaged and minority students who could not afford to live in high-income catchment areas (Goldhaber and Eide, 2002).

In the UK, Gray (1992) supported the liberating power of the market while retaining welfare rights, in preference to simple egalitarianism or socialism. The research director of the centre-left Fabian Society has suggested that diversity leads to improvement. Thus, we should allow parents more choice, and schools more selection. This is argued to be meritocratic since it would, in principle, allow everyone the same advantages as the existing private sector (Pollard, 1995). This is particularly important for education, for while the National Health Service has traditionally drawn the public and the private provision together, state education policy has traditionally enforced a rigid separation of the two. Only a 'super class', plus some professionals, use private schools and thus opt out of the state system altogether (Adonis and Pollard, 1998). The remainder of the more privileged classes have access to the most desirable schools because of the link between school reputation and the cost of local housing, and because their children gain access to selective education in disproportionate numbers. The Performance and Innovation Unit (2001: 39) cites catchment areas as the greatest barrier to social mobility in the UK. It proposes instead 'reducing the weight given to geographical catchment area as a determinant of access to the best State schools'. This would counteract the scope for middle-class parents to 'buy' a good education for their children by moving to areas adjacent to desirable schools. Some commentators, including many in the UK government, therefore, believe that choice and diversity will increase equity of provision, and others believe that it will decrease it. This is important, since the relative composition of schools can have both short- and long-term impacts on students' lives (Mickelson, 2001). It also seems a relatively simple thesis to test. What does the existing research evidence say?

Evidence for segregation

The introduction of programmes of parental choice of school, linked to funding arrangements where finance follows students, has been shown by several studies to have implications for school intakes and their social class composition. It has been claimed that social segregation between schools is increasing, leading some disadvantaged schools into a 'spiral of decline', and creating a system of winners and losers. The findings of small-scale empirical studies of school choice in urban areas of England have found evidence that supports these predictions (Blair, 1994; Gewirtz et al., 1995), and the results from studies of school choice in England, Scotland, Israel and New Zealand have provided some confirmation (Woods et al., 1997; Willms and Echols, 1992; Goldring, 1995; Waslander and Thrupp, 1995; Lauder et al., 1999; also see Gorard, 1999a, for fuller discussion of this issue). British research by Levacic and Hardman (1998) suggests that, within a system of choice, the schools with high levels of students from poor families tend to lose numbers, and therefore budget share, over time. Levacic and Hardman (1999) also suggest that the policy of allowing grant-maintained schools to opt out of LEA control has increased polarisation between institutions, because they 'covertly select students by ability'. Bagley and Woods (1998) report that the families in their study were avoiding schools on the basis of the current student background characteristics such as race, religion and ability, suggesting that socio-economic segregation is linked to segregation in terms of other indicators as well.

Hook (1999) describes how schools with low pass rates in examinations gain poor local reputations, which then have a strong deterrent effect for many residents. These so-called 'sink schools' also have a high proportion of transient students, who may be both partly the cause and partly a symptom of the problem (Berki, 1999). Families in their areas who have high aspirations therefore tend to move away (or use alternative schools), leading to a cycle of decline in inner urban areas, and an ever-increasing gap between the schools servicing the rich and those used by the poor. Worpole (1999) observes that the average length of trips to and from schools has increased from 2.1 to 2.7 miles over the last decade, and that the increasing use of family cars further exacerbates the educational divide between the haves and the have-nots. 'Schools which are left behind can get trapped into a vicious circle of decline' (p. 17). Markets in education apparently lead to a waste of effort in marketing rather than teaching and learning, and an increase of selection, and their beneficiaries are the middle classes rather than the poor (Finkelstein and Grubb, 2000). Successful schools are limited by the size of their classrooms, and therefore do not generally grow to accommodate the demand as a business would. Instead, they become more selective and it is this that leads to stratification (Astin, 1992). Fisk and Ladd (2000: 10) reported that 'the most obvious negative consequence of the Tomorrow's Schools reforms is that enrolment in New Zealand . . . became increasingly stratified'.

In the UK, it is reported that choice leads to 'the polarisation of schools, with those in more working-class areas sucked into a spiral of decline'. 'This polarisation has happened on a massive scale in England, especially in London' (Macleod, 2001: 7). After the Greenwich judgement in court (which ruled that the market could operate across LEA boundaries) some children could not get schools in their own LEA (Ealing), and had to be taught temporarily in a public library. In summary, after 13 years of relatively unrestricted choice policies, many commentators would agree with the TES (2002: 20) in concluding that: 'As every international comparison has shown, English schools are more socially differentiated than any others in Europe. Some hardly warrant the description "comprehensive" at all, thanks to the parental choice policies pursued by successive governments. They may be even more socially stratified than the old grammar and secondary moderns they replaced.'

Commenting on experiments from the USA, Powers and Cookson (1999: 109) suggest that 'perhaps the most consistent effect of market-driven choice programs across the studies . . . is that choice programs tend to have the effect of increasing stratification to one degree or another within school districts'. The advent of charter schools – state schools outside the control of school districts – has reportedly permitted greater racial and ethnic segregation (Cobb *et al.*, 2000). Miron and Nelson (2002) claimed that charter schools run by educational management organisations have employed their autonomy to select their student populations by ability, motivation and first language.

Evidence for equity

However, the cumulated conclusions about choice and equity are confusing (see Lee *et al.*, 1994). There have been many small policy experiments in the US, but the resulting information is very limited, and the outcomes, in terms of equity, (as well as standards) are still in dispute

(Archbald, 1996). This 'controversy exists for a reason' (Witte, 1998: 248) because different studies have produced different answers to what is apparently the same research question. Sometimes the reasons for these differences could be the nature of the choice programme being studied, and sometimes the nature of the methods used, the sample selected, or the timing. A voucher scheme is not the same as a policy of open enrolment, while a few hundred interviews cannot encapsulate socio-economic movements within a national school system, and a change of policy can produce markedly different effects in the early and more established stages of implementation, for example.

There have been studies in many countries showing different patterns to those above – either no increase in segregation or even some decrease after an increase in choice. Why these studies might be different from the majority academic view is examined later in this chapter. Some commentators see less evidence of any change over time as a result of choice policies, and for two main reasons. First, because of the importance of geographical location and local factors in the implementation of any national policy (Herbert, 2000). Second, because much of the work cited above has a missing comparator in that no data are provided from before the onset of choice policies. The current systems in operation may not be very good for social justice, but there is no evidence that their precursors were any better (Brighouse, 2000).

Stillman (1990) suggests that there has not been much increase in the active choice of schools or the use of out-of-catchment schools since the reforms of the 1980s. This may be partly due to the number of school closures stemming from surplus places in the system, and partly because so many significant elements of choice already existed. As the use of school allocation procedures involving an 11+ examination declined from 1968 to 1977, so the number of LEAs allocating places via choice schemes increased from 20 per cent in 1968 to 27 per cent in 1977, while the number using a catchment or feeder school system rose from 53 per cent to 70 per cent (Dore and Flowerdew, 1981). According to Forrest (1996), in 1985 61 per cent of LEAs operated catchment area systems, and 39 per cent used a system of open preference. By 1996, despite the interim 1988 Education Reform Act, the number of LEAs using catchment areas had only dropped to 41 per cent. This kind of evidence, of some stability over time and the prevalent continued use of neighbourhood schools, suggests that market-driven impacts may be muted.

In Scotland there was rise in placement requests (out of catchment) from 8 per cent of school transfers in 1985 to 11 per cent in 1991. This was especially marked in urban areas (Willms, 1996). Most people in this survey gained a place in the school they wanted. Using the dissimilarity index (see Appendix), the study found no sustained rise in segregation over the period.

In England and Wales different social classes have long been substant-ially segregated from each other by residence, which has made any attempt to create a good social mix in 'local' comprehensive schools very difficult (Dore and Flowerdew, 1981), and the evidence presented later in this book suggests the situation does not seem to be improving. In fact, residential segregation may itself be reinforced by the rising cost of property in desirable catchment areas, leading to selection by postcode and the continuance of educational 'ghettoisation' (Association of Teachers and Lecturers, 2000), the so-called 'Belfast model' of mutual determination of segregation. Advocates of increased school choice have suggested choice as a partial antidote to this self-sustaining cycle of residential segregation, and there is some, albeit limited, evidence that this is possible. For example, Parsons et al. (2000) found that while there has been a pro-gressive rise in the use of schools further away from home, this has not had the polarising effect suggested above. Out-of-catchment schools have been chosen by more children from 'struggling' neighbourhoods than 'prosperous' ones, and this is likely to reflect a greater dissatisfaction with their local school among those living in poorer areas.

An institutionally desegregated system is anyway largely pointless if schools create tracks, bands or sets within schools (Mickelson, 2001). In fact, a small 'superclass' and a smaller group of nonconformist/non-traditional families have always avoided publicly-funded schools in the UK by paying for private education or educating their children at home. A few local authorities have retained a system of selection for grammar schools, some families have always used faith-based schools and, in Wales, some have elected to use Welsh-medium education. The remainder, the vast majority of students, have always attended a school close to the family residence. Thus, the segregation in the school system is largely a result of wider residential segregation, and where you live therefore becomes a key determinant of your life chances (Pacione 1997).

US choice programmes which give greater emphasis to access to fee-paying schools are claimed by some observers to be especially popular with those disadvantaged sections in many communities, such as immigrant, minority and one-parent families, who have been deserting some large inner-city schools (Levin, 1992; Wells, 1995). Witte (1998) reports that a voucher scheme in Milwaukee attracted mostly very low-income families, with considerably below-average incomes for local publicly-funded schools (even below the average of those eligible for free lunches). These families were mainly Black or Hispanic in origin, and often had one parent, suggesting that choice might therefore lead to successful desegregation by income and ethnicity over time. Cobb et al. (2000) confirm these findings, in a review of the Milwaukee scheme. Choice students were disproportionately Black or Hispanic, from low-

gle-parent families on welfare. Other well-founded studies
that choice can lead to greater integration in the US (Greene,

Methodological issues

The methods used, and the timing of research, into the impact of markets
are crucial. Mainstream educational research in the UK has been primarily 'qualitative' and small-scale in nature, focusing on the process of
choice, and methodological debates have developed over the validity of
some of the most prominent results (see Appendix). The problem for
small-scale studies is that changes in socio-economic segregation between
schools may have arisen simply from changes in the number of schools in
many authorities since 1988, coupled with changes in the socio-economic
characteristics of the families in each area. Most studies involve samples
rather than populations, are limited geographically, and are missing a
direct comparator with which to compare a pre-market system with the
same one operating under a market regime. For this reason alone, they
are unable to demonstrate the stratifying (or otherwise) effects of markets,
and their conclusions are therefore unwarranted.

To take the argument one stage further, consider the following scenario.
A school principal may have witnessed a significant increase in the
number of children eligible for free school meals in one school, for
example. Even if this growth takes into account changes in the number
on roll, bearing in mind that schools may have changed in size for a
number of reasons (including the closure of adjacent schools) this school-
level rise in indicators of disadvantage is not evidence of increasing
segregation. Even if the school is now taking a larger share of disadvantaged children compared to its neighbouring schools than it used
to, this is still not evidence of greater segregation. For example, the school
in question may have started the period with less than its 'fair share' of
poor students and be simply catching up with its more disadvantaged
neighbours, so leading to less segregation in fact. Indeed, our own figures
suggest that it is likely that the great majority of school principals have
witnessed a rise in indicators of disadvantage over the last 10 years. This
problem, in disguised form, appears in Bradley et al. (2000), for example.
Segregation can only be said to increase when all of the changes in the
numbers of students of all types are calculated relative to other schools in
the region of analysis. In short, we need to separate the effect of changes
arising from demographic shifts from the results of market-based policies
(and this is precisely what our method allows, see Appendix).

What has been generally missing until now has been a robust
comparator, of the kind which would enable researchers to track, over
time, the stratifying effects of markets in comparison with the situation

pre-1988. By implication, post-1988 markets in education have been compared with the *status ante*, which has been variously referred to as 'state monopoly schooling' (Chubb and Moe, 1990) or 'selection by mortgage', whereby the housing market effectively determines who is entitled to go to school where (Hirsch, 1997). There has been no direct comparison of the extent to which social stratification, which undoubtedly occurred under the catchment or neighbourhood area system, has been transformed by the post-1988 impact of market-led principles for educational provision. In practice, it would be possible for markets to have a clearly stratifying effect but for them to still lead to less stratification than a pure catchment area system. A limit case of this claim is the relatively rapid desegregation by ethnicity following the replacement of apartheid with more liberal market policies in the universities of South Africa (MacGregor, 1999).

As Greene (200(chols
(1992) snapshot stu   vhich
advantaged peopl   n the
absence of this pro;   vhere
choice is still not ɑ   /illms
and Echols also oc   : this,
the *status ante* of a   often
been assumed to be   learly
preferable to a sy   1995;
Reay and Ball, 199;   valid
(Brighouse, 2000).

[handwritten annotation across centre of page: "example of Methodology"]

Standards and diversity

The other main debate about markets in public policy concerns driving up standards. In fact, the drive to improve standards in education is probably the key one for legislators (Friedman and Friedman, 1980). As Witte (1998) and others point out there are clearly questions about the long-term benefits that accrue to families who participate in school choice programmes, such as the Milwaukee scheme, and the extent to which students achieve grades higher than those they might have achieved had they remained within publicly-funded schools. Indeed, it is proper that choice programmes are examined in these terms for it can be argued that there is little point in public investment in these schemes, even where they lead to different principles of student allocation, if there are no concomitant increases in student performance.

Choice programmes are thought to drive up standards by rewarding successful schools with increased numbers and funding, while forcing unsuccessful schools to change or face extinction (through closure). This can be implemented in a variety of ways, including vouchers and per capita funding with open enrolment. Increasing the range of schools, through diversity, is thought to allow education to break free from unsuccessful approaches, and to allow new forms of schools to be rewarded through choice, where they are successful. This push for diversity is based on the perceived failure of state-funded monopolies of schools, and the differential effectiveness of sectors and school types. A related consideration concerns trends in the polarisation of results, whatever happens to patterns of equity in school compositions.

While this book focuses on the impact of choice policies over the past 13 years in the UK, the future importance of policies aimed at diversifying state schooling (at time of writing) cannot be overstated. US cities such as Boston are breaking up their secondary schools to encourage innovation and diversity, and to drive up standards (Marcus, 2002). This approach is likely to be copied in the UK, where the Minister for Schools is considering the use of vouchers, subsidies for parent-run private schools, and incentives such as payment by results (Canovan, 2002). Private, non-profit making, companies are taking over the running of some schools, especially those that have received poor inspections (Shaw, 2002; Fitz and Beers, 2002). City Academies have recently been introduced to 'buck up' schools and to solve specific problems in London (Kelly, 2002). In fact, a recent Green Paper on education creates a portfolio of diverse schools in England which include 33 new City Academies, 300 advanced schools, and 2,000 specialist schools. According to the Minister for Education 'the model of comprehensive schooling that grew up in the 1960s and 1970s is simply inadequate for today's needs . . . the keys are diversity not uniformity' (DfES, 2002: 6). According to the UK government, 'a culture of under-achievement still has its mark on the system' (Mansell 2002a, p. 6), and the comprehensive system is 'bedevilled by a culture of under-achievement' (Mansell *et al.*, 2002: 1).

'Spirals of decline'

Commentators opposed to the increase of market forces in education have not tended to suggest that standards will fall as a result. Rather, opponents have tended to focus on arguments about equity (see above), without explicitly accepting (or denying) the thesis about standards. Nevertheless, both the advocates and the opponents of the greater use of market forces in compulsory education have predicted that some schools will enter what is termed here a 'spiral of decline'. This is a condition in which a school both loses student numbers (and therefore a proportion of its resources) and increases the proportion of socio-economically disadvantaged students in its intake. The spiral stems from the relationship between these two characteristics in a market driven by student-funding and raw-score performance indicators. Schools improve by changing their intakes, leaving others with more disadvantaged students (Myers, 2000). A depressing and vicious circle emerges as less popular schools become disproportionately disadvantaged, and aspirational parents leave. As schools become more socially disadvantaged their 'league table' position tends to decline, so more local families might prefer to use alternative schools. The school in decline loses both numbers and presumably more of the relatively socially advantaged families in its potential catchment, since the latter are deemed more likely to be the 'alert clients' using their powers of 'exit' (Hirschman, 1970). This leads to even poorer league table results since there is a clear relationship at an aggregate level between socio-economic status and raw-score school outcomes. This leads to fewer students, smaller budgets and so a 'spiral of decline'.

Some advocates of market forces see this as a temporary, but necessary stage in systematic improvement based upon a mechanism where good schools will be popular and bad schools will either reform or eventually close through lack of numbers. Opponents see this as a crucial component of their opposition to the concept of allowing families the freedom to choose schools for their children, since the system will penalise those who do not, or cannot, make 'good' choices. Hardman and Levacic (1997: 123) analysed the change in recruitment of 276 secondary schools from across six local education authorities between 1990/1991 and 1993/1994. They found that 100 had increased the size of their intake, 145 remained relatively constant and 31 saw a decrease in their intake. This, it was argued, 'suggests that the redistribution of the annual intake cohort amongst groups of competing schools reflects the differential popularity of those schools'.

The ensuing movement away from particular schools has two suggested impacts. One is that the number of students on roll falls, leading to a decline in the level of resources that those schools obtain (Whitty *et al.*, 1998). It has been estimated that 75 per cent of funding under Local Management of Schools (LMS) is based on numbers on roll within a school (Congdon and McCallum, 1992), while the variations in funding remain considerable – ranging from £2,390 per primary student per annum in South Gloucestershire to £4,143 in Tower Hamlets (Mansell, 2002b). In addition, the social mix of declining schools becomes increasingly problematic such that the prevalence of less able students, i.e. 'at-risk' students (Tomlinson, 1997a) or the 'wrong' students (Lauder *et al.*, 1999), places extra pressure on their already declining resources. Critics of the new education market argue that giving parents the opportunity to state a preference for particular schools will throw some schools increasingly into this position. Our research tests this thesis.

Improved standards?

As with the debate about equity, the impact of school choice on educational standards is still unclear. Some studies, especially in the US, show higher school performance in areas with higher proportions in private education (Geller *et al.*, 2001). Is this evidence that competition works? There is a correlation between the introduction of choice policies and improvements in reading and maths (Powers and Cookson, 1999). In general, where choice has an impact on attainment in the US, this appears to be a positive one (Jeynes, 2000), but sparse. Perhaps it is simply more effective for ethnic minority groups who have the greatest need.

In the UK, Levacic (2001) argues that there will be greater competition between schools where there are more local schools, and concludes that the growth in GCSE scores has been higher in such areas. Bradley *et al.* (2000) suggest that current school results are related to those in the previous year in nearby schools, and that this could be the effect of competition. Borland and Howsen (2000) cite a growing body of evidence that market competition leads to higher student achievement. If degree of competition is an input and test scores are an output in a production–function approach, then attendance policies, student/teacher ratios and levels of teacher education are relatively insignificant in terms of improvement (as well as being quite costly to ameliorate). Degree of competition is the most important manipulable variable that can lead to any improvement in test scores.

However, as is shown in Chapter 5, it is very difficult to establish whether tests and examinations are of equal standard over time (or place). Without this certainty, it is very difficult to establish genuine improvement over time (or place). In fact, the most commonly agreed finding from all studies of school effectiveness and improvement is that schools account for very little of the difference between students in terms of attainment. In addition, it is not clear that market forces are being allowed to operate freely in the UK. For example, schools are not being closed purely on the basis of poor results (Mansell and Henry, 2000). In this case we would be unlikely to detect any impact.

School types

Although the advocacy of choice and diversity is generally based on a theory of 'different but equal' for a variety of school types, in practice many claims are made that one type of school is intrinsically superior to others. As with claims about changes in standards over time, claims about the differential effectiveness of school sectors are difficult to substantiate. Data analysed at the school and student level can give apparently conflicting results, but hierarchical models suggest that selective schools are more effective than non-selective schools with equivalent students (Kreft, 1993). Schagen *et al.* (2002) found some indications that specialist schools in the UK are superior to standard comprehensive schools in value-added terms, especially for high ability children. However, they also point out that the local competitors to specialist schools performed worse than expected, so that there is no overall gain to the system. They also found evidence that religious-based schools, especially Jewish schools, do better than expected. A similar claim has also been made by a junior UK education minister who noted that all faith-based schools perform better than their counterparts (TES, 2001), and the gap between them is widening (although this argument is based on a misunderstanding of the figures, as shown in Chapter 5). Related claims, based on similar reasoning have been made for schools in designated Educational Action Zones (TES, 1999).

Other commentators believe that it is less clear whether there are genuine differences between school types (Cobb *et al.*, 2000). It is difficult to disentangle the effects arising from new forms of school organisation and curriculum change from effects generated by the social composition of the school population, the mere perception of improvement in survey/interview work, a Hawthorne effect, and the lack of a suitably agreed control group. There is considerable dispute whether specialist schools, for example, add value or not (Schagen and Goldstein, 2002; Jesson, 2002; Edwards and Tomlinson, 2002). Yang and Woodhouse (2000) found that once the prior attainment of students was accounted for at student and institution level, there was no difference between the effectiveness of the grammar and comprehensive sectors (as well as little stability in any school effect over time). Similarly, Yang and Woodhouse (2001) found no difference in performance between any school types.

Is there a school effect?

In light of the above, it is possible, therefore to wonder whether there is any systematic school 'effect' at all (Gorard, 2000a). For one commentator, 'Over the past 25 years . . . studies show that individual and family background traits explain the vast majority of the variance in student test scores, and observable school characteristics, such as per student spending, teacher experience, or teacher degree level, have at best a weak relationship with student outcomes' (Goldhaber *et al.*, 1999: 199). Bynner and Joshi (2002) drew on two successive longitudinal cohort studies that commenced in 1958 and 1970 respectively, constituting perhaps the most powerful UK datasets linking social background and modes of schooling to educational achievement. These demonstrate the extent to which social class remains the strongest determinant of student attainment and school performance. Social class rather than, for example, systemic change from selective to comprehensive education emerges as the greatest influence on the age at which students left school, their leaving qualifications and their chances of entering higher education. It is therefore easy to exaggerate the impact of schooling and the capacity to transform long-standing differences in achievement between middle-class and working-class students (Hutton, 2001). If this is so, we would not expect the introduction of choice to have any appreciable impact on overall school standards either way. At best, the market will be a zero-sum game, with some schools gaining better scores or more students and other schools losing by an equivalent amount.

Many large studies conclude that the school attended has little or no impact on student achievement, and that most apparent improvement over time is counterfeit (Suter, 2000). There are considerable difficulties in establishing measures of student progress in school, and therefore making fair comparisons between schools (Prais, 2001). When this is attempted, it is claimed that the differences between outcomes in schools are largely attributable to student background (McCallum and Demie, 2001). The variation between school outcomes is small, even smaller than within each school (Plewis, 1999). Therefore, school-based choice policies are unlikely to raise standards of attainment in the way its advocates claim. They are certainly going to be less effective than broad social policies that tackle important issues for individuals, such as poverty.

Is there a school-mix effect?

An even harder phenomenon to establish empirically is the so-called school-mix (or halo) effect. This refers to the proportions of middle- and working-class children or high- or low-ability children in a school. The argument is that if the proportion of one category is increased in any school it may have an impact over and above the change due to those individuals alone. For example, Wilby (2001) claims that countries with genuinely mixed schools – such as Finland, Canada, and Korea – have a higher performance in literacy tests. In fact, the least privileged 25 per cent by SES in these countries have higher reading scores than the average across 28 countries. If this is true, then the school-mix effect is crucial in understanding the potential impact of market forces in education.

Some research suggests that if we control for student-level background characteristics in each school, then there is some evidence of a halo effect whereby students do better in schools with higher attainment (Schagen and Morrison, 1998). But, if we control for school-level background variables, such as FSM, then students with higher prior attainment than their school average do better than would be predicted (like a big fish in a little pond). These differences are similar to the idea of the types A and B school effects suggested by Willms (1992). Type A denotes how well we expect a student to do in a particular school compared to the average of all schools. This is like the big fish example, and should be of more interest to parents when choosing a new school. Type B concerns how well a school performs in relation to similar schools, and is of more interest to policy-makers and school improvers.

Conclusion

These two debates provide the structure for much of the rest of this book. Chapter 3 explains how it is possible to test more definitively the changes in segregation caused by school choice policies, and Chapter 4 summarises the results of this test. Chapter 5 explains how it may be possible to test whether school choice policies have led to an improvement in standards, and Chapter 6 summarises the results of these approaches. The remainder of the book then attempts to explain the surprising findings stemming from our tests of these two debates.

Part II

School choice and equity

Chapter 3

What is social segregation and how do we measure it?

In order to begin answering the questions posed in Chapter 1 and considered in more detail in Chapter 2, this chapter discusses the nature and measurement of social segregation between institutions, such as schools. We commence with a discussion of what is meant by 'segregation' and how we employ the term in this study. Conceptualising and measuring the differences in the social composition of two or more institutions or communities is a longstanding activity amongst social scientists, economists and policy-makers who have an interest in health, employment, criminal justice and education (among other areas of public policy). Our discussion in this chapter draws upon that tradition in order to think through how we can measure changes, if any, in the social composition of schools in the period after markets were introduced into British education. If there were measurable changes then clearly that could count as evidence for markets having at least one of the effects that advocates and critics have suggested. We introduce the idea of proportionate analysis, and go on to show its applicability in education, as well as in other areas of social research. In the second part of the chapter we describe the datasets used in our own research, and relate these to the measures of segregation we introduced earlier. In particular, we describe the measures of disadvantage we used throughout this study and show how these measures, used in combination, can provide a robust account of the differences between the social composition of schools. The chapter concludes with a description of our more detailed data collected from documents and expert respondents. Further technical information about methods of assessing segregation appears in the Appendix.

What is segregation?

The term 'segregation' has been most frequently used in a political sense to refer historically to the USA, mainly in the south, where under so-called 'Jim Crow' regulations black and white populations were assigned to separate schools, recruited into different units in the US army, or were required to sit in different parts of buses and trains. Moreover, these communities received not only separate but also unequal resources in a society that systematically disadvantaged black families and their children. A landmark ruling in education in the Brown v. Board of Education case, 1954, overturned much of that and paved the way for fully integrated schooling. In social science, segregation has a broader meaning denoting measures of the extent to which institutions and communities have shared different social characteristics, and that is the way we use the term in this study to examine questions of equity.

Our discussion of segregation starts from four important assumptions. First, in many respects an analysis of segregation between schools is very similar to an analysis of segregation involving any other type of institution or organisational category, and to more general analyses of societal inequality. Second, there are many different interpretations of the term 'segregation'. Third, there are consequently many alternative methods of calculating the level of 'segregation' in an institution such as a school. Fourth, the indices are used with official statistics and other census-type data. Thus, there is no need to consider sampling variation or confidence intervals.

For our study, the key characteristic of segregation is unevenness. Segregation, here, is a measure of the unevenness in the distribution of individual characteristics between organisational units. In this we are in agreement with many of the major writers in the field. James and Taeuber (1985: 24), for example, describe segregation as referring 'to the differential distribution of social groups among social organizational units', and writing of occupational segregation Blackburn et al. (1995: 320) state that 'segregation is the tendency for women and men to be employed in different occupations. Such segregation creates gendered occupations which are disproportionately "female" or "male"'. This is certainly the type of increasing inequality (unevenness of distribution) between schools in terms of disadvantaged students that has been described by many UK researchers in the field of school choice (see Chapter 2).

To illustrate this point, imagine a society with only two schools, each having the same number of students (100, for example). If one school contains all of the female students and the other contains all of the male students, then we could describe this school system as totally segregated in terms of sex. Scaling the number of female students in both schools (by doubling to 200 for example) does not change this total segregation, nor does scaling the number of males in both schools (by decreasing to 50 for example). These situations are summarised in Tables 3.1 and 3.2. Segregation is unaffected here by the actual numbers of female or male students in the society, and any measure of this segregation should therefore be 'composition invariant'.

Table 3.1 Example of total segregation 1

School	Females	Males	Total
School 1	100	0	100
School 2	0	100	100
Total	100	100	200

Table 3.2 Example of total segregation 2

School	Females	Males	Total
School 1	200	0	200
School 2	0	50	50
Total	200	50	250

On the other hand, the situation of no segregation by sex occurs when each school has its 'fair share' of both groups of students. In our original example, if both schools contained 50 female and 50 male students then there is no segregation. Doubling the number of female students in both schools leads to no change in this pattern, nor does halving the number of males for example. These situations are summarised in Tables 3.3 and 3.4. Again, segregation is unaffected here by the actual numbers of female or male students in the society, and any measure of this segregation should therefore be 'composition invariant'.

In making this statement of invariance, of course, there is no suggestion that nothing has changed in the two schools systems. The situation in Table 3.1 changes from one of gender balance overall, but with total segregation, to gender imbalance with more female students in the

Table 3.3   Example of no segregation 1

School	Females	Males	Total
School 1	50	50	100
School 2	50	50	100
Total	100	100	200

Table 3.4   Example of no segregation 2

School	Females	Males	Total
School 1	100	25	125
School 2	100	25	125
Total	200	50	250

system, still with total segregation in Table 3.2. It is also true that in Table 3.4 males are now less likely to meet other male students than they were in Table 3.3. These differences could be important social science findings but they are not ones that are relevant to our pursuit of measures of segregation. In real life, of course, both of the above extremes are unlikely. Any system of allocating students to schools, in the UK at least, is likely to lead to some but not total segregation.

Measuring segregation

In our study, the raw figures for each indicator per school are converted into a segregation index (S). For a school system such as that shown in Table 3.5 using a particular indicator of disadvantage then:

$$S = 0.5 * (\sum | A_i/A - C_i/C |)$$

where: A_i is the number of disadvantaged children in school i; C_i is the total number of children in school i; A is the total number of disadvantaged children in the chosen area; C is the total number of children in the chosen area.

S is an area-based figure that reflects the proportion of a particular minority group that would have to exchange schools for there to be an even distribution of the minority group between all schools, relative to their size, in the given area. It is therefore easy to interpret. Technically, it measures plain disproportionality. We have extensively considered the use of this measure along with other commonly used indicators of segregation (see Taylor *et al.*, 2000; and Gorard and Taylor, 2002a). In brief, this measure has been chosen since it is strongly composition invariant. Changes in the levels of segregation are not artificially affected by changes in the overall size of the minority group, such as occurs in England when records change from take-up to eligibility for free school meals (see below).

We have also analysed our data using a variety of other indices, partly for comparison, and partly because no one index can fully describe the patterns uncovered. All proportionate indices of unevenness we have used show the same basic pattern over time (i.e. the changes we describe in later chapters are sufficiently robust to appear whatever method one uses). The

Table 3.5   Distribution of students' characteristics between schools

School	Disadvantaged	Advantaged	Total
School 1	A_1	B_1	C_1
School 2	A_2	B_2	C_2
...	...	...	...
School n	A_n	B_n	C_n
Total	A	A	C

problems we have encountered with many other recognised indices, especially the dissimilarity index (D), are described in the Appendix. Once its calculation has been understood, S can be seen to be precisely what is meant by the term 'segregation' in this context. It is the strict exchange proportion, showing what proportion of disadvantaged children would have to exchange schools for there to be no segregation. It can be used to decide whether schools are becoming more or less mixed in terms of parental income, or any other indicator of social disadvantage, such as ethnicity, stages of English, special needs, or eligibility for free school meals.

Selecting the appropriate level or area for analysis using S is relatively unproblematic. For example, if we wanted to know the proportion of disadvantaged school children across the whole of England who would need to exchange schools to attain complete equity, then the appropriate level of analysis would be England. The calculation would use the number of disadvantaged children and the number of children in each school in England, and the number of disadvantaged children and the number of all children across the whole of England. Similarly, if we wanted the measure to tell us how much segregation there was at the LEA level then the area used in the calculation would be changed (with an LEA substituted for England in the calculation above). Consequently, the segregation index can be calculated at many levels of analysis in order to reflect the overall degree of segregation at the respective level, such as the country, the economic standard regions, the LEA, or the school district. The level of analysis is chosen according to the scale at which one wishes to discuss the results; all are equally appropriate and equally valid.

To examine and explain changes in the proportion of disadvantaged students in schools we have also used a segregation ratio (SR). This is the number of 'disadvantaged' children in any school divided by the number of children in the school, in proportion to the number of disadvantaged children in the district divided by the number of children in the district. This gives a proportionate measure of the level of social stratification in the school compared to its surrounding schools. The segregation ratio (SR) provides a school-level measurement reflecting changes in the distribution of a particular group of children in each school. It is defined as the proportion of disadvantaged children within a school over or below its 'fair share', where SR would be equal to one for all schools if there was no segregation in a particular year. Consequently, SR can be used to trace the trajectory of segregation for individual schools over time.

$$SR = (A_i/A) \, / \, (C_i/C)$$

where: A_i, the number of disadvantaged children in school i; C_i, the number of children in school i; A, the total number of disadvantaged children in a subarea; C, the total number of children in a subarea.

A critical element of this measurement is that the SR of a school is mutually determined with the relative levels of segregation in other schools. If the SR of one school was equal to 1.5, indicating that this school had 50 per cent above its 'fair share' of a particular subgroup of children, then there would have to be at least one other school with SR less than one, i.e. with a proportion of the subgroup less than its 'fair share'. The 'fair share' could be based on the proportion of disadvantaged children in all schools in England. In this case the SR would indicate the proportion of such children in a school relative to the overall proportion in England. Alternatively, the 'fair share' could be based on the proportion of disadvantaged children in a local education authority. The choice of scale will alter the value of each schools' segregation ratio, but not their local rank order in terms of disadvantage.

The nature of our sample

Our sample is a complex one, composed of three levels. At the highest level it contains records for each state-funded school in England and for each school, whether state-funded or fee-paying, in Wales, all for as many years as these have been available (from 1989–2001 for the most complete fields). These records contain school organisation information (such as size, sector, method of entry), local context figures (such as population density), and school outcomes (such as GCSE results). They also include student composition figures, such as gender, unauthorised absences, the number of students on roll, the number eligible for and taking free school meals, and the number from each ethnic group, first language, and measures of special educational need. These figures apply to around 4 million students per year. While the dataset refers to both primary and secondary schools, our emphasis here is on secondary schools. The Education Reform Act 1988 came into force in 1989, so the school census figures for January 1989 represent the situation before choice was available nationally (i.e. they are our status ante figures for school composition). The first cohort to enter secondary school in the era of extended choice was counted in the January 1990 census, and would have taken terminal examinations aged 16+ by June 1994. The 1994 census would also have been the first year where all students in compulsory secondary schools had enrolled during the era of choice.

To provide a clear picture of what has happened to between-school segregation over time we analysed the social composition of schools from 1989 to 2001 at five levels: England and Wales; by standard economic region; by LEA; by school district or competition space (where available); and by school. Much of our data was provided from the annual schools' census by DfEE (now DfES) via Form 7, and the Welsh Office (now NAfW) via Stats 1. Some data, such as school names and types, and details of local government reorganisation, came from the series represented by The Education Authorities Directory and Annual (1998). The rest, such as LEA-level data on number and types of schools, figures for independent schools and CTCs, ethnicity, exclusions and SENs, came from the series DES (1990, 1991, 1992), DfE (1993, 1994, 1995), DfEE (1996, 1997a, 1977b, 1998a, 1998b, 1999b, 2000, 2001a) and DfES (2001a, 2002).

At the next level of the sample, 40 LEAs from Wales and England were selected for further in-depth study. These LEAs were chosen to be as diverse as possible on the basis of the results of the first stage, within the limits set by the successful negotiation of access and constraints imposed by travel. The variation was geographic (north/south, England/Wales, urban/rural, political control, ethnic diversity), educational (selective/nonselective, GM/LEA), and based on segregation (high/low, increasing/decreasing/static). These LEAs provided brochures on their school admission and allocation procedures for as many years as these had been retained. We also conducted an in-depth taped interview with one or more people in each LEA responsible for the annual admissions process. In some LEAs (usually urban) this involved a team including the director of education (a post abolished in many LEAs during the period of the study), in others (usually rural) this involved only one officer and represented only a small part of their duties (since admissions were seen as such a simple task).

Level three of the sample was based on more detailed consideration of three contrasting LEA clusters emerging from level two. Each cluster consisted of several contiguous LEAs with cross-flows of students (nine LEAs in total). One was in west inner- and outer-London, one was a county to the southwest of London, and one in west Wales. Our earlier interviews had suggested schools in these clusters that were in 'competition' with each other, and we interviewed the headteacher (or other school manager responsible for year 7 entry) in 21 of these schools.

To provide an international perspective, we also present an analysis of the PISA (Programme for International Student Assessment) database figures on school compositions and outcomes (www.pisa.oecd.org). The PISA study was conducted by the Organisation for Economic Cooperation and Development in 2000. It covered 265,000 15-year-old students from 32 countries (OECD countries plus others). The survey items included tests in literacy, maths and science; as well as student and school questionnaires on aspects of student motivation, use of ICT, school organisation and so on. For the UK, the survey covered 9,340 students in 362 schools. We compare the UK results with those of the other 14 countries in the European Union (EU). The aim of our analysis is to consider the distribution between schools of groups of students who fall into the lowest categories, or the lowest 10 per cent, in terms of poverty and other factors associated with educational achievement.

Indicators of disadvantage

The following discussion is necessarily technical but also central to an understanding of this chapter. Previous major studies of the social composition of schools, going back to the comparative studies of grammar and secondary modern schools, and of state and fee-paying schools (Halsey *et al.*, 1980) have employed occupationally based categories of social class as the unit of comparative analysis. These demonstrated that working class students were under-represented in those schools that conferred an advantage on their students in relation to the labour market. In much the same way, major studies of school choice research also employed social class as the unit of analysis (Edwards *et al.*, 1989; Fitz *et al.*, 1993; Gewirtz *et al.*, 1995; Gorard, 1997b; Lauder *et al.*, 1999). Social class is conceptually powerful because it denotes the financial standing, status and cultural attributes of those social groups to whom it refers. Social classes are by definition economic, social and cultural entities. For these reasons class is often the preferred measure for social scientists when discussing patterns of socio-economic advantage and disadvantage. However their over- or under-representation in phases or sectors of education, for example, can become highly political because this is taken as evidence or a system being unjust and therefore requiring either intervention of reform. These previous studies have been based on samples. In the case of some school choice research the samples amounted to no more than 100 or so families. In this new study we have not employed social class to talk about the social composition of schools, because social class data on the individual students who entered and attended the 24,000 schools that feature in this study do not exist. Instead we have used other measures, such as the take-up of and eligibility for free school meals, special educational needs, language and ethnicity.

Free schools meals

In the absence of unique student identifiers and related social class data for school populations in England and Wales, and in order to pursue our objective of large-scale analysis, we employed free school meals (FSM) as the chief means to examine changes in the social composition of schools over time. To calculate levels of between-school segregation we obtained the number of children eligible for (or taking) free school meals for every secondary school in England and Wales, and for every year between 1989 and 2001. Free school meals are only available to school children from very low-income families. FSM is a widely used and understood instrument to measure the proportion of relatively socially disadvantaged children in a school or local education authority, for which complete longitudinal data sets are available. It represents the most appropriate and convenient measure of social disadvantage, according to Rutter and Madge (1976). Overall, about 18 per cent of the student population fall into this group, although they are unevenly distributed geographically and by institution. The use of FSM then as a proxy indicator of poverty and social disadvantage has been long-standing within the political arithmetic tradition of social research.

FSM is the most consistently collected indicator of the social make-up of schools that is now available retrospectively to 1989. The Social Security Act 1986 (in force 1988) abolished the discretion of LEAs to allow FSMs for deserving cases, and deleted family credit (the successor to family income supplement) as a criterion for eligibility. Therefore, during the period of this study (1988–2001) the only criterion for FSMs was families receiving income support (the successor to supplementary benefit). It has the advantage for research of being an unambiguous and consistently applied dichotomy (unlike social class, for example). It is the indicator of social and educational need most usually used by LEAs in allocating scarce resources (Smith and Noble, 1995).

There are some minor methodological problems in using free school meals (FSM) as an indicator of low income. In Wales, the Welsh Office STATS1 forms have asked schools for the number of students eligible for FSM every year, while the DfEE Form7 asked schools about FSM take-up on a particular day until 1993, and since then has asked for eligibility. Figures are not available on the proportion of families potentially eligible for FSM who do not register for income support, and some LEAs suspect that there are individuals outside the system. Nevertheless, it is likely that eligibility is a much safer measure than take-up, which could be affected by systematic regional variation, such as special dietary requirements. We use eligibility for FSM, rather than take-up, wherever possible, and accept that there will be some cases of students from families on income support unknown to the schools. The change in record-keeping in 1993 makes regional comparisons and year-on-year comparisons more complex. Abrupt changes in the number of FSMs may be due to policy changes or changes in methods of collecting the statistics, as well as being produced by external 'social effects', such as the local economy or changes in patterns of school choice. However, by converting the number of students eligible for (or taking) FSM in each school, to a measure of how far that number is away from what would be the school's fair share of such students, the resulting ratio has the same metric and the same theoretical distribution whichever measure is used. This makes cross-year and cross-border comparisons feasible.

Our method of calculating a segregation index therefore overcomes any problem caused by differences in the actual numbers taking and eligible for free school meals, in a way that simply presenting percentages per year does not. When calculated for both eligibility and take-up in those years for which both figures are available, the results are in close agreement. Perhaps the most important evidence that either measure is equally useful at this level of aggregation lies in the similarity between the overall results for Wales (where only eligibility is used) and England (where take-up is used until 1993).

Several schools and LEAs (including Essex and Hampshire), while admitting that there was no way of knowing for sure how many 'eligibles' they were unaware of, believed the annual census to be reasonably accurate especially since school formula-funding and the category for 'value-added' assessment of results (PANDA) could rest on it (Midgley, 1999). Most schools conduct simple checks, such as comparing the records of two children from the same family, for example. An officer in a London LEA with high turnover of residents said of their records for FSM and ethnic background: 'We are quite on the ball here and have got ourselves . . . almost a 100 per cent response rate'.

Another London officer pointed out:

> Some of the church schools, for instance, decided that they wanted to push families to let them know they were on income support, even if they didn't want to take up the free school meals, so that they could be included in the funding.

An officer in a rural LEA felt that even this was unnecessary:

> In rural primary schools, where everybody knows everybody else, the secretary usually knows who is on income support. There may be a few each year who are not claiming [but even these are asked to do so in order to complete the Form7].

The Child Poverty Action Group has also been working to get comprehensive coverage of FSM eligibility, and to encourage take-up (Campaigns 2000). Therefore, although there are probably more families on incomes low enough to qualify for income support than actually claim it (Gordon, 1999), the biggest limitation of these figures of disadvantage is that they apply only to a minority of the school population. However, in previous debates about the impact of markets, it has not generally been the potential struggle between the middle-class and the super-rich that has concerned commentators. Rather, the focus has been on precisely the disadvantaged 20 per cent of the population that FSM attempts to measure. It is not perfect, but it is available with complete coverage for 13 years, based on an unchanging legal definition leading to a binary classification (FSM or not), which is more robust and reliable than an occupational categorisation.

Other indicators of disadvantage

There are other measures that can add to the FSM picture and give alternative estimates of any social movement. Unfortunately no LEA has been able to provide a complete history back to 1989 of most of these indicators in the way that they can for FSM. For example, the figures for statements of special educational need (SEN) are less complete, not being required in the annual returns from schools until 1994 (1995 for Wales). It should also be borne in mind that the figures for SEN (now additional educational needs (AEN)) are likely to be less accurate than those for FSM. There are several indications of discrepancies in the completion of Form7 and STATS1 by schools. Thus, significant annual changes may be produced by a simple change in the procedure of recording. In Bristol LEA, for example, the number of cases of SEN recorded on the Form7 in the first year that the question was introduced was of a different order of magnitude to those in any subsequent years, possibly due to a confusion over the distinction between columns A and B SEN (those with and without a statement of need). Nevertheless, the analysis of these figures is important because it triangulates with the other findings. Around 2.5 per cent of the school populations have a statement of special educational needs.

Similar comments can be made about the figures for ethnicity and first language. Around 20 per cent of students are non-white, and 8 per cent speak English as a second language. The figures are not available back to 1989 (we have no status ante), and like SEN but unlike FSM their definition has changed over the period of the study. Even where the census tries to use a consistent metric for ethnicity, consistency of interpretation or co-operation may be lacking. In Hounslow LEA (near Heathrow airport):

> We used to have a distinct kind of minority ethnic group . . . but with this influx from former Yugoslavia . . . it is not as clear cut as it was before [and 'White' achievement is declining as a result of East European immigration] . . . London schools are refusing to use the 'White Other Europeans'.

Geography of disadvantage

For purposes of comparison we used the number of unemployed adults as an indicator of local residential differentiation. In precise terms this included the number of males aged 16 to 65 and the number of females aged 16 to 60 who were economically active but who were reported to be unemployed in the 1991 UK Census. In the case of any educational measure schools provide the obvious unit for which to measure segregation. For residential segregation the choice of unit is more complicated (see Chapter 7). For ease, above all else, the 1991 enumeration districts (ED) were chosen as the organisation units for the residential differentiation measure (and then aggregated to LEA or school catchment level as appropriate).

We also compared the intake composition of schools with the socio-economic characteristics of their immediate locale. The data used to reflect the school composition was the number of children eligible for free schools meals as a proportion of each school's total intake in 1993. The data used to indicate the socio-economic characteristics of residential neighbourhoods was Townsend's Index of Deprivation, calculated from variables in the 1991 UK census at the Ward level. In order to identify the residential characteristics for each school a point-in-polygon analysis was conducted. Once each school was assigned to a Ward, the respective Townsend Index score was calculated for that particular school. The study incorporated methods of quantifying levels of market activity and participation by parents using a geographical information system (GIS). This uses the home postcodes of one year's (1995/1996) secondary school admissions from seven LEAs in England, representing urban and rural locales. We calculated the straight-line distances between students' homes and the schools they attended in order to quantify the degree to which parents had exercised their ability to choose a school (see Taylor, 2002). We used this method to differentiate between those parents who sent their child to their nearest secondary school and those parents who sent their child to an alternative. Aggregated to the level of the LEA this is then used as an indicator of the propensity for parents in different areas of England to choose an alternative to their local, and perhaps traditional, school.

One way of identifying a school in a state of 'decline' is changes in their student roll relative to other schools. In other words they would not need fewer students to be losing their 'market share' if all other local schools had increasing rolls. However, the use of 'market share' has significant limitations here. This is because a school is limited to the number of students it can admit by their published admission number (PAN). Therefore, a very popular school that is consistently oversubscribed would appear to be losing its 'market share' if unpopular schools nearby managed to increase their rolls by any amount. As a consequence, in searching for spirals of decline, we focused on schools with an absolute fall in student numbers. This is simpler and can be measured more accurately over a period of time (PANs can change from year to year, shifting the basis for changes to their 'market share'). This temporal feature was necessary, for it would be unscientific to attempt such judgements without knowing relatively long-term trends in admissions. Because of these potential problems we also attempted to identify schools in 'spirals of decline' from alternative perspectives. We concentrated our search on two other, not wholly distinct, groups of schools; those under special measures ('failing' schools as defined by OFSTED inspections) and those that had been closed during the last 4 years.

Semi-structured interviews

Within the selected LEAs, we collected more detailed data on admission procedures, and the background and prior attainment of school intakes. These were complemented by the views of LEA officials and school administrators. A content analysis was carried out of LEA school admission brochures, such as Cardiff County Council's 'Admission to schools: information to parents 1998/99'. In all we examined 80 such brochures. The participating LEAs were selected partly by their own expression of interest, partly for convenience (plans for fieldwork were taken into consideration), but chiefly to represent variation in the national dataset: Wales (11) and England (29), urban (25) and rural (15), GM school rich (15) and GM poor (25), highly and less segregated (maximum 33 per cent segregation index in Wokingham, minimum 7 per cent in Islington), declining (24) and increasing (16) in segregation from 1989 to 1999. Although they only represent around 25 per cent of the authorities in these two home countries, this is a much larger number than reported in previous studies of this type.

Each LEA provided documentation of its school admissions arrangements, including details of the application procedures to be followed by parents and guardians and the criteria used to allocate places. Where possible, such documentation has been provided for several previous years, thus allowing a consideration of local changes over time. Although, for analytic clarity, the admissions arrangements are broken down into two components, 'application procedures' and 'allocation criteria', it must not be forgotten that these two constituent parts will act together in producing any effect on school admissions or compositions. The procedures which parents have to go through in order to allow their child to transfer from primary to secondary education could affect not only the number of secondary schools they apply for, but even whether they apply to any alternative institutions at all or merely accept a 'default' choice that, in some cases, is made for them. Only then, after this initial decision has been made and the application completed, do the specific allocation criteria set down by different LEAs (and/or schools) come into effect. The process of application defines the parameters within which the allocation criteria (if any apply) operate. It is for this reason that the former cannot be ignored in any examination of the latter.

Taped, open-ended, interviews were held with the officers responsible for admissions from each LEA, and with the heads (or alternates) from each school. The interviews were semi-structured based on an interview schedule appropriate to the findings from the first stage of the study for LEAs, and from the LEA interviews for heads. Data were collected in the form of field-notes and observations throughout the investigation, from negotiation of access to feedback of results to end-users.

The interview data were transcribed, entered, coded and analysed in the light of the national and regional findings. The narratives from interview and other on-the-ground observations, and the details of admissions procedures in place in each LEA, were employed to help explain the changes and local variations in our measures of segregation. We see these second-stage interviews as vital to further our understanding of the processes by which local institutional arrangements mediate the impact of national policies.

Explaining segregation

In trying to explain patterns of segregation, we focused particularly on 3 years of segregation figures:

(1) 1989 marks the beginning of the period under analysis and the last annual school census before the impact of ERA88;
(2) 1995 is the year after all compulsory-age students had entered their secondary school since 1989, and national levels of segregation plateaued out before changing direction;
(3) 2001 is the year for the most recent figures we have.

We used the segregation index based on free school meal students as our dependent variable(s) in a regression analysis (Gorard, 2001a). Our explanatory variables included figures for the following educational and background themes:

Education characteristics:
   Fee-paying sector or not
   Funding arrangements
   Number and size of secondary schools
   Number of admission appeals per school
   Number of students with special educational needs
   Number of surplus places per school
   Number of unauthorised absences per school
   Types of schools (by control, such as county, VA and GM; and by type, such as grammar and comprehensive).

Background characteristics:
   LEA political control
   Local population density

Local residential segregation
Local unemployment rates
Number of students from each ethnic group
Number of students using English as an additional or second language.

As we were examining levels of segregation since 1989 we obtained these data over as long a period of time as possible. For variables that we generated from our school-level database this was generally straight-forward. However for many variables this was more difficult, due variously to changes in what was collected by central government, changes in the definition of the variables (for example, from 'English as a second language' to 'English as an additional language'), changes in policy (such as the funding formulas), the lack of repeated data (such as unemploy-ment figures by enumeration districts from the UK Census, used to calculate residential segregation), the availability of data over such a relatively long period of time (such as the number of elected councillors by political party for each local authority), and changes in the structure of local government.

This last factor is significant for the analysis, as the geography of local government has changed considerably and gradually during the 1990s. This has meant that between 1995 and 2000 every published piece of data was based on a different set of LEAs. In order to overcome this the data have been re-aggregated, where possible, to what we have termed 'old' LEAs and 'new' LEAs. The 'old' LEAs are those that existed prior to local government reorganisation, characterised by metropolitan boroughs and counties, the latter based on a three-tier system of governance. The 'new' LEAs are those that existed in 2001. The key difference was the creation of unitary authorities and the reduction in size of the former county LEAs. This has meant that the number of LEAs in England has increased from just over 100 to 150, and in Wales from 8 to 22. In some cases re-aggregating the data has been impossible, i.e. there are no raw figures, or these are otherwise meaningless, such as the average spending per student by the LEA. Consequently we have undertaken our regression analyses for both sets of LEAs, 'old' and 'new' in parallel. The key ele-ments, as described in the rest of this book, are common to both analyses.

Chapter 4

Changes in the social composition of schools

Introduction

In Chapter 2 we outlined the claims that educational markets provide further opportunities for financially and culturally advantaged families to secure their choice of schools. A social justice argument would suggest that we should aim for schools with broadly similar intakes, rather than allowing some schools disproportionately to serve children from families in poverty. If market forces have the effect on schools that their critics predicted, then we should be able to detect their impact through an examination of changes in the number of schools and changes in their social composition. The rest of this chapter is devoted to that task, using the segregation measures described in Chapter 3.

Put simply, the logic of our argument is that if markets have their predicted effects on the social composition of schools then these can be detected and measured by examination of between-school changes in the proportions of the children entitled to free school meals (in poverty). These were calculated for a period just prior to the implementation and impact of market policies and for the decade after them. In any one LEA, for example, this might be reflected in a growing concentration of FSM students in one school, and an increasing inequality in its social composition relative to other schools. Alternatively, FSM children could become more evenly distributed across schools. In either case, our segregation index would measure the extent to which this movement occurs.

As will become clear in the account that follows, the situation is complicated by three features of British education. The first is that schools were already segregated before the introduction of market polices, and this has to be taken into account. Second, the size and composition of school intakes were already variable before the introduction of choice policies. Third, the number of schools and their compositions are regulated by demographic features such as the expansion or contraction of local populations, and by transformations in the economy. We show how we have considered these features in our analysis of segregation, while they have been largely ignored in previous work in the UK. So, in the period since the introduction of school markets in the form of choice and admissions policies did schools become more unequal in their socio-economic composition? We address this question at four levels of enquiry: national, regional, local education authority, and school level. We turn first, however, to situate UK school segregation in a wider European context.

The social composition of schools

International comparisons

Table 4.1 shows the segregation indices for all EU countries in terms of three indicators from the PISA study described in Chapter 3. The figures in brackets are the proportional differences between each score and the score for the EU as a whole. Although it is commonly presumed that schools in England are more segregated than in equivalent European countries (e.g. TES, 2002), this table demonstrates that the UK has one of the least segregated school systems in terms of parental occupation, family wealth, and non-native students. In fact, the UK is one of only three countries that has below EU-average segregation on all three indicators. For more on this see Smith and Gorard (2002) or visit www.cf.ac.uk/socsi/equity.

Table 4.1 Segregation index (S) for lowest 10 per cent score on parental occupation scale, lowest 10 per cent score on PISA index of family wealth, and students born outside country of residence

Country	Parental occupation	Family wealth	Country of origin
All EU	33	28	48
Austria	36 (+0.04)	24 (−0.08)	49 (+0.01)
Belgium	36 (+0.04)	26 (−0.04)	45 (−0.03)
Denmark	33	28	42 (−0.07)
Finland	36 (+0.04)	21 (−0.14)	55 (+0.07)
France	31 (−0.03)	31 (+0.05)	47 (−0.01)
Germany	36 (+0.04)	33 (+0.08)	41 (−0.08)
Greece	43 (+0.13)	26 (−0.04)	48
Ireland	29 (−0.06)	30 (+0.03)	45 (−0.03)
Italy	30 (−0.05)	27 (−0.02)	55 (+0.07)
Luxembourg	24 (−0.16)	23 (−0.10)	24 (−0.33)
Netherlands	30 (−0.05)	23 (−0.10)	41 (−0.08)
Portugal	40 (+0.10)	36 (+0.13)	35 (−0.16)
Spain	32 (−0.02)	28	57 (+0.09)
Sweden	27 (−0.10)	29 (+0.02)	40 (−0.07)
UK	31 (−0.03)	26 (−0.04)	46 (−0.02)

National figures

Figure 4.1 shows the level of between-school segregation in all state-funded secondary schools in England from 1989 (the last year before open enrolment) and 2001. These values of our segregation index are calculated for each school in relation to the national figures for families in poverty. The first thing to note is that schools in England were, and remain, socially segregated, though not to the same extent as other national systems (see above). In any year, around one third of students would have had to change schools in order for there to be an even spread of 'poor' children between schools. The period before open enrolment was not, therefore, some kind of golden age of equity. What our research confirms is that, prior to the introduction of market-driven policies, secondary schools in England (and Wales, see below) were socially stratified, and this is in line with about 40 years of research in the sociology of education. On the basis of these new findings, though, it appears that whatever the stratifying effects of market forces and competition may be the effects of pre-existing catchment areas or zoning and 'selection by mortgage' may have been worse. In fact, the segregation index for 1989/1990 is the highest for the years for which school census data still exist. Some commentators have commenced their analysis as though the education system was somehow less stratified before 1988 in England and Wales (in Gorard and Fitz, 1998a). One might only expect the introduction of schemes of choice to lead to segregation if they started from a relatively well-integrated system. They

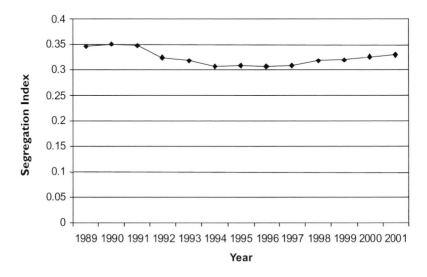

Figure 4.1 Change in FSM segregation over time in England.

did not (Hirsch, 1997). Local patterns of use and preference already led to clear segregation by income and social class.

The second thing to note is that, when policies of choice and competition were superimposed on the prior pattern of school use, there was a slight temporary increase in the segregation index. We had previously observed this phenomenon in some LEAs in Wales, and tentatively explained it in terms of a policy-related 'starting-gun' effect. The figures for Lambeth and Wandsworth Local Education Authorities are used here as typical examples of this phenomenon (Figure 4.2). After an initial rise, segregation then declines and settles at a lower level than before, as the market becomes 'established'. If some sections of society are more aware of changes in policy and more attuned to their new rights as 'consumers' ('alert clients'), one might expect that they would produce a shift towards stratification in the immediate aftermath of choice reforms whatever the long-term outcomes. Put simply, after any change in legislation, some sections of society will be quicker off the mark in utilising any new-found rights, and it is likely that these sections will comprise those who are already more privileged in some sense. This is what we term the 'starting-gun effect'.

However, in the longer term, choice is also likely to be exercised by the less advantaged sections of any community (Echols *et al.*, 1990; Cookson, 1994). The Alum Rock study in the US showed how information on options became much more widely spread over time (Powers and Cookson, 1999). Policies, such as the Assisted Places Scheme which offered places at fee-paying schools to academically-able children from financially less well-

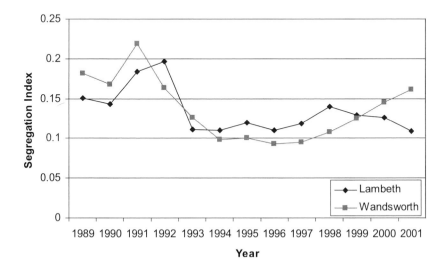

Figure 4.2 Segregation in Lambeth and Wandsworth LEAs.

off families, extended rights, in principle, to other groups that have always been available to the socio-economically privileged. It is also the case that choice policies undermine the prevailing source of social stratification in education, namely the residence-based system of allocating school places.

From 1990 to 1994, segregation in England broadly declined from a high of above 35 to around 30 per cent. These changes over time represent important and long-term shifts in the socio-economic composition of schools. It is worth noting that the most important drops come in 1991/1992 and 1992/1993 before the change in recording from take-up to eligibility for free school meals in England to which they cannot, therefore, be related. In terms of our operational definition, we have a definitive answer to one of the questions posed in Chapter 1. The introduction of open enrolment and increased parental choice in the Education Reform Act 1988 is associated with lower, rather than higher, socio-economic segregation between schools.

In 1995, 1996 and 1997, segregation in England stayed at around 30 per cent. This suggests that the imposition of school choice on a system with the level of segregation found in 1989 led to progressively less segregated schools (in general, but see below) as successive cohorts moved from primary to secondary school. Once the starting-gun effect was over, and all of the students in secondary schools had entered since 1989, this trend ceased and the position stabilised. In essence, the impact of choice policies (if that is what it is) was limited and relatively short-lived.

The national change in figures for all primary schools is almost identical to those for secondary, while the figures themselves are higher, presumably because primary schools serve even more narrowly defined residential areas. Segregation between all schools in terms of families in poverty decreased after 1989/1990. Where other indicators are available, segregation by ethnic group, first language, and additional educational need has also declined since 1989, but unlike segregation by FSM continues to decline until 2001. Unlike other measures of educational disadvantage, such as family poverty, this decline is not related to the overall increase in the number of disadvantaged children (see below). For example, although in Bolton LEA statements of special educational need increased from a total of 213 in 1994 to 473 in 1997, in Cornwall they declined from 2,515 to 1,497, while in Wrexham they remained steady at 365 to 368. Despite these differences all three LEAs experienced substantial desegregation in terms of SEN students over time.

There is no evidence then, on the figures presented here, to link education markets with increasing segregation. These polices are not associated with increasing concentrations of disadvantaged children in some schools and their absence in others, rather the reverse. The relevant legislation, enacted in 1988, only began to take effect in schools after 1989 and had increasing impact for successive cohorts. In the year following the 1988 Act, which allowed every family to request a place at any school, there was a slight increase in between-school stratification, followed by a marked decline representing a very large social change involving hundreds of thousands of students. This appears to have flattened out and settled at a lower level by 1995, which continued until 1997. Subsequently, from 1998 to 2001 segregation in England increased every year to around 33 per cent, after a change of government in the UK in 1997, and the introduction of the School Standards and Framework Act 1998. Why this might be so is examined further below, and in later chapters of this book we consider the implications of this recent rise in segregation for current and future policy.

Regional figures

This overall pattern of reduced segregation between schools in 1989–1995 also appears in every economic region in England (and Wales) as we show in Table 4.2. These values are calculated as the total for each school in relation to the relevant regional figures for families in poverty. The greatest proportionate decreases were in the south east and outer London. These represent densely populated regions, with large numbers of secondary schools and with transport links that make the idea of choosing from a range of schools a feasible proposition for parents from across the socio-economic spectrum. They are, therefore, perhaps the most likely to show change in a market-like situation. It would be expected that offering choice of schools, or any other change in the policy of allocating school places, would have less impact on patterns of enrolment in rural areas with fewer candidate schools within a reasonable travelling distance for most families.

In Wales a slightly different pattern of national segregation has emerged (Gorard and Fitz, 1998b). Not only is the level of segregation significantly lower in Wales (22 per cent) than in England, but also the rate of change over the same period is smaller (the variation in the early figures is likely due to discrepancies in the Welsh Office figures). In other words, schools in Wales are more mixed in socio-economic terms than their counterparts in England.

Moreover, segregation in Wales continued to decline to the end of the 1990s. Similar trends, using different datasets and methods of analysis, have emerged from Scotland (Paterson, 2001). These differences between the home nations and the variation of trends over time in England would suggest that there are several factors affecting between-school segregation. In accounting for the patterns we observed in school segregation over time, both demographic and socio-economic changes have to be factored into the analysis alongside changes in policy. We cannot naively

Table 4.2 Change in FSM segregation over time in the economic regions of England and Wales

Standard Regions	1989	1990	1991	1992	1993	1994	1995	1996	1997	1998	1999	2000	2001
North east	0.24	0.24	0.25	0.23	0.24	0.23	0.23	0.23	0.23	0.24	0.24	0.24	0.25
North west	0.31	0.32	0.33	0.31	0.31	0.29	0.29	0.29	0.28	0.29	0.29	0.29	0.30
Merseyside	0.25	0.24	0.26	0.27	0.27	0.26	0.25	0.25	0.26	0.26	0.25	0.26	0.25
Yorkshire and Humber	0.32	0.33	0.34	0.32	0.30	0.30	0.29	0.29	0.29	0.29	0.29	0.29	0.29
East Midlands	0.32	0.32	0.32	0.30	0.29	0.28	0.28	0.28	0.29	0.29	0.29	0.30	0.31
West Midlands	0.34	0.35	0.35	0.34	0.32	0.31	0.31	0.32	0.31	0.32	0.32	0.33	0.33
Eastern	0.29	0.30	0.30	0.29	0.27	0.26	0.26	0.27	0.27	0.27	0.28	0.28	0.28
Inner London	0.18	0.18	0.19	0.19	0.16	0.16	0.16	0.15	0.15	0.16	0.15	0.16	0.17
Outer London	0.29	0.31	0.30	0.29	0.28	0.26	0.26	0.25	0.25	0.26	0.26	0.27	0.27
South east	0.34	0.34	0.34	0.32	0.32	0.30	0.30	0.30	0.30	0.31	0.32	0.32	0.31
South west	0.26	0.27	0.26	0.24	0.23	0.22	0.22	0.23	0.24	0.24	0.25	0.25	0.26
Wales	—	0.23	0.25	0.24	0.25	0.22	0.23	0.22	0.23	0.22	0.22	0.21	0.22

attribute any and all changes in segregation to the introduction of choice and competition in the state-funded education system, as other researchers have done (e.g. Gewirtz *et al.*, 1995).

Another observation, also confirmed at a local level (see below), is that segregation is generally lower in regions like inner London where population density is greatest (and rich and poor areas of housing are closer together), and in the north east and Wales where the population – unlike London and the south east – is less variable in terms of class structure, income and other socio-economic indicators. The suggestion here is that segregation depends on the local variability of potential school users as much as their allocation to schools.

For example, despite the strongly composition-invariant nature of our index (see Appendix), it would appear that an increase in poverty is empirically related to a decrease in school segregation. If an increase in the raw figures is equivalent to a decrease in variability (or perhaps increasing polarisation by income) then at least part of the desegregation can be explained as a form of 'equality of poverty'. That is, as the volume of children eligible for FSM increases, there are more to be distributed across the secondary school system, and this distribution has taken place in a way that smoothes out differences between school socio-economic populations. Although the total school population of secondary schools grew from 2,958,268 students in 1989 to 3,216,135 in 1997, the number of students eligible for free school meals grew from 506,066 in 1993 (the first year in which eligibility was returned by all schools) to 590,379 in 1997. At least part of the desegregation could therefore be due to this increase from 17 to 18 per cent of students eligible for free schools meals, which represents a considerable increase in the official assessment of children from families in poverty. This would be similar to the economic phenomenon of greater income inequality in periods of economic growth, whereas 'a recession means negative economic growth, so we might expect to see back-pedalling in the way of less income inequality' (Kacapyr, 1996: 3).

School numbers

Previous research concerned with the impact of choice and competition policies on schools has claimed that these policies would force some schools to close (e.g. Lauder *et al.*, 1999). In our research we investigated school closures in the period after educational markets were established. We were interested in the idea that markets drive some schools into 'spirals of decline', where schools experienced greater disadvantage in their social composition, loss of numbers and loss of resource. Our findings suggest no strong connection between markets and the changing rates of school closures, nor schools going into 'spirals of decline'. The demographic features of the secondary school system may well explain the muted effects of markets.

To examine whether markets cause schools to close it is important to recognise that schools, anyway, closed under previous regimes of school admission and planning. Figure 4.3 shows that the number of children per secondary school in England has generally been increasing since 1947 (the earliest figures available). This is partly due to population growth and urbanisation, partly due to successive raising of the school-leaving age, and more recently due to school closures. In the period of our investigation, 1989–2001, the number of students per school dropped slightly in the first year after the 1988 reforms, but has grown steadily since. This would lead us to expect that schools in 'spirals of decline' would be rare, since even 'unsuccessful' schools might be expected to grow in numbers (or at least maintain their size). In addition, the closure of schools leads to mixing students from previously distinct catchments, and could lead directly to less socio-economic segregation. As above, economic growth (in this case of numbers of schools) would tend to lead to segregation, while declining numbers leads to desegregation. The change in school numbers is, therefore, a partial explanation for the decrease in between-school segregation since 1989.

The most recent fall in the average number of students per secondary school was in 1990. Note that Figure 4.4 shows that there has been no overall growth in use of independent schools, which remains at less than 8 per cent for England and less than 2 per cent for Wales (Gorard, 1996),

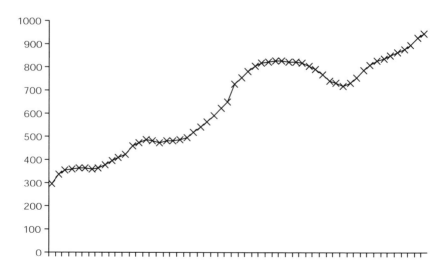

Figure 4.3 Average number of students per secondary school in England, 1947–2002.

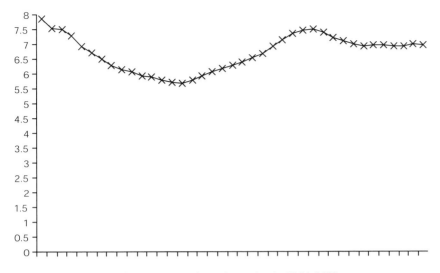

Figure 4.4 Percentage of students in independent schools, 1964–2002.

except in 1990 and 1991. Between 1989 and 1991 there was a temporary growth that matches the drop in the number of students per secondary school in the maintained sector. It may well be that the starting-gun effect (see above) reflected fear and uncertainty about the 1988 Education Reform Act, especially the National Curriculum Orders and associated testing regime (Gorard, 1997c). By 1995, however, this had reversed and the proportion of students in independent schools was at its lowest for a decade. It is also important to note that the slight growth in numbers at independent schools started around 1986, before the 1988 reforms, and stabilised by 1991. This is likely to reflect economic and employment cycles as much as the public view of state schools. Many more families than this report that they would consider a private school if they could afford it, so in times of prosperity numbers tend to grow (Abrams, 2001).

Despite a growth over the same period in the number of students with registered special needs, Figure 4.5 shows a steady decline in the number of designated special schools (perhaps as a result of the Warnock Report (Howson, 1999). There was a corresponding decline in the proportion of students at special schools, as these were integrated into mainstream schooling (from 1995, students in referral units but not in mainstream school were recorded separately, and this figure remains at around 8,000 with no evidence of a trend over time).

Over the period 1990 to 1995, therefore, when segregation between schools was declining, the number of maintained schools was also falling and so the school population was divided into fewer units. At the same

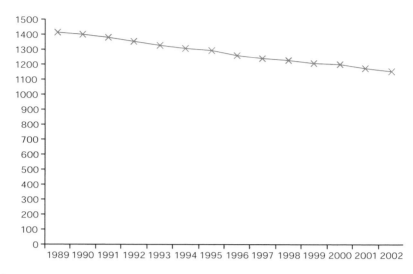

Figure 4.5 Number of special schools 1989–2002.

time, fewer students from higher income families attended fee-paying schools and fewer students with special needs attended separate schools. Between these factors, all of which may or may not be related to market forces, we may be able to explain much of the drop in segregation.

LEA-level figures

Of course, it could be argued that the national and regional picture of overall socio-economic segregation between schools is too highly aggregated, and that we may be chiefly representing here little more than socio-economic convergence of the residents in different parts of the country, whereas markets in schools are local in nature. For this reason we also present the results of similar calculations at LEA, district and school level. A local analysis may also be of assistance in identifying the determinants of these powerful changes since, despite national legislation, local variations in segregation patterns could be due to the existence of differences in the ways in which contested places at schools are actually allocated (see Chapter 9).

There appear to have been two major phases, the first of desegregation between 1989 and 1995 and then the more recent phase of increasing segregation between 1996 and 2000. It is worthwhile, therefore, to examine the rates of change for these two periods separately. Analysis at an authority level shows that 87 of the LEAs in England and Wales had a marked decline in socio-economic segregation between secondary schools from 1989 to 1995 (Table 4.3). The final column in each of Tables

Table 4.3 LEAs desegregating, 1989–1995

LEA	1989	1990	1991	1992	1993	1994	1995	Change
Portsmouth	0.36	0.33	0.29	0.26	0.20	0.18	0.17	−35.2
West Berkshire	0.28	0.19	0.19	0.19	0.14	0.19	0.13	−35.1
Southwark	0.14	0.13	0.12	0.13	0.09	0.10	0.07	−33.3
Knowsley	0.12	0.10	0.11	0.14	0.08	0.08	0.06	−31.5
Brent	0.29	0.27	0.26	0.26	0.19	0.17	0.16	−30.7
Windsor and Maidenhead	0.33	0.21	0.22	0.19	0.17	0.16	0.18	−29.1
Wandsworth	0.18	0.17	0.22	0.16	0.13	0.10	0.10	−28.7
Bath and NE Somerset	0.31	0.29	0.27	0.20	0.17	0.17	0.17	−28.0
Tower Hamlets	0.15	0.17	0.19	0.18	0.12	0.12	0.09	−27.3
Waltham Forest	0.26	0.27	0.29	0.29	0.17	0.15	0.15	−25.4
Milton Keynes	0.48	0.54	0.19	0.21	0.27	0.26	0.29	−24.2
Stockport	0.30	0.32	0.32	0.28	0.25	0.23	0.19	−22.2
Westminster	0.22	0.17	0.21	0.21	0.17	0.15	0.14	−21.8
Wiltshire	0.25	0.26	0.21	0.19	0.14	0.15	0.16	−21.7
Isle of Wight	0.18	0.17	0.17	0.16	0.12	0.11	0.12	−21.6
Islington	0.10	0.15	0.11	0.11	0.10	0.09	0.06	−21.3
Cornwall	0.17	0.18	0.18	0.17	0.13	0.12	0.12	−18.7
Leicestershire	0.32	0.29	0.30	0.27	0.20	0.21	0.22	−18.1
Camden	0.22	0.17	0.16	0.18	0.18	0.15	0.16	−17.1
Nottingham City	0.23	0.20	0.21	0.20	0.17	0.15	0.16	−17.1
South Gloucestershire	0.22	0.20	0.22	0.15	0.16	0.16	0.16	−16.8
Manchester	0.15	0.16	0.17	0.17	0.14	0.11	0.11	−15.9
Bexley	0.30	0.28	0.31	0.27	0.21	0.21	0.22	−15.7
Trafford	0.35	0.28	0.29	0.26	0.27	0.26	0.26	−15.2
Swindon	0.33	0.32	0.31	0.25	0.26	0.23	0.24	−14.9
North Tyneside	0.25	0.26	0.30	0.27	0.21	0.17	0.18	−14.8
Swansea	0.35	0.35	0.33	0.31	0.30	0.28	0.26	−14.8
Luton	0.30	0.34	0.31	0.31	0.24	0.23	0.22	−14.7
Doncaster	0.24	0.23	0.25	0.21	0.18	0.18	0.18	−14.0
Greenwich	0.13	0.16	0.14	0.11	0.10	0.10	0.10	−14.0
Northamptonshire	0.33	0.31	0.30	0.31	0.27	0.27	0.25	−13.8
Wakefield	0.28	0.29	0.30	0.29	0.24	0.21	0.21	−13.6
Rochdale	0.24	0.25	0.18	0.22	0.19	0.20	0.18	−13.5
Bridgend	0.21	0.21	0.21	0.21	0.19	0.18	0.16	−13.5
East Sussex	0.23	0.25	0.21	0.19	0.19	0.17	0.18	−13.1
Rotherham	0.24	0.24	0.24	0.21	0.21	0.18	0.19	−12.5
Sandwell	0.18	0.23	0.24	0.23	0.20	0.17	0.14	−12.5
Cambridgeshire	0.26	0.22	0.26	0.24	0.22	0.22	0.21	−12.3
Somerset	0.20	0.21	0.22	0.23	0.17	0.15	0.16	−12.0
Lewisham	0.11	0.11	0.10	0.10	0.12	0.11	0.09	−11.4
Lambeth	0.15	0.14	0.18	0.20	0.11	0.11	0.12	−11.4
Gloucestershire	0.33	0.33	0.33	0.32	0.28	0.28	0.26	−11.0
Middlesborough	0.19	0.20	0.18	0.20	0.15	0.16	0.15	−10.4
Hampshire	0.27	0.26	0.28	0.25	0.22	0.23	0.22	−10.2
Oxfordshire	0.38	0.36	0.35	0.32	0.31	0.30	0.31	−10.1
Bradford	0.31	0.31	0.32	0.31	0.28	0.26	0.25	−9.8
Southampton	0.17	0.15	0.18	0.16	0.13	0.13	0.14	−9.4
Devon	0.16	0.20	0.14	0.17	0.13	0.14	0.13	−9.3
Merton	0.23	0.26	0.23	0.26	0.19	0.19	0.19	−9.3

Table 4.3 (continued)

LEA	1989	1990	1991	1992	1993	1994	1995	Change
Dorset	0.18	0.20	0.14	0.18	0.15	0.17	0.15	−9.2
Kent	0.35	0.37	0.36	0.34	0.34	0.30	0.29	−9.1
Bracknell Forest	0.29	0.23	0.20	0.32	0.25	0.22	0.24	−9.1
City of Bristol	0.19	0.21	0.23	0.17	0.15	0.16	0.16	−8.7
Worcestershire	0.28	0.26	0.28	0.29	0.26	0.24	0.24	−8.3
Barnet	0.25	0.28	0.24	0.26	0.25	0.24	0.22	−8.2
North Lincolnshire	0.22	0.21	0.21	0.18	0.21	0.20	0.19	−8.0
North Somerset	0.26	0.20	0.22	0.23	0.23	0.23	0.22	−7.8
St Helens	0.27	0.23	0.23	0.25	0.25	0.22	0.23	−7.7
Sefton	0.32	0.29	0.30	0.33	0.31	0.30	0.28	−7.2
North East Lincolnshire	0.25	0.21	0.27	0.23	0.22	0.22	0.22	−6.9
Ealing	0.14	0.13	0.12	0.11	0.11	0.11	0.12	−6.8
Wigan	0.24	0.23	0.23	0.23	0.24	0.19	0.21	−6.5
Surrey	0.28	0.27	0.29	0.28	0.27	0.23	0.24	−6.3
Salford	0.25	0.25	0.27	0.27	0.29	0.24	0.22	−6.2
Tameside	0.19	0.19	0.20	0.23	0.20	0.17	0.16	−6.1
Hertfordshire	0.32	0.30	0.31	0.29	0.30	0.28	0.29	−5.9
Croydon	0.27	0.29	0.28	0.24	0.27	0.23	0.24	−5.9
Richmond-upon-Thames	0.19	0.19	0.18	0.18	0.20	0.16	0.17	−5.7
Warwickshire	0.28	0.30	0.29	0.27	0.25	0.25	0.25	−5.7
Redbridge	0.24	0.26	0.28	0.24	0.22	0.23	0.22	−5.6
Wokingham	0.28	0.34	0.36	0.37	0.33	0.27	0.25	−5.6
Cheshire	0.34	0.32	0.31	0.29	0.31	0.30	0.30	−5.5
York	0.31	0.29	0.28	0.28	0.27	0.29	0.28	−5.4
Leeds	0.34	0.35	0.37	0.34	0.31	0.30	0.31	−5.4
Lancashire	0.28	0.29	0.30	0.28	0.28	0.26	0.25	−5.2
Northumberland	0.30	0.31	0.29	0.30	0.30	0.26	0.27	−5.2
Solihull	0.43	0.43	0.43	0.40	0.43	0.39	0.38	−5.2
Hillingdon	0.27	0.24	0.19	0.23	0.25	0.25	0.25	−5.1
Staffordshire	0.22	0.24	0.24	0.23	0.22	0.21	0.20	−5.1
Leicester City	0.20	0.19	0.22	0.16	0.20	0.18	0.18	−5.0
Barking and Dagenham	0.09	0.19	0.12	0.08	0.11	0.09	0.08	−4.9
Bedfordshire	0.28	0.30	0.33	0.28	0.25	0.25	0.26	−4.7
South Tyneside	0.15	0.14	0.15	0.15	0.13	0.13	0.13	−4.5
Liverpool	0.19	0.18	0.20	0.19	0.18	0.17	0.17	−4.0
Calderdale	0.29	0.30	0.31	0.31	0.27	0.30	0.27	−4.0
Birmingham	0.25	0.27	0.27	0.25	0.24	0.24	0.23	−3.5
Suffolk	0.24	0.28	0.27	0.26	0.22	0.20	0.22	−3.5

4.3 to 4.5 shows the proportionate change in LEA segregation from 1989 to 1995. The desegregating LEAs include urban and rural, English and Welsh, large and small, but many are middle-sized urban areas with relatively high population densities (and therefore mostly in England). None of the very small or sparsely populated areas appear in this list, nor do many predominantly rural counties with very large numbers of schools (e.g. Essex). Middle-sized urban LEAs are perhaps precisely the

Table 4.4 LEAs with little or no change in segregation, 1989–1995

LEA	1989	1990	1991	1992	1993	1994	1995	Change
Norfolk	0.20	0.20	0.22	0.19	0.21	0.19	0.19	−2.9
Harrow	0.17	0.16	0.14	0.16	0.15	0.15	0.16	−2.9
Rhondda Cynon Taff	0.18	0.18	0.18	0.18	0.18	0.19	0.17	−2.9
Kirklees	0.30	0.33	0.32	0.30	0.30	0.28	0.29	−2.7
City of Kingston-upon-Hull	0.17	0.20	0.23	0.20	0.16	0.16	0.16	−2.6
Walsall	0.26	0.26	0.28	0.26	0.25	0.24	0.24	−2.5
Lincolnshire	0.31	0.34	0.33	0.31	0.32	0.29	0.29	−2.3
Sutton	0.36	0.37	0.41	0.37	0.34	0.34	0.35	−2.2
Nottinghamshire	0.21	0.23	0.22	0.20	0.18	0.19	0.20	−2.0
Brighton and Hove	0.11	0.15	0.11	0.10	0.10	0.10	0.11	−1.5
Hackney	0.11	0.13	0.13	0.11	0.08	0.08	0.10	−1.4
Cardiff	0.35	0.35	0.35	0.34	0.36	0.34	0.34	−1.4
Stockton-on-Tees	0.26	0.30	0.28	0.26	0.26	0.24	0.26	−1.3
Slough	0.32	0.37	0.31	0.39	0.35	0.31	0.31	−0.9
Warrington	0.26	0.30	0.31	0.27	0.28	0.26	0.26	−0.8
Coventry	0.20	0.21	0.21	0.19	0.20	0.20	0.20	−0.5
Halton	0.16	0.15	0.18	0.19	0.19	0.19	0.16	−0.5
Wrexham	0.14	0.14	0.14	0.14	0.14	0.14	0.14	0.0
Merthyr Tydfil	0.13	0.13	0.13	0.15	0.13	0.12	0.13	0.0
Clwyd	0.16	0.16	0.16	0.16	0.16	0.16	0.16	0.0
Dyfed	0.15	0.15	0.15	0.15	0.15	0.15	0.15	0.0
Conwy	0.14	0.14	0.14	0.14	0.14	0.14	0.14	0.0
Isles of Scilly	0.00	0.00	0.00	0.00	0.00	0.00	0.00	0.0
Rutland						0.00	0.00	0.0
Gateshead	0.25	0.26	0.28	0.25	0.24	0.23	0.25	0.5
Newcastle-upon-Tyne	0.21	0.23	0.23	0.23	0.23	0.22	0.22	0.8
Redcar and Cleveland	0.22	0.21	0.24	0.20	0.23	0.23	0.23	0.9
Wirral	0.24	0.23	0.25	0.28	0.26	0.26	0.25	1.3
Shropshire	0.18	0.20	0.21	0.21	0.18	0.19	0.19	1.5
West Sussex	0.21	0.21	0.27	0.24	0.21	0.22	0.22	1.6
Wolverhampton	0.17	0.22	0.18	0.20	0.17	0.19	0.17	1.7
Dudley	0.24	0.24	0.29	0.26	0.27	0.24	0.25	2.2
Kingston-upon-Thames	0.24	0.23	0.28	0.26	0.23	0.21	0.25	2.3
Stoke-on-Trent	0.15	0.13	0.16	0.15	0.17	0.16	0.16	2.7
Flintshire	0.17	0.17	0.17	0.17	0.17	0.18	0.18	2.9
Sheffield	0.24	0.23	0.24	0.25	0.24	0.25	0.26	2.9
Medway	0.22	0.27	0.29	0.24	0.29	0.27	0.23	2.9

kinds that contain local markets with a large number of schools within relatively easy reach of all families. The reason why these 87 LEAs, rather than others, showed such large decreases in segregation is therefore likely to be market-related. They are among those in which a market is capable of operating.

A partial explanation may also lie in the extent to which changes in local populations and school numbers have muted any unintended

Table 4.5 LEAs segregating, 1989–1995

LEA	1989	1990	1991	1992	1993	1994	1995	Change
Thurrock	0.09	0.13	0.11	0.15	0.18	0.20	0.20	38.1
City of Derby	0.12	0.13	0.15	0.16	0.22	0.20	0.22	30.8
Torbay	0.13	0.18	0.15	0.16	0.19	0.22	0.24	28.0
Hammersmith and Fulham	0.13	0.16	0.17	0.19	0.20	0.21	0.23	26.4
Hartlepool	0.11	0.13	0.12	0.14	0.15	0.14	0.18	21.4
Southend	0.20	0.28	0.22	0.25	0.32	0.31	0.30	21.0
The Wrekin	0.15	0.16	0.22	0.24	0.23	0.23	0.23	20.1
Derbyshire	0.16	0.17	0.22	0.24	0.21	0.23	0.23	19.4
Poole	0.20	0.20	0.30	0.26	0.36	0.23	0.28	16.3
Bournemouth	0.19	0.16	0.28	0.27	0.25	0.24	0.26	14.5
Blackpool	0.10	0.12	0.13	0.09	0.14	0.12	0.13	13.0
Hounslow	0.14	0.18	0.16	0.19	0.17	0.17	0.18	13.0
Havering	0.26	0.30	0.30	0.32	0.31	0.30	0.33	12.1
Durham	0.16	0.17	0.18	0.17	0.18	0.19	0.20	12.0
Neath Port Talbot	0.12	0.12	0.15	0.14	0.12	0.14	0.15	11.1
Essex	0.20	0.21	0.21	0.24	0.22	0.25	0.24	10.8
Cumbria	0.24	0.28	0.27	0.29	0.30	0.30	0.29	10.7
Darlington	0.15	0.19	0.19	0.20	0.22	0.19	0.18	10.5
Haringey	0.13	0.09	0.15	0.20	0.15	0.17	0.16	10.0
Barnsley	0.17	0.20	0.20	0.19	0.18	0.19	0.21	9.7
Herefordshire	0.17	0.15	0.17	0.28	0.22	0.20	0.20	8.6
Sunderland	0.13	0.14	0.19	0.15	0.17	0.16	0.16	8.2
East Riding of Yorkshire	0.19	0.24	0.21	0.15	0.20	0.23	0.22	8.0
Kensington and Chelsea	0.15	0.18	0.13	0.25	0.25	0.16	0.18	7.6
Buckinghamshire	0.41	0.41	0.43	0.47	0.51	0.47	0.47	7.2
Pembroke	0.13	0.18	0.15	0.15	0.15	0.15	0.15	7.1
Enfield	0.22	0.23	0.25	0.25	0.27	0.27	0.25	6.7
Blackburn	0.22	0.23	0.19	0.19	0.16	0.24	0.25	6.3
Caerphilly	0.09	0.08	0.08	0.09	0.10	0.09	0.10	5.2
Carmarthenshire	0.19	0.19	0.19	0.19	0.19	0.19	0.21	5.0
Newham	0.11	0.12	0.12	0.13	0.11	0.11	0.12	4.9
North Yorkshire	0.25	0.26	0.25	0.25	0.27	0.27	0.28	4.7
Bury	0.20	0.23	0.25	0.27	0.27	0.21	0.22	4.6
Oldham	0.28	0.31	0.32	0.35	0.31	0.29	0.30	4.5
Bromley	0.29	0.37	0.37	0.33	0.30	0.31	0.31	4.3
Reading	0.23	0.27	0.24	0.31	0.33	0.34	0.25	3.9
Plymouth	0.25	0.28	0.25	0.26	0.26	0.27	0.27	3.5
Peterborough	0.14	0.11	0.08	0.07	0.16	0.14	0.15	3.3
Bolton	0.27	0.28	0.30	0.26	0.28	0.29	0.29	3.2

impact of the choice policies. For example, several of these LEAs have reduced the number of their schools as part of a reorganisation to reduce the number of surplus places. Some also contain significant numbers of families who use schools in adjacent LEAs. Both of these phenomena could reduce segregation – the first by forcing the redistribution of students among schools, and the second by reducing variation among the families using local schools. This hypothesis is backed up by the strong link between the level of segregation, its change over time, and the initial percentage FSM figure for each LEA. Areas with a higher proportion of students taking FSM tend to have lower levels of segregation (R = −0.54), and to show a greater proportionate drop in segregation over time (R = −0.27). This is interesting because it is contrary to the authors' pre-conception that segregation would be worse in areas with high levels of poverty. However, these can only be partial explanations, since substantial reorganisation for most LEAs has been a one-off event. Segregation in the whole of England and Wales has declined, and this could not be due to families shuffling between LEAs, any more than it is due to an increase in using schools in Scotland or paying for places in independent schools.

Another 37 LEAs showed little or no change in segregation between 1989 and 1995 (Table 4.4), although it should be noted that in the majority of these segregation has declined marginally, and that the remainder show years in which segregation has been lower than it was in 1989. In some cases the lack of change is due to a lack of alternative schools (the Scilly Isles with only one school being the most extreme case) or low population density (Dyfed being the most extreme case with an average 0.2 persons per hectare). In other cases, such as Halton or Gateshead, the reason for the lack of change is harder to find. A partial explanation lies in the LEA procedures for allocating contested secondary school places since 1989 (see Chapter 9). In Cardiff, for example, secondary schools used matched primary schools whose leavers were guaranteed a place. As these primary schools themselves ran a catchment area system so, effectively, did the secondary schools. It is not surprising to find that Cardiff LEA appears in this group (although it should be noted that many LEAs in England and Wales run a similar system). Another example involves the rule that siblings of those already in school take priority. This would lead to a slight inhibition in the year-on-year socio-economic variation within a school. Similar considerations apply to LEAs who are only prepared to fund free travel to the closest school from a child's home. In effect, these LEAs are saying to poor families, the government claims you can choose any school you like but if you choose a non-adjacent one you must pay for the travel. In sum, many of the LEAs in Table 4.4 are those in which a market for schools is incapable of operating – for structural, geographical or political reasons.

Only 39 LEAs showed an increase in segregation of 3 per cent or more between 1989 and 1995, and it should be noted that even several of these show years in which segregation declined below the 1989 figure as well (Table 4.5). These 39 include all types of LEAs, urban and rural, English and Welsh, large and small. Four showed very substantial increases – Thurrock, City of Derby, Torbay, and Hammersmith and Fulham – only the latter of which showed a regular year-on-year increase. Many of the

LEAs that have become increasingly segregated share some similarities as 'suburban' areas of a capital city (e.g. Thurrock, Hounslow and Havering). Some of these LEAs, such as Bromley and Buckinghamshire, run an overtly selective system of grammar schools, while others, such as Haringey, are deeply affected by the policy of grant-maintained (foundation) schools. These schools control their own admissions policies and therefore draw their intake from wide areas that often extend beyond the boundaries of LEAs. If these schools are drawing in a more privileged intake than surrounding neighbourhood schools then this would show up as increasing segregation. These factors may explain part of their difference to the majority of the LEAs in this analysis.

In general, urban areas have shown the greatest change over time (in either direction). In the case of some inner-London LEAs that change has meant that there was almost no segregation by poverty, for example (see www.cardiff.ac.uk/socsi/markets for LEA maps of levels of segregation and their changes over time). Milton Keynes and Solihull head the most segregated LEAs in 1989, closely followed by Buckinghamshire, Oxfordshire, Sutton, Portsmouth, Trafford and Kent. At the other end, areas with the least segregation were Thurrock and Thameside (formerly part of Essex), Barking and Dagenham, Islington, Blackpool and Hackney. It is important to note that urban and metropolitan LEAs feature both as very high and very low segregated areas. However, there were few county LEAs with very low levels of segregation. The exceptions tended to be in the most remote areas of England: Cornwall, Devon, Herefordshire, Derbyshire and Durham.

By 1995, the pattern of segregation looked very different. There were fewer LEAs at the extreme ends of high and low segregation, indicating that segregation levels across LEAs had homogenised. Buckinghamshire was now the most segregated LEA, followed still by Solihull. Three outer London Boroughs, all to the south, had become relatively more segregated than other LEAs in the country: Sutton, Bromley and Havering. Knowsley had become the least segregated LEA along with the London boroughs of Southwark, Islington, Barking and Dagenham, Lewisham and Tower Hamlets.

After 1995, a new and different pattern of change emerged. LEAs such as Southwark, Wandsworth, Westminster, Bath and North East Somerset, Peterborough, Manchester, Brighton and Hove, Torfaen and Blaenau Gwent became more segregated. These were closely followed by an even more unlikely set of LEAs such as Cornwall, East Sussex, the west coast of Wales, South Gloucestershire, Wiltshire, Hertfordshire, Trafford, Rotherham and Wigan. This suggests that the two phases in national segregation were being driven by changes in segregation by two different sets of LEAs, and that the factors underlying these changes are different for the two time periods.

By 2001, inner London LEAs continued to have low levels of segregation while the outer London boroughs remained relatively high. The urban areas of south Wales and the south coast of England were highly segregated compared with their neighbouring, more rural, local authorities. The counties surrounding London and those along the commuter belts of the M4, M40 and M1 and, towards the north of England, the large counties of Lincolnshire, North Yorkshire, Cumbria and Northumberland also had relatively high levels of segregation. But other urban areas outside London were more mixed, some with very low levels of segregation, such as Manchester, Oldham and Knowsley.

These differences between LEAs reinforce the importance of considering regional differences in the sociology of education (Gorard and Rees, 2002), and highlight the danger of attempting to generalise from a small-scale study. An analyst working in only one LEA, for example, may select a London or Metropolitan borough near the head of Table 4.5, and erroneously lead their readers to believe that a national picture can, therefore, be deduced.

District-level figures

In the original six LEAs used for the study in Wales (Gorard and Fitz, 1998b), it was possible to use our detailed local knowledge to group the schools into districts within LEAs. Analysed at the district level the same picture of overall desegregation after 1989 (with minor variations) was obtained. It is, therefore, worth emphasising here that the level of aggregation used in analysis cannot obscure variations at any other level (see Chapter 7). It would be impossible for desegregation at LEA level to arise mainly from cross-border movements between adjacent LEAs in London, for example, since this would show up at the regional level. It would, for the same reason, be impossible for segregation to increase at a sub-LEA level and not show up at a higher level of aggregation unless balanced by a superior and opposite process of desegregation elsewhere. Therefore suggestions, such as those of Gibson and Asthana (1999), that segregation is actually increasing at one level of analysis while decreasing at another are necessarily incomplete until there is an explanation of how such a paradox could be resolved.

School-level figures

In trying to decide what is producing the overall desegregation and its local variations, our first step was to look at the history of individual schools. Do some LEAs display 'polarisation' whereby most schools are moving towards a more equal share of FSM students, but one or two schools are becoming 'sink' institutions taking the surplus students from a disadvantaged background? The first thing to note that such a process would not be new. Polarisation happened already, even under conditions where LEAs had a greater say in the allocation of students to places. The question then is, did polarisation happen more frequently under market conditions? In fact, this possibility is catered for by the method used to create the findings so far, and the answer is clearly 'no'. The number of schools moving away from the 'ideal' of a proportionate share of children from poor families, and the size of that movement, are directly related to the segregation index for their LEA. For example, the London borough of Haringey has nine schools which collectively show an increase in segregation from 13 per cent in 1989 to 19 per cent in 1997. It should, therefore, be no surprise to discover that seven of these schools moved further from an equal share of FSM, while only two moved closer to equity (using the segregation ratios described in Chapter 3). But none of these schools became anything like a 'sink' school in a spiral of decline (at least in terms of segregation). In fact, the most disadvantaged school in 1989, which was the closest to a sink school in 1989, was the school showing the largest shift towards an even share of FSM students (all relevant figures appear in Gorard and Fitz, 2000).

Islington LEA is a near neighbour of Haringey with the same number of schools, but an overall drop in segregation from 15 to 5 per cent by 1997. In Islington, only one school moved away from an equal share of FSM (and this was a voluntary-aided one moving towards a decreasing share of disadvantage). The other eight all move closer to parity in terms of segregation. As in Haringey, the most disadvantaged school in 1989 showed the largest shift towards an even share of FSM students, matched by an equal and opposite shift by the most advantaged school which started with nearly half of its fair share of FSM students and ended up with slightly more than its fair share. In every LEA that has been examined in detail a similar picture emerges. As with England and Wales overall, the regions, the LEAs and the districts within them, the schools themselves generally moved towards an even spread of FSM students.

School size and spirals of decline?

In 1988, the General Secretary of the National Association of Headteachers gave voice to the widespread fear that "... the operation of market forces will inevitably mean that oversubscribed schools will quickly fill up to the limit of their capacity and disappointed parents will be offered under-subscribed schools. At the same time severely under-subscribed schools will have to close because surplus places will have to be taken out of use" (Hart, in Haviland, 1988: 168). The remainder of this chapter is devoted to a summary of our evidence concerning the existence of schools in spirals of decline. There has been little research on school rolls prior to the expansion of market forces in education. One study, by Butel (1988) who examined the changing rolls of 45 secondary schools in one LEA, calculated that the average school size had fallen from 861 students in 1978–1979 to 820 students in 1985–1986. This is an overall drop of 4.8 per cent. Butel also analysed the differential impact of change across the LEA, and observed a pattern of declining urban school intakes and growing rural school intakes. The magnitude of change in this one LEA before the introduction of the 1988 Education Reform Act makes it difficult to interpret many of the changes throughout the 1990s as being market-related. From the 1970s to the 1980s the number on roll of many schools declined, leading to the surplus places that motivated at least part of the reforms in the 1980s. This decline was demographic, and as far as we can tell, unrelated to school allocation procedures. From the 1980s onwards the number on roll of most schools increased (by 20 per cent from 1989 to 1999). Again this has a demographic cause, exacerbated by the school closures stemming from the earlier decline.

We found no clear evidence that the process of school choice has led some schools into 'spirals of decline' in which they lose both market share and become increasingly stratified in terms of indicators of disadvantage (Gorard et al., 2002a). The number of children in secondary schools increased during the period while the number of schools decreased. Therefore, most schools have increased their average number of students even where they are seen as less desirable in their local 'markets'. These average increases are clearly not evenly distributed across all LEAs (Figure 4.6). Nearly three-quarters of all current English secondary schools increased their student rolls between 1989 and 1999. Only 28 per cent of all English secondary schools saw a decrease in size during that time. The latter schools, plus those closed or merged in the interim, are candidates under our operational definition for being in spirals of decline. It should be noted that of those schools declining in student numbers, two-thirds experienced a fall of only 0 to 10 per cent. A few schools saw much larger falls in their school rolls (17 schools declined in size by 30 per cent or more). For example, Fryern Community College (Essex) declined by 63 per cent and Kingsland Community College (Bedfordshire) fell by 43 per cent.

Changes in size cannot be assessed simply in raw figures, nor as percentage point differences for the reasons discussed further in Chapter 5 (not least because urban and rural schools tend to be of different orders of magnitude). In order to produce an estimate of the change in size in each area (or school) which can be appropriately compared across areas, we find the difference between the number on roll in 1989 and in 2001, and divide this by the original size of the school. This yields a range of +1 to +84 per cent. The largest increase in school sizes from this sample of LEAs was in Brent where the average school increased from 605 full-time

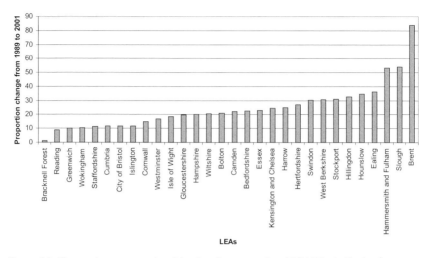

Figure 4.6 Change in average school intakes for a sample of 30 LEAs in England, 1989–2001.

students in 1989 to 1,114 in 2001. A programme of school closures and amalgamations lies behind this very large increase. For example, in 1989 there were twenty-two schools in Brent but by 2001 this had fallen to thirteen. In searching for 'spirals of decline' it is therefore important to take these results into account. For example, not all closed schools were in decline before they ceased operation, and some schools only went into decline after their closure was announced. LEAs tend to close schools over an extended period, phasing out one year group at a time, so producing a decline in overall numbers which we then need to separate out in analysis. What we are searching for instead are schools which have no clear demographic reason for a drop in numbers, but which show such a drop in conjunction with an increasingly disadvantaged intake.

One difficulty lies in distinguishing a 'spiral of decline' (in numbers) from the usual flux in school sizes both before and after 1988. In Hounslow LEA for example, as in several other LEAs at the right-hand end of Figure 4.6, no schools ended the period with fewer students. The picture for Slough LEA is slightly different. Again there is variation between schools with some increasing at a faster rate than others, but there is one school which ends the period with a smaller number on roll. This school dropped from 650 students in 1989 to under 500 by 1992. It is, therefore, a candidate for a school in a terminal spin, losing both 'market share' and raw numbers of students to other local schools. The timing of this significant decline is also interesting, taking place in the years immediately following the Education Reform Act 1988. It is important to note, however, that the school is no longer in decline since it recovered in size to 630 by 2001.

It is also interesting to observe what has happened in Bracknell Forest LEA, since this was the LEA from the sample with the smallest increase in size of the average school intake (see left-hand end of Figure 4.6). The relatively small increase in the ratio of students to schools should make at least some of the schools susceptible to decline. However, only two schools ended the period with fewer students on roll than in 1989, and in both cases they increased their roll considerably over a number of years during this period. This is particularly noteworthy as Bracknell Forest has been selected here as the extreme case from our subsample.

School closures

Another group of schools that we considered in terms of spirals of decline were those that were closed or merged before 2001. There were 86 fewer secondary schools in England in 2001 than in 1995 (which is as far back as we have accurate identification for every single school – due to problems with reorganisation, loss of archives, official transcription errors, changes in DfES numbering, etc.). The combined effect of closing some schools, opening new schools and amalgamating others means that it is possible to identify a total of 90 school closures over the same time period. This represents just over 2 per cent of the total number of second-ary schools that were open in 1989. Around 40 per cent of these schools faced a significant drop in size in the final year(s) before closure. Once an LEA has decided to close schools they often incrementally reduce a school's intake by not admitting a new year of students. The effect of this is to make the school fall in size irrespective of any other factors. However, our interviews with those responsible in the LEAs also show that any school considered for closure generally goes out for consultation with the local community as well as to the Secretary of State, making closure a protracted process (Pollock, 2000). A decline in recruitment for the year or two preceding closure, but after publication of the proposals, could be due to a lack of confidence in the school being open for the duration of a child's full schooling. While clearly an outcome of choice, it should be argued that the consequent drop is not a symptom of a 'spiral of decline'. Nor is it market-driven since the prior decision to close the school is made centrally. Although the school loses numbers and is closed, the notification of closure precedes the loss of numbers. What we wish to identify, rather, is a school closed due to lack of numbers.

None of the schools closed in our sample of 30 LEAs meets this criterion. Five of the six closing schools in this subsample actually increased in size in the mid-1990s before their planned and phased closures. Only St Mark's Church of England School stands out from this analysis as a clear candidate for a 'spiral of decline', showing a year-on-year decline in numbers from 1989. Of course, we cannot tell if St Mark's Church of

England School was already in decline before the introduction of greater open enrolment in 1988. Indeed, the relative size of all schools in 1999 is strongly related to their relative size in 1989, a very similar conclusion to that drawn by Butel (1988) in an earlier study in one LEA. Consequently, any change seen in rolls between 1989 and 2001 might simply be an extension of demographic changes that began to affect school recruitment prior to marketisation. It is also noteworthy that LEAs, in which a significant number of school closures took place ended up with a lower level of socio-economic segregation than previously (see above).

'Failing schools'

The final group that we considered were those placed under Special Measures by the school's inspectorates (OFSTED in England, and Estyn in Wales). The notion of Special Measures was first introduced in the 1993 Education Act and reinforced in the School Inspections Act 1996. After an inspection and an unsatisfactory report by an inspection team schools may be deemed as failing and placed where 'Special Measures are required to be taken in relation to a school if the schools is failing or likely to fail to give its students an acceptable standard of education' (Section 13,9). Riley (1996) claimed that schools deemed as 'failing' were affected by the measures introduced in the 1988 Education Reform Act, and argued that such schools tended to lose 'able' students to other schools, who in turn attempted to exclude 'troublesome' students from attending their school. Our analysis was based on two sets of schools placed under Special Measures by OFSTED and the DfEE Inspection teams from two different time periods. The first set of 20 secondary schools were those under Special Measures in June 1996. The second set of 61 secondary schools were those under Special Measures further into the inspection cycle, in August 1999.

Some of these schools in Special Measures increased and some decreased in size after the announcement, but their tendency to decrease was more marked in the first set of 'failing schools' in 1996. This is because several schools in the first batch were closed down (including St Richard of Chichester and the Waterfield School). The points made earlier about the procedure for closing schools apply here also. In the second set of 'failing schools' no schools were closed, but the greatest declines were observed in Abbotswood and Merryfield Schools, which were only opened in the mid-1990s. In the first group, it is observable that the greatest fall in rolls, even among those schools falling consistently through-out this period, came at around the time of the OFSTED inspections, and particularly for schools that were eventually closed. Otherwise, the changes in size of schools in Special Measures is no different from changes in schools more generally. Only in a short period at the time of the

OFSTED inspections does there appear to be any effect on school rolls. Clearly many parents may use this information in making their school choice. This suggests that it is not the market, in general, but the announcement of the label of 'failing' that is the cause of falling numbers for the short term (i.e. the policy of inspection may be having the opposite effect to that intended, see Weiner, 2002).

Changes in composition

In all, from our detailed sample of 835 schools in 30 English LEAs, we identified 12 schools above that were prime candidates to be in a spiral of decline on the basis of intake size, whether falling rolls, closed schools, or those in special measures. We then investigated whether the candidate schools also increased their proportion of students with socio-economic disadvantage?

Six of these schools actually became less segregated over time, taking an increasingly 'privileged' intake. Therefore, only half of these 12 candidate schools saw an increase in their segregation ratios, calculated for eligibility for free-school meals, over the period. But even these showed considerable volatility in the composition of their intakes. Schools in trouble financially, due to falling rolls, or with poor academic reports appear to have very changeable intakes, in contradiction to the more commonly-held belief that such schools would simply take more and more socially disadvantaged students. Three of these schools started the period with less than their 'fair share' of children in poverty anyway. A fourth did not open until 1996. A fifth increased segregation in 1989/1990 but decreased substantially thereafter. Therefore, only one school in our sample, Fryerns Community, has a profile of a true spiral of decline – losing both numbers (and therefore budget) and having a growing proportion of students from families living in poverty. Even with Fryerns, two caveats should be noted. The school actually showed decreases in segregation from 1991 to 1992 and again from 1994 to 1998. The common notion of how market forces could lead schools into spirals of decline rests heavily on two key components: a fall in numbers and an increasingly disadvantaged intake of children. Occurring iteratively these factors could have serious implications for the distribution of resources, the ability for schools to improve standards, and social justice in general. From our database we have been able to identify only one school that both lost market share and had a growing proportion of students from families in poverty. There is no reason to assume that such rare patterns of change have not always occurred, irrespective of the policy in operation. As would be predictable from the decline in number of schools and the overall drop in segregation, spirals of decline are not one of the impacts of school choice in the UK.

Conclusions

Having considered changes over 13 years in all of the state-funded schools in England and Wales, in terms of their student intake as assessed by four different measures of socio-economic disadvantage, and at differing levels of aggregation, it is clear that segregation between schools did not increase as a result of marketisation. There was a slight increase from 1989 to 1990, but by 1995, once all students of compulsory school age had entered in an era of open enrolment and choice, segregation between schools was substantially lower than in 1989, the last year when all students had entered before open enrolment. The reduction was progressive, as new cohorts entered secondary schools, and those cohorts who had entered before open enrolment left schools. This interpretation is reinforced by findings from the early part of this study where we were able to calculate segregation for each cohort separately (Gorard and Fitz, 1998b). In Swansea LEA, for example, each year group in schools after 1990 was less segregated by eligibility for FSM than the year above it. Both in England and Wales, by 1995 the intake to each school was generally a better reflection of the wider society from which it recruited (at least in terms of the most disadvantaged sections of each community). In concluding this, the study both challenges the findings of, and to some extent questions the methods of, several previous small-scale studies. Other large-scale studies have, like ours, shown no drop in equity associated with increased parental choice (e.g. Bradley and Taylor, 2002). The changes in school enrolment observed in previous small-scale studies would seem to be partly explicable in terms of socio-economic and demographic changes in society rather than changes in school admissions. By questioning the simple thesis of 'markets lead to segregation' this work leads to a more complex picture of the determinants of social change (Chapters 7 to 10).

It is often assumed that with open enrolment, as long as there are enough surplus places in the education system, 'popular' schools will increase the size of their intakes year-on-year and those that are 'unpopular' will see a fall in numbers year-on-year. But popular schools can only keep increasing as long as there are places available in the school and, therefore, more popular schools will eventually become oversubscribed. It should be noted, however, that there are exceptions to this where schools have successfully admitted students over their planned admission number (PAN), and in Wales where the Popular Schools Initiative has allowed a few schools to expand in the face of growing demand for their places. Unpopular schools will only see a fall in the size of their intakes as long as there are places available in other schools. If schools closures, rising birth rates or other factors combine to keep school rolls high then, by definition, spirals of decline in terms of simple numbers cannot take place. It may seem scientifically perverse to seek a reason for the absence of a phenomenon, but we still feel that this requires further explanation for the particular benefit of readers who were convinced that these spirals would be evident. The concept of 'spirals of decline' is so deeply embedded in much writing about markets in education that the lack of empirical support for their existence is a surprise. To some extent, of course, the increase in parental choice took place in an era of generally increasing school rolls and this is likely to provide much of the explanation. We feel that much of the rest of the solution lies in the role of the LEAs in their handling of school closures, and the allocation of places (see Chapter 10).

It is, of course, also important to consider systematic differences within the groups considered here. For example, although indicators of poverty are more evenly spread, it could be that the more motivated, or better educated, or 'artificially poor' parents among these are still being segregated from the others. Similar considerations apply to the majority of the population not encompassed within the measures of socio-economic disadvantage used here. It would be non-parsimonious to assume such a position, but unwise not to consider it as a possibility (along with many others). Consideration of the in-depth data for a stratified subsample of LEAs, schools and their users is therefore a key task (see Chapter 7 for a full discussion of the possibility of segregation occurring at some other level). Before doing so, it will also be interesting to begin to examine how far the changes noted above have impacted on school performance.

Part III

School choice and standards

Chapter 5

What is school performance and how do we measure it?

One of the justifications advanced for increasing the role of markets in education was the possible contribution this could make to raising the standard of teaching and the quality of learning. It was argued that where schools had to compete for students it would force them to focus on performance, as measured by student attainment in public examinations, and thus contribute to driving up standards of teaching and learning. While there is an accessible logic in this argument, is there any evidence that educational markets have had such an impact on levels of student attainment? The other side of this argument is that school may well have sought to improve their performance and pursuit of market advantage by changing the character of their intake rather than improving the quality of teaching and learning. As a result, have schools polarised or moved apart in terms of performance? In this chapter and the next, we assess the relevant evidence.

But there is a broader question that is examined in this chapter, namely how can we judge school performance, educational achievement and the question of 'standards' over time? Our first task then is to address the general problem of 'comparability'. The first part of the chapter describes the background and methods that can be employed in the investigation of this complex area. We move on to describe the importance of contextualised performance measures, and then create a 'natural' experimental design, and introduce methods for assessing academic polarisation. These methods are employed in Chapter 6 to decide whether ERA88 has had an impact on school standards. Our datasets are largely the same as those described in Chapter 3 for use in describing patterns of socio-economic segregation between schools, but with the addition of school-level variables representing key stage and GCSE results. It should be noted that historical student-level records were not available, and that our analysis is, necessarily, conducted at the school level.

Problems of comparability

Although there have been attempts to express school performance in terms of efficiency or value-for-money, the key issue for us concerns educational standards as revealed by the test performances of students. To make a claim that one student, school, sector, region, or year produced 'better' or 'worse' results than another, assumes that we have a benchmark that is valid for comparison over time and place. This assumption is easy to disprove.

Perhaps the most easily overlooked problem is that knowledge is not a static commodity. There has been a drop in archery standards among the UK population over the last millennium. Is this evidence of poorer education today? Presumably not, since the skill is now less relevant than it was. If the number of children knowing the meaning of the word 'mannequin' is less today than in the 1950s, is this evidence of poorer education today? Presumably not, because linguistic usage changes. Because children of yesteryear did not know the word 'cyberspace' does this mean they were under-educated? So when the National Commission on Education (1993) complained that number skills have deteriorated for 11–15-year-olds, why should this be construed evidence of poorer education today? Perhaps this is simply evidence that words and number skills have changed in their everyday relevance. On the other hand, if the items or the wording in any test are changed to reflect these changes in society, then how do we know that the test is of the same level of difficulty as its predecessor? In public examinations (UK O-levels, for example), by and large we have until now relied on norm-referencing. That is, two tests were declared equivalent in difficulty if the same proportion of matched candidates obtain each graded result on both tests. The assumption is made that the actual standards of each annual cohort are equivalent, and it is these that are used to benchmark the assessment (Baird *et al.*, 2000). How then can we measure changes in standards over time since there cannot be any, by definition? But, if the test is not norm-referenced we cannot tell that apparent changes over time are not simply evidence of differentially demanding tests (e.g. Hackett and Kelly, 2000). As exam systems become more familiar then scores rise through greater teaching to the test (Henry, 2001).

There are numerous additional and well-documented hurdles to be overcome in comparing examination standards over time. For example, it is not clear that the level of attainment required to gain level 4 at KS2 has remained the same over time (Cassidy, 1999a), nor an A-level in mathematics (Kitchen, 1999), nor that the same grade is comparable across different subjects, nor the same qualification presented by different examining boards (Noah and Eckstein, 1992). Scripts are lost and test scores are added up incorrectly (Cassidy, 1999b). Markers are sacked because of unreliability, and as many as 2 per cent of papers are upgraded after remarking (Cassidy *et al.*, 2000). In one test in Northern Ireland over 71 per cent of candidates might well have been misgraded in an 11+ examination (McGill, 2000). Interested parties fiddle the figures (Mansell, 2000). Teachers, students, parents and examiners may increasingly connive in 'cheating' the system since schools are their own exam centres, are judged by exam success, and exam boards are commercial organisations seeking to maintain and increase their custom (Davies, 2001). In sum, exams are neither accurate nor particularly reliable in what they measure (Nuttall, 1979).

International comparisons

International comparisons of school performance share all of these problems and more. The issues include the comparability of different assessments, the comparability of the same assessments over time, using examinations or tests as indicators of performance at all, the different curricula in different countries, the different standards of record-keeping in different countries, and the competitiveness (especially) of developing countries (see O'Malley 1998). Yet what international comparisons such as those of Reynolds and Farrell (1996) claim to do is solve not one but all, and more of these problems at once. An observer who claims that on the basis of a standard test, one country has performed better than another, is also saying that the test involved similar children, who had followed a similar curriculum, that the test was a useful indicator of educational progress, and that it was administered in the same way in both countries. It is not clear that either the PISA or TIMSS studies, for example, can genuinely make these claims (Brown, 1998; Black and Atkin, 1999; Gorard, 2001b; Wang, 2001). Even home international comparisons (between England and Wales for example) require more than simply comparing two sets of scores (Gorard, 1998a). Given these difficulties, is there any way that we can make sensible statements about how schools have fared in terms of performance, both as a system and in relation to each other? One challenge is to find a reasonable comparator, something that might act like the control group in laboratory-based experiments, against which a system can be measured and compared. One way is to take two sectors of an existing education system, where the contextual characteristics – primarily the social composition of the student populations – are known and to compare changes in performance in each. The long-standing existence of fee-paying and state-school sectors in the UK provides such an opportunity.

A natural experiment

The most commonly used measure of school outcomes in the UK is the General Certificate of Secondary Education (GCSE) and its equivalents.

At least one GCSE is taken by over 95 per cent of the 16-year-old age cohort each year. Around 90 per cent of the cohort obtain at least one GCSE at the lowest grade (G), and around 50 per cent obtain five or more 'good' passes (grade A*–C). These scores have increased every year since ERA88. We are, however, unable simply to attribute any changes in these raw-scores to market forces for there were many policy changes all taking place at the same time. Treating our analysis as a 'natural experiment', we would say that there are important confounding variables (Gorard, 2003a). These include changes in the collection of figures over time, in the definition of the relevant age cohort, and in the nature of the qualifications themselves. Most notably the introduction of the GCSE (to replace the separate GCE and CSE examinations) in 1986/1987 heralded an increase in coursework at the expense of terminal examinations, and the abolition of strict norm-referencing which had previously worked to maintain results at a relatively constant level (Foxman, 1997). It is at least possible therefore that the improvement since 1988 is based on what has been termed, perhaps rather uncharitably, 'counterfeit excellence' (Zirkel, 1999), where indicators of examination success rise regardless of genuine improvement in performance. There is some evidence in the UK that the standards required for any grade in some subjects have declined (Tymms and Fitz-Gibbon, 2001).

So we turn to our natural experiment. Our control group is the private or fee-paying sector (Newsam, 1998). Around 8 per cent of students in England and 2 per cent in Wales attend fee-paying schools. These schools have always existed in a market – a very real and volatile one in which money changes hands and schools are forced to close through loss of students (Gorard, 1997b). Legislation such as the ERA88 had no direct effect on fee-paying schools. The 'experimental' treatment is the introduction of the limited market that affected only state schools, whereas the changes in the nature of assessment, described above, affected both groups equally. Possible confounds to this natural experiment include changes in the type and proportion of fee-paying users over the period in question. The results are in Chapter 6.

School outcomes and context

The major undisputed theme of all work on school outcomes is that these are related to non-school context factors, most notably the socio-economic backgrounds of the students. National systems of education, school sectors, schools, departments and teachers combined have been found to explain approximately zero to 20 per cent of the total variance in school outcomes depending upon the study (see Coleman *et al.*, 1966; Jencks *et al.*, 1972; Reynolds, 1990; Daly, 1991; Creemers, 1994; OECD, 1995; Stoll and Fink, 1996). The remainder of the variance in outcomes is explained by student background, prior attainment and error components. The larger the sample used, the weaker is the evidence of any school impact on attainment at all (Shipman, 1997), especially as 'outlier' scores such as those from children with special needs are routinely eliminated before analysis (Hamilton, 1998). Even the school impact that has been recorded cannot be seen as a unitary trait applying to all subjects, departments, ages, and abilities, and to both genders (Nuttall *et al.*, 1988), nor is it necessarily consistent over time, or for different kinds of outcomes (Sammons *et al.*, 1996). In fact 'the real challenge for educators and policy-makers today is to avoid the myth that schools make no difference' (Rothstein, 2002: 12).

The importance of this is two-fold. First, it suggests that we are unlikely to be able to detect any improvement in school performance over time as a result of market forces. If schools have little detectable impact anyway, then finding variation in that part of the impact attributable to school placement policies will be almost impossible. Second, it means that we should look carefully at input and contextual factors when evaluating any claims for the superiority of one school system or sector over another. This is particularly important in an era of increasing diversity of schools.

Another way of assessing changes over time is based on the changing relationship between background variables (socio-economic context) and school attainment (outcome scores). For example, it is clear that measures of student poverty such as eligibility for FSM are strongly negatively related to student achievement, even though both sets of figures have risen over the period of this study. One reasonable interpretation of a genuine improvement in an era of increasing raw scores would be that outcomes are no longer as socially determined as they were previously. Children from poor families would now be more likely to obtain their 'fair share' of the qualification spoils than they were in previous cohorts. We tested this idea by using multiple regression models with the school GCSE benchmark as the dependent variable, and a basket of indicators including student ethnicity, poverty, first language, gender, school type, and additional educational needs as independent predictors of performance. We created one model for each year from 1993 (before the first choice cohort ended compulsory schooling) to 2000. Again, the results are summarised in Chapter 6.

A related issue is that of the differential effectiveness of different types or sectors of schools (which are similar to, and share many of the same problems as, international comparisons). Evidence that one sector or another is performing better is often claimed, but rarely substantiated (see Gorard, 1998b). The importance of student background factors in assessing relative performance is paramount. Jesson (2001: 29), for example, suggested via value-added analysis that nonselective specialist schools out-perform other nonspecialist schools. Jesson also suggested that the level of added-value that these schools can generate should be seen against the fact that they are representative of the education system at large, 'many of them are sited in inner-city areas and other areas of relative or absolute social disadvantage. The success of these schools, sometimes described as "against the odds", is very encouraging and offers "signs of hope" for others schools similarly placed' .

However, Jesson not only ignored the differential funding available to specialist schools, but also the fact that proportionately more designated specialist schools were of single-sex, ex-grammar, and foundation status than would be expected. Yet he felt able to compare the performance of, for example, secondary modern schools (taking those unwilling or unable to pass 11+) with that of specialist ex-grammar schools. As we show in Chapter 8 the socio-economic composition of the two groups is very different. While this does not completely invalidate the value-added analysis, it does suggest an alternative explanation not involving the specialism. Similarly, the fact that many specialist schools are sited in inner-city and disadvantaged areas does not, in itself, mean that they serve a representative section of the local community. The siting of a school is not always a good guide to the social composition of its student body (see Appendix). Therefore, it is important to consider the actual composition of specialist schools, and the same argument would apply to city academies, faith-based schools, and educational action zones.

Assessing academic polarisation

Our final concern in this section is academic polarisation. Are the results of 'good' and 'bad' schools or students diverging? In order to answer this question we needed to consider more carefully than is usual what such divergence would look like. Imagine a country of 100 million adults, of whom 50 million are male and 50 million are female. There are 1000 members of parliament (MPs), and all of these are male. The employed workforce is 50 million of whom 25.5 million are male. This imaginary country has a considerable political bias towards males. The country also has a slight employment bias towards males, but the political bias is much greater than the employment bias. None of the female half of the population are MPs, while 49 per cent of women are in employment. Of the male population 0.001 per cent are MPs, and 51 per cent are in employment. The ratio of male to female MPs is 1,000:0 (equivalent to an infinite amount) whereas the ratio of male to female employed is 25.5:24.5 (equivalent to 1.04). Therefore the inequity among MPs is far greater than among the general employed workforce. However, the most common 'method' used to analyse such data comes to the opposite and totally wrong conclusion. It is the purported method of differences between percentages.

The argument goes like this. The percentage of male MPs is 0.001 per cent and the percentage of female MPs is 0 per cent, so the difference between them is 0.001 per cent. The percentage of males in employment is 51 per cent and the percentage of females is 49 per cent, so the difference between them is 2 per cent. Since 2 per cent is much larger than 0.001 per cent the lack of equity in general employment is greater than among MPs. This is a very poor argument. In order to decide what is happening we cannot simply subtract two sets of percentages and compare the results (Fleiss, 1973). Since all numbers change from one case to another, the question is not whether any percentage point difference has grown, but whether it has grown more or less than the numbers between which it is the difference. Or, put more elegantly, 'the drawback with using the absolute difference in proportions to evaluate social reforms, however, is that the measure is largely driven by changes in the overall totals'. But similar arguments, using precisely these types of figures, are commonplace in the media and in research reports (e.g. Gillborn and Youdell, 2000; for further examples see Gorard, 1999b).

A junior education minister in England recently made the mistake of pointing to a growing gap between the performance of faith-based schools and their LEA-controlled counterparts (TES, 2001). The faith-based schools do tend to have higher examination scores (but with different student compositions). But the minister, Ivan Lewis, claimed that faith-based schools are doing better than ever, because the gap with other schools has grown to 7.5 from a 7.1 percentage point difference in students obtaining five or more good GCSEs passes. In fact, faith-based schools scored 49.4 per cent compared with 42.3 per cent for the other schools in 1997, whereas by 2001 the scores were 55.3 and 47.8 per cent. Thus, contrary to the minister's claim, the scores actually show a slight drop in the gap from 17 per cent (or 49.4/42.3) to 16 per cent (or 55.3/47.8).

Similarly, Bradley and Taylor (2002: 13) suggest from their Table 2 that the faith-based (VA/VC) schools in their sample are improving their standard GCSE benchmark scores faster than other comprehensive schools (Table 5.1). They base their claim on the fact that the gap was 10.4 points in 1992 and 13.4 in 2000 or, put another way, the change for LEA schools was 9.4 points, whereas for faith-based schools it was 12.4. In fact the proportionate gap between the groups was 32 per cent (or 43.1/32.7 or 55.5/42.1) in both years. Put another way, the proportionate change for both groups was 12.5 per cent. Again, these figures do not support the conclusions originally drawn from them.

We overcome this problem, at least in part, by use of an achievement gap, which is a special two-by-two case of the segregation ratio (see Chapter 3, and Gorard, 2000b). Calculation of an achievement gap between two groups requires a preliminary analysis of the different group patterns

Table 5.1 Comparing LEA-controlled and faith-based schools (from Bradley and Taylor, 2002)

School type	N	%5 A–C 1992	%5 A–C 2000	Change 1992–2000	Relative change
LEA	2030	32.7	42.1	9.4	12.5
VA/VC	603	43.1	55.5	12.4	12.5

Source: from Bradley and Taylor, 2002.

of entry for any test, giving rise to an entry gap. The entry gap for an assessment is defined as the difference between the entry for group A and group B. Formally the gap is:

Entry gap $=(E_a-E_b)/(E_a+E_b) * 100,$

where E_a is the number of group A entered for the test, and E_b is the number of group B.

The achievement gap for each grade within an assessment such as GCSE is defined as the difference between the performance of group A and group B relative to the performance of all entries, minus the entry gap. Formally the gap is:

Achievement gap $=(P_a-P_b)/(P_a+P_b) *100 -$ Entry gap,

where P_a is the number of group A achieving that grade or better, and P_b is the number of group B. The achievement gap for equal entries is an expression of how much better (or worse) one group does than the other. A gap of 10 per cent, for example, refers to the proportion of group A attaining a specific outcome over and above what would be expected if there were no gap. The groups can be defined by country, ethnicity, gender, social class, income, or school types for example.

Since 1994, the DfEE have published the average GCSE points scores for all students in the appropriate 15-year-old cohort in England, disaggregated by ranked twentieth parts (e.g. DfE, 1995). In other words, the points score of the top twentieth of the population (as measured by GCSE outcomes) can be compared to the bottom twentieth, and to every 5 per cent of the population in between. Each twentieth part represents around 22,000 students per year. These figures are also broken down by type of school, and from 1995 the figures have been presented for boys and girls separately. The advantage of the GCSE point score (where G=1, F=2, E=3, etc.) over the more usual GCSE benchmark is that it measures across all levels of attainment better, rather than focusing unduly on GCSE grade C. The disadvantage is that it is an artificial measure created by converting an ordinal value (ranked grades) into a pseudo-interval value in which a C grade is worth five times that of a G grade. There is no mathematical, philosophical or educational justification for this. It is simply convenient, and therefore any conclusions based on such a measure must always be tempered with caution (see Fielding, 1998). These scores, aggregated to 25 per cent and 50 per cent groups, are used in Chapter 6 to test the notion that student scores across schools are becoming more polarised over time.

Describing trends in school performance

International comparisons

To put what follows into context, and to reassure readers that the UK does not face any particular crisis in terms of school outcomes, we first look at the figures for polarisation by school outcomes in a number of developed countries. Of the 23 countries in a 1992 OECD comparison only Germany, Norway, Switzerland and USA had a clearly higher proportion than the UK of their population educated to upper secondary level. The situation remained the same in 1996 and is predicted to remain so until at least 2015 (CERI, 1997). The net entry rate for university-level education was 41 per cent in the UK, the fourth highest of 18 countries in the study (CERI, 1998). In 1996, the UK had one of the largest number of 'expected' years of education, and the third highest ratio of university-level graduates to population, along with perhaps the most balanced figures for participation by gender at all levels of initial education (Eurostat, 1998).

Table 6.1 shows the segregation indices for all EU countries in terms of the results indicator (reading test score) from the PISA study described in Chapter 2. The figures in brackets show the proportionate difference between the score for each country and that for the EU as a whole. The UK is one of the least segregated school systems in terms of reading scores (the only outcome measure comparable across all PISA schools). Some conclusions can be drawn from these figures in relation to the characteristics of national school systems. The most segregated school systems in terms of student reading scores tend also to be the most selective, either by ability (e.g. Netherlands) or family religion (e.g. Belgium). The least segregated tend to have little selection (e.g. Denmark), or systems of choice without much diversity of schooling (e.g. Ireland, and the UK at time of writing). For more on this, see Smith and Gorard (2002) or visit www.cf.ac.uk/socsi/equity.

Table 6.1 Segregation index (S) for lowest 10 per cent on reading score

Country	Reading score
All EU	49
Austria	62 (+0.12)
Belgium	66 (+0.15)
Denmark	39 (−0.11)
Finland	27 (−0.29)
France	56 (+0.07)
Germany	61 (+0.11)
Greece	58 (+0.08)
Ireland	39 (−0.11)
Italy	58 (+0.08)
Luxembourg	41 (−0.09)
Netherlands	66 (+0.15)
Portugal	48 (−0.01)
Spain	40 (−0.10)
Sweden	29 (−0.26)
UK	43 (−0.07)

National figures

In so far as it is possible to ascertain, school examination results have risen since 1989 in absolute terms (Figure 6.1). All such indicators have risen since the introduction of ERA88 (which also created a system of national testing in four key stages from ages 7 to 16, based on a common curriculum). The percentage obtaining five good GCSE passes has increased from 22.6 in 1975 to 46.4 per cent in 1998 (DfEE, 1998c). The same source also shows larger increases from the late 1980s, after the introduction of school choice. However, as we explain in Chapter 5, so many changes were taking place in education and assessment at this time that the increased growth in exam scores cannot be attributed to market forces without using a comparison group.

Our comparison group is the independent or fee-paying sector. It is clear that state-funded schools have been catching up with fee-paying schools at all levels of attainment, and other accounts confirm this trend (Howson, 2000). In England, maintained secondary schools have been slowly catching up with independent schools in terms of good GCSE passes since 1995 (Figure 6.2), and have now overtaken independent schools in terms of the lowest level of GCSE qualification (Figure 6.3).

In Wales, maintained schools have closed the gap with independent schools since 1992 at the lowest level of GCSE, at the 5+ good GCSE benchmark, and at A level (Table 6.2). This can be seen by considering the achievement gaps, as described in Chapter 5. For example, 70 per cent of students at independent schools gained five good GCSEs in 1992 compared to 34 per cent in maintained schools. This gap is 35 per cent (or 36/104). By 1997 the gap has dropped to 32 per cent (or 40/126).

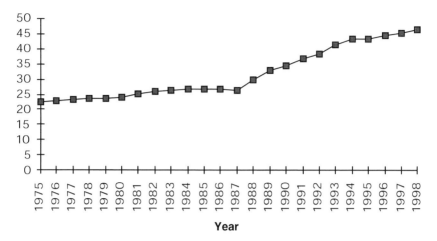

Figure 6.1 Percentage attaining 5+ GCSE A*–C equivalent.

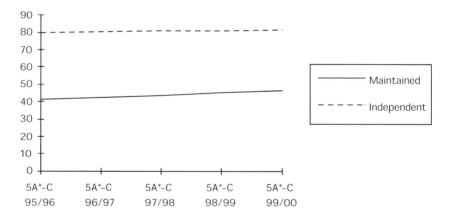

Figure 6.2 Percentage attaining 5+ GCSE A*–C equivalent in maintained and independent schools, England 1995/1996 to 1999/2000.

Of course, it may be argued that the 'degrees of freedom' for independent schools are fewer than maintained schools even in 1992. Their results are already nearer the 100 per cent limit and, therefore, have less room to improve. But this argument could not be made about the starting points for Figure 6.3 for example. Both sectors start at roughly the same point. We seem, therefore, to have evidence of a specific improvement in

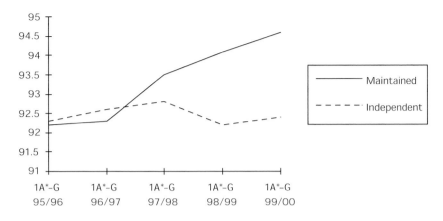

Figure 6.3 Percentage attaining 1+ GCSE A*–G in maintained and independent schools, England 1995/1996 to 1999/2000.

Table 6.2 Comparison of results by sector in Wales

| | % 1 GCSE A*–G | | % 5 GCSE A*–C | | A level points | |
	Maintained	Independent	Maintained	Independent	Maintained	Independent
1992	76	86	34	70	13.4	17.3
1993	77	86	36	73	13.6	17.7
1994	80	87	39	75	14.5	20.0
1995	80	90	40	80	14.9	19.2
1996	80	91	41	79	15.5	19.3
1997	81	89	43	83	16.0	19.9

the maintained sector from 1992/1993 onwards (the last year in which the standard entry cohort for GCSE had been recruited prior to the ERA88).

In this we are in agreement with some other analysts. The QCA (2001), in their 5-year review of standards, suggest no support for the view that recent increases in exams are linked to any drop in standards (i.e. the improvement is, at least, partly genuine). Similarly, an analysis of successive GCSE cohorts from 1994 to 1996 found a significant improvement in their performance over time (Schagen and Morrison, 1998). But such evidence can do little more than suggest that this is an impact of market forces, for there are so many other confounding changes over the same time. Bradley and Taylor (2002) suggest that good schools (in terms of examination scores) have taken a larger share of school numbers over time, which, they say, shows that there is a genuine market in schooling. Their econometric analysis suggests that exam scores have risen as schools try to outdo the scores of their neighbouring schools from last year. However, there are some technical difficulties with this analysis. Bradley and Taylor (2002) use the number of students with five good GCSE passes per teacher as their dependent variable. This may be unfair to rural and small schools who tend to have necessarily higher teacher: student ratios. They also divide their sample of schools into tiers by their year 2000 level of FSMs, but they compare GCSE scores for 1992 with those of 2000. Because socio-economic composition of schools is so important, and they do not use the FSM scores for 1992, any change in apparent performance over time could be FSM-related and zero-sum in nature.

School figures

Despite these improvements in examination scores, the strength of the statistical link between the socio-economic background of students and examination results has not weakened since 1989, and the scale of the difference between the top and bottom performing students remains very large (dwarfing the more commonly cited difference between boys and girls for example). The R^2 values from the regression analysis described in Chapter 5 remained at very close to 90 per cent for all years, with no indication at all of an improvement (reduction) over time. In each year the key predictor of school outcomes, using a forward stepwise approach, was the local level of poverty for each school. Therefore, whatever the improvements in raw scores over time, it is clear that these have not broken the well-established link between student background and school outcomes (Gorard and Taylor, 2002b). In apparent confirmation of this, a study at the Centre for Longitudinal Studies in London has reported that children from particularly poor families are just as likely to leave school with no qualifications as they were 20 years ago (Hackett 2000). Similar conclusions, but for different reasons and using different methods, have also been drawn in France (Duru-Bellat and Kieffer, 2000).

Around 90 per cent of the variation in school outcomes can therefore be explained by student background characteristics and the nature of their school (or else by prior attainment figures), and this figure is relatively constant over time. Given that these models also include an error component, there is little variance (from 100 per cent) left to attribute to a school, or even a school system, effect. The possibility of discovering any improvement in this relatively small school effect over time would seem difficult enough. To identify a part of this improvement that is a direct result of market forces would appear nearly impossible. In this we agree with the conclusion of Plewis (1999) that the most effective way to tackle inequality in education is by addressing poverty itself. The variation between school outcomes is very small (much smaller than within schools), so that strategies like the market which are aimed at schools (or even larger units), rather than individuals, are likely to be ineffective. 'Over the past 25 years . . . studies show that individual and family background traits explain the vast majority of the variance in student test scores, and observable school characteristics, such as per-student spending, teacher experience, or teacher degree level, have at best a weak relationship with student outcomes' (Goldhaber *et al.*, 1999: 199).

Student-level analysis

The overall growth in indicators of attainment (see above) has had the side effect of reducing differential attainment in terms of social groups, such as those defined by poverty and ethnicity. We have dealt with this decline in more detail elsewhere (e.g. Gorard *et al.*, 2001b). Using valid pro-portionate analyses, differences in attainment have declined as measured between: ethnic groups, boys and girls, economic regions, and school sectors (Gorard, 2000a). Despite the continued importance of socio-economic, as opposed to educational, determinants of school outcomes, the system as a whole is therefore becoming more equitable in the distribution of qualifications.

However, there is a possibility that student outcomes became more polarised within institutions even though the schools themselves became more mixed. Perhaps the introduction of targets and public performance indicators has created a situation where increasing polarisation is taking place within schools, but is not discernible between them. For example, schools may be encouraged to concentrate their resources on those students on the 'cusp' between GCSE grade C and D (or between G and fail). The long-term impact might be to improve the results of relatively high 'ability' students at the expense of relatively low achievers, produc-ing 'winners' and 'losers' in each school.

DfES figures for the GCSE points score of each twentieth part of the age cohort give no support to this idea at all. Although the variation between the absolute GCSE point scores for each twentieth of the popula-tion is large, and indicative of a highly polarised examination system, this in itself is no surprise. In a sense the examination system is based on discriminating between the performance of individuals. The key finding for present purposes is that over time the differential attainment of the highest and lowest scoring groups is decreasing. This is true for all students, and for each school type, for both boys and girls, and at all levels of aggregation.

Tables 6.3 and 6.4 show differences in GCSE point scores for the top and bottom 25 and 50 per cent of students, respectively. They show a remarkably consistent pattern. The gaps in attainment between the top and bottom groups, whether quarters or halves of the school population, are closing at about the same rate. The improvement in the lowest attaining group is markedly greater than for the highest. While these findings may come as no surprise to those who have read our findings so far, it is worth recalling here that we are talking about points per student, and that the figures can be used to decide whether the attainment of students within schools is becoming increasingly polarised. It is not. In this, our analysis agrees with that of earlier cohorts from 1900–1919 to 1960–1969 by Heath (2000), where differences in O-level attainment by class, gender and ethnicity were all seen to have declined. We have no reason to suppose that what we are picking up here is the result of market forces. It could be a longer term trend. The point, rather, is that market forces have not interrupted or reversed this trend towards equity. Our findings therefore disagree with those of West and Pennell (2000), among others, who used similar figures from 1992/1993 to 1996/1997, but made the mistake of only examining simple differences between percentage points (see Chapter 5).

Conclusion

The thrust of the last two chapters has been to suggest that a consideration of the standards or effectiveness of a school system is not a simple matter of counting and comparison. Even where simplifying assumptions are made about the outcomes from schools, such as a concentration on statutory assessment and test results, philosophical and methodological difficulties persist. In fact, it is sometimes difficult to discover what difference schools actually make to attainment even in these very restrictive terms.

Table 6.3 Changes in gap between top and bottom 20 per cent by GCSE points

	1993	1994	1995	1997	1998	1999	2000	Growth
Lower 20%	5.0	5.3	5.7	6.0	6.7	7.6	8.2	160%
Top 20%	59.0	61.0	62.3	62.8	64.3	65.3	66.1	112%
Gap	84%	84%	83%	83%	81%	79%	78%	

Table 6.4 Changes in gap between top and bottom 50 per cent by GCSE points

	1993	1994	1995	1997	1998	1999	2000	Growth
Lower 50%	17.0	18.3	18.8	19.2	20.3	21.4	22.1	130%
Top 50%	49.3	51.4	52.1	52.6	53.8	54.9	55.6	113%
Gap	49%	47%	47%	46%	45%	44%	43%	

As schools became more similar in composition in the early 1990s, their overall results converged, and the results within schools continue to converge (apparently as part of a longer term trend). An argument can also be constructed that the increase in public examination scores post-1988 in the maintained sector relative to independent schools means that market forces have been effective in driving up standards. However, the limits on improvement imposed by the 100 per cent limit for any indicator and the complex nature of policy changes post-1988 mean that this argument must be tentative. In any case, there is no evidence that this improvement (if that is what it is) has reduced the link between socio-economic background and school attainment. The relative composition of schools continues to play a key role in understanding the nature of the school system in England and Wales. The next chapter, therefore, returns to a consideration of the nature of this segregation between schools, and its relationship to geography.

Part IV

Explanation and case studies

Chapter 7

The role of geography

Introduction

This chapter looks in more detail at the geographical variation in between-school segregation within England and Wales, as described in Chapter 4. For children from families in poverty, England and Wales has a socially divided secondary education system. These divisions are lowest in urban areas with good transport, low residential segregation, and mostly LEA-controlled comprehensives (and banding). Divisions are highest in mixed rural/urban authorities with poor public transport, high residential segregation, and a large number of schools that are their own admission authorities (and selection by ability). The first type tended to decrease segregation further after the Education Reform Act 1988, while the second tended to remain static or increase in segregation. The key variables of population density, residential segregation, poverty, ethnic diversity, school diversity, school selection and admissions arrangements, all help to explain the variation between levels of segregation across LEAs. Our regression models are able to explain both levels of and changes in segregation in all LEAs with around 100 per cent accuracy. The levels of segregation between schools for three key years (1989, 1995 and 2000) were all explicable from the available contextual characteristics in the 149 LEAs in England ($R^2=1.00$). We describe this model in the next three chapters with the help of our in-depth data based on interviews, observation and documentary analysis. Of the indicators in the model, clearly the most important, as judged by the proportion of variance in segregation that they explain, are those relating to local geography. They are discussed here in terms of three overall themes: the most appropriate level of aggregation at which to conduct our analysis, the nature of the population in each LEA, and the role of housing.

Modifiable areal unit problem

Our findings are consistent at all levels of aggregation from school to national, yet the possibility has been raised that the indicators we have used are not sensitive enough to distinguish the increased segregation that must surely have taken place between schools after 1989 at some level. Having been surprised that schools became less segregated by poverty, class, ethnicity, first language and special need, some commentators have posited a set of differences that lie beneath the surface of these grosser indicators (e.g. Lauder, 1999). Elmore and Fuller (1996), like Willms and Echols (1992) before them, presented evidence that choosers (those who do not accept allocation to their nearest school) differ systematically from nonchoosers. A common observation is that single-mothers from poor families in voucher schemes in the US, or the (defunct) Assisted Places scheme in Britain, were more frequently better educated than mothers in equivalently poor families not using the schemes. A potential explanation is that they are part of a growing 'artificially poor' (Edwards *et al.*, 1989) who have become single through death or divorce. Of course, even if this were true, and it may well be, this does not lead to segregation unless it is a more stratifying process than that of allocation to residence. In support of their notion of segregation by stealth, both Elmore and Fuller (1996) and Witte (1998) cite Wells (1995). This claim has had a large impact and has propagated through the research literature as a social science fact. However, the conclusions of the Wells paper, the only primary published evidence, are not warranted by the patterns in the 24 cases involved (Gorard, 2000c). Nevertheless, there remains a problem to be faced (Taylor *et al.*, 2003). Does the precise definition of the area of analysis affect the results? In practical terms, should we use economic and administrative borders or would it make a difference if we used natural 'markets' or 'approximate areas of competition' for each school instead?

The spatial unit of enquiry is a key aspect of all research. This could be the household, a school, a village, a city, a local education authority, or the whole of the UK or beyond. Any empirical analysis uses data aggregated to such geographical zones, often based on an arbitrary decision. For example, the UK census collects individual household level data and then aggregates up to a variety of larger zones, such as the enumeration district, ward or local authority. However, these zones, determined primarily for ease of enumeration, may bear little resemblance to the real social geography of the people they contain. This anomaly could be crucial if the analysis of such data in different zones, or levels, alters the resulting pattern of aggregated observations. This is known as the Modifiable Areal Unit Problem (MAUP) and its possibility has long been recognised and debated by geographers (Openshaw, 1984; Tobler, 1991; Wrigley, 1995). Two components of this affect the interpretation of data: a scale problem and a zoning problem. The scale problem relates to the variation in results due to the progressive aggregation of smaller zones into larger zones, whereas the zoning problem describes the variation in results due to different arrangements of a fixed set of zones, whilst keeping the scale fixed (Kitchen and Tate, 2000).

The modifiable areal unit problem is also a potentially important factor in territorial justice – 'the just distribution of resources among political or administrative units in accord with some normative criteria' (Pinch, 1985: 41). The relationship between the allocation of resources and their corresponding spatial access underpins many key public services, such as schools, local authority services, public transport, GP practices, and National Health services. The modifiable areal unit problem could also be critical for measures of segregation. For example, Wong (1997) argued that a segregation measure, in this case the dissimilarity index, was sensitive to scale because of the relationship between the physical clustering of particular population groups and the zoning pattern of enumeration districts used in the measure. The results of measuring segregation could, therefore, change as a result of using different levels of analysis (Wong, 1999).

Clearly, as with all measures of segregation, the level of analysis is an important component of the segregation index and the segregation ratio (SR) – the chief indices used in this book. Both measures use some form of geographical zone in the calculation of segregation. We have already explained that this is unproblematic for the segregation index as it is, by definition, an area summary – the choice of area will be consistently appropriate at whatever respective spatial scale this summary calculation represents (see Chapter 3). But, in the case of SR, changing the basis of the 'fair share' could affect the results. A straightforward example of this would be in the use of an England-derived SR in comparing the levels of segregation between two schools, one located in a northern de-industrialised city and the other located in a relatively affluent suburb in the south east. This comparison might be considered inappropriate because the overall level of poverty in these two areas is significantly different to start with. In the context of the modifiable areal unit problem this would constitute a scale problem; the use of England as the aggregate basis from which to calculate the 'fair share' might ignore significant regional variations such as the north–south divide.

A potential solution to this could be to use the schools' respective economic standard regions as the basis for calculating the 'fair share'. Consequently the resulting segregation ratios would indicate any trends in segregation in relation to the overall proportion of disadvantaged children in that standard region. Again, it could be argued that using economic standard regions will hide disparities in the distribution of poverty within such regions, and, therefore, underestimate the levels of socio-economic polarisation in schools. As before, reducing the scale of the geographical zone to the LEA might appear to overcome this problem. If one were to accept this criticism of the segregation ratio then this line of argument would eventually lead us to ask at what scale the impact of overall intraregional variations in poverty on trends in school segregation would be minimised.

The answer to this question may depend on the nature of the research being conducted. One could argue that when measuring changes in the level of disadvantaged children in a school the 'fair share' should reflect the overall level of disadvantaged children in schools that are competing with each other. This argument appears to make a great deal of sense, particularly if we are interested in the effects of the market on the social mix of school intakes. Since any impact of market forces on changes in the composition of a school concerns the movement of children between schools, then the relative composition of a school should only be measured against the schools that it gains from or loses to. If this argument is accepted then the use of a defined 'competition space' would appear to be the most appropriate geographical zone to use in the calculation of the segregation ratio. This seems to provide a neat solution as the scale of the chosen geographical zone would simply reflect the spatial extent of competition. Therefore, calculating the segregation ratio of an urban school would probably require more schools to be incorporated into the calculation of the 'fair share' than in the case of rural schools.

Let us assume, for the present, that the segregation ratio should be calculated at the level of competition between schools. In other words, the segregation ratio of a particular school is measured against the overall proportion of disadvantaged students in only the schools it gains from and loses students to. To do this requires us to identify the schools that each and every school competes against. This is a complex task since each school's competition space can be very different, even if the schools are located in the same LEA. Figure 7.1 shows the locations of every student admitted to three schools in the same LEA in one year. These real examples illustrate the different spatial extent of school intakes, for these three schools compete with a different set of other schools. School A has a very localised intake on the edge of the LEA boundary, indicating that this school competes chiefly with nearby schools from the same LEA. School B is dramatically different in that its intake comes from across the entire LEA, suggesting that it competes to some extent with all of the schools in the LEA. This contrasts with school C whose intake extends across the LEA boundary into two other LEAs, while only competing with some of the schools from its own LEA. These three examples clearly illustrate the differences in competition spaces even though they are all from the same LEA.

To help identify competition spaces, schools themselves can state what they believe are the other schools they compete with, but competition between schools is often not spatially confined. An individual school may be able to define all of the schools it competes with, but it has been

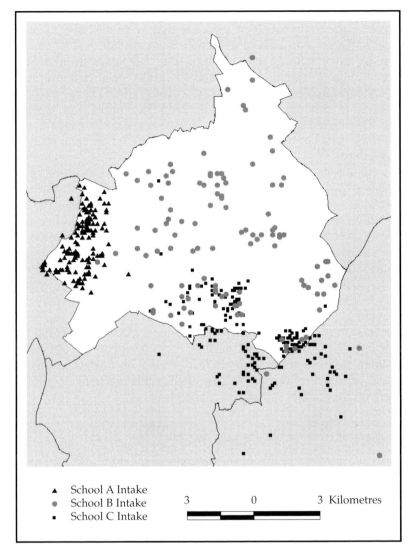

Figure 7.1 Students' home locations in three secondary schools.

shown that some of these competitor schools themselves compete with a different set of schools (Taylor, 2002). This 'linked' competition is illustrated in Figure 7.2. In school A's case it only competes with school B. Therefore, using school A's competition space in order to calculate its segregation ratio would only be based on changes in the composition of these two schools. However, changes in the composition of school B are also affected by exchange of students with school C. Consequently, even though there is no direct competition between school A and school C, changes in the composition of school C may have an impact upon the level of segregation for school A. In such cases it might make more sense to use all three schools in calculating the 'fair share' from which to measure the segregation of each school's intake, even though school A does not consider itself in competition with school C. However, consider the effects of this argument if many school's competition spaces are linked, in a causal chain, to other competition spaces. It might therefore make more sense to use all of the schools from a larger area, such as an LEA anyway.

A second methodological problem in defining the competition space of a school is that it is liable to change. Therefore, when calculating the segregation ratio over time it may be inaccurate to use the same competition space in 1999 as for 1989. Some catchment areas overlap, as in the case of foundation, VA and community schools. In some rural areas, as observed by one LEA officer, 'certain areas where they might live are in the traditional catchment area of the school, but where they live is actually closer to another school'. This shows that concerns over the level of analysis in the calculation of the segregation ratio may not be warranted in practice. It would be a pretence to suggest that we, or other commentators, can truly identify discrete local markets. Potential critics of our approach so far would need to be much clearer about whether they wish to argue simply about the number of schools in any areal analysis, or whether they are talking about actual exchange of students. The importance of this is demonstrated below.

The effects of scale on the segregation ratio

We use two case studies from our larger analysis to illustrate how their respective segregation ratio calculations are affected by using different levels of analysis. The first example is of a boys' Roman Catholic school in a western outer London borough. Figure 7.3 illustrates the segregation ratios over time of this school using four levels of analysis: England, outer London, the LEA and a hypothetical competition space. The first

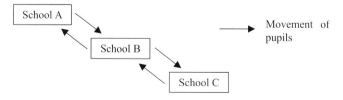

Figure 7.2 'Linked' competition.

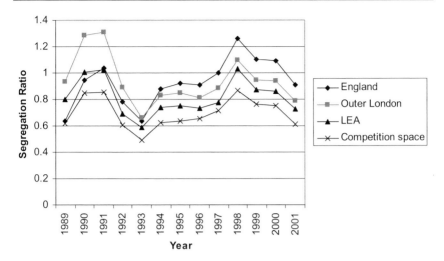

Figure 7.3 SR trends for a boys' Roman Catholic school.

three are easily defined geographic zones. As the headteacher himself pointed out, the boys attending this school came from across six neighbouring London boroughs. Defining the competition space of this school is therefore problematic. It could be argued that the school is actually only in competition with other Roman Catholic schools in these six LEAs, or maybe only just boys' RC schools in this part of London. However, as the headteacher pointed out, the boys who do not get a place in this school can go in three different directions. They may go to alternative local (based on the students' home location) community schools, to other denominational schools, or to one of a number of fee-paying schools. Accurately identifying the competition space of this school is not straightforward. The segregation ratios illustrated in Figure 7.3 under the 'competition space' label are based on the proportion of FSM students in all schools from across the six identified LEAs.

In 2000 this school had a proportion of FSM students in its intake slightly above average compared to the rest of England (i.e. the segregation ratio 'England' is above 1.00), yet when measured at the other three levels of analysis it has slightly below its 'fair share' of FSM students. Even though it might appear that this offers two different conclusions they are both valid. As discussed earlier if we wanted to know how this school compared against all schools in England then the England SR would tell us. If we wanted to see how the intake of this school had changed while allowing for, say, changes in the north–south divide then the other three calculations would be more useful. The point to note is that the ratios at all levels tell the same story about trends over time.

The next example is of a mixed community school located in the very centre of a western outer London borough. Figure 7.4 shows the segregation ratios for this school based on six levels of analysis: England, outer London, the LEA and three distance-based competition spaces. The head teacher of this school found it difficult to identify a competition space. This was because for several years during the 1990s the school was undersubscribed and, therefore, took any students from right across the LEA who did not get into any of the other community schools. By the end of the period this school could fill its places with first choice applicants, hence the spatial extent of its intake differed to that at the beginning of the 1990s. Because of this, and largely for comparison more than anything else, the three competition space segregation ratios illustrated in Figure 7.4 are determined by using the overall proportion of FSM students in schools at incremental distances from this school. In other words competition space 1 uses the nearest 12 schools to this school, competition space 2 uses the nearest eight schools and competition space 3 uses the nearest two schools.

Again, the point to note is that the SR trends over time are similar for all levels. By 2001 this school took more than its 'fair share' of FSM students and more than it did in 1989, whichever level of analysis was used in the calculation. As with the previous example the change over time was greater for the England SR than the other calculations. This example differs from the previous case as the intake of this school moved away from its 'fair share'. But these two examples illustrate that even under very different circumstances the segregation ratios at all levels of analysis point to the same conclusions.

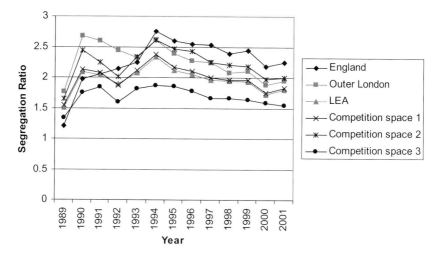

Figure 7.4 SR trends for a mixed community school, west London.

The use of different levels of analysis focuses attention on different levels of the segregation pattern, but without affecting trends over time. Theoretical considerations suggest that the most appropriate level of analysis would be at a scale where there is actual movement of students between schools. However, defining such competition spaces, both theoretically and practically, is highly complex and perhaps impossible. The inaccuracy in defining such a zone in reality surely outweighs the accuracy perceived in theory. There may be some examples where an easily identifiable competition space can be used. But in many more the complexity of competition between schools and the changes over time would actually suggest that a small unit of analysis produces less accurate results. There is often an easy assumption that the smallest scale of analysis should be employed. Nevertheless, it must be remembered that calculations at any scale produce equally valid conclusions for that scale. If we wanted to know to what extent schools were segregating against one another, while incorporating regional demographic change, then it would be perfectly valid to calculate the scores at a national level.

In the great majority of LEAs, for the great majority of families, the LEA is the arena of choice. LEAs as a unit of analysis are linked by relatively similar admissions procedures (see Chapter 9). The number of cross-border applicants is greatest in London and the south east, but these patterns cannot be projected on to the rest of the LEAs in England and Wales. In our southeast England case study, 50 per cent of applicants are from out of county for some schools. Some schools have very low numbers of local LEA children in the intake – 9 per cent in one school in Hammersmith and Fulham – and no doubt there are other spectacular examples. According to our interviewees however, these patterns are long-standing, pre-dating the 1988 legislation relevant to parental choice.

Local population differences

In 1989, there was already a high level of segregation in the schools of England and Wales. There was also significant variation in the levels of segregation between LEAs, and this variation largely continues to 2001. Attempting to understand why such variations existed, even before open enrolment, highlights the other factors that determine divisions between schools. Repeating this exercise for levels of segregation in later years then shows how the impact of these factors has changed, and if further explanations for the levels of segregation need to be pursued.

Population density

The considerable variation in levels of segregation between LEAs and in changes over time are described in Chapter 4. Not all local education authorities (LEAs) experienced any desegregation, and a few have even experienced increased segregation throughout. In general, Wales has less segregation than England, and urban areas have less segregation than rural ones (Gorard, 1998c). The scale of these geographical variations is not always clear to commentators and policy-makers based in London. In urban areas there is generally less physical space between middle-class and working-class residential areas. Since families living in urban areas, particularly in London, are characterised by their 'cheek-by-jowl' existence, there is a greater likelihood that they will attend similar state schools (especially where proximity criteria are used in allocating places). This would contrast quite significantly with the physical divide in county shires. There is greater school choice for parents, with fewer problems of access to a greater number of schools, in cities than in remote rural areas of England. Therefore, urban parents from all socio-economic backgrounds have access to an alternative school other than their nearest. This helps ensure that school intakes are more socially mixed.

One LEA officer remarked:

> [Urban areas stand out] because of the comparative ease of getting to an alternative 'cause our transport policy only allows for transport in a majority of cases if you're going to your catchment school. . . . So in rural areas unless you've got transport it's more difficult to move.

In rural LEAs it is more common for families simply to use their nearest, and only viable, school. Some rural LEAs only have a part-time school admissions officer, who can tidy up the few cases to be decided in an afternoon, and many would probably agree with one who said: 'We haven't really got a problem with admissions'. Several said that they had never had an appeal (against placement) and hoped never to have one. Even where things are more complicated: 'It's always a major headache at transfer time fitting all the children in . . . but come September it goes away somehow.'

What was clear from our rural respondents was that the whole issue of choice in the 1988 Act and the subsequent School Standards and Framework Act was not intended for them. It was seen as a London-based solution to a perceived London problem. One LEA officer commented: 'It does seem a lot of it is aimed at solving problems in London that don't exist in other parts of Britain.'

Rural LEAs have always co-operated in the admissions process. Now, because of the need for admissions forums, this officer has to formally but pointlessly consult with 13 authorities about their admissions, and all of them simply say 'no comment, no comment, no comment'. 'Just because there is a problem with four London boroughs with different types of schools . . . why impose nationally a system to deal with that and it has been a total and utter waste of money?'

Poverty

Another indicator of relevance to patterns of segregation is the actual level of local poverty and unemployment. As would be expected, areas with more similarity among inhabitants (where there are no 'rich' or 'poor' for example) have less segregation by schools. When these geographical factors change, through the provision of new housing estates or the closure of local industry, the levels of segregation in local schools are affected. Chapter 4 outlined how changes in the levels of poverty impacts upon schools. Two related factors that are important in the resulting regression models are the overall levels of poverty (i.e. the absolute proportion of children eligible for free school meals) and the levels of unemployment in each LEA. The greater the levels of poverty the less socio-economic segregation between schools there tends to be. Note that this is an empirical finding, not a compositional effect which might occur with other indices, but which would anyway work in the opposite direction – e.g. higher levels of poverty lead to higher levels of segregation using the dissimilarity index. Instead, this finding is related to the point made above regarding the geography of residential areas. In essence, areas with a sizeable proportion of residents living in poverty are more likely to be evenly distributed than in areas where only a small proportion of the population are living in poverty. As overall levels of poverty rise the population in poverty are likely to be more evenly distributed. Conversely, as overall levels of poverty fall the population 'left' in poverty are likely to be more concentrated in space, at least in the short term.

There is extreme bifurcation of income in some LEAs. One admissions officer in inner London said: 'Well, the key socio-economic issue for this borough is that you have extreme levels of poverty and wealth. There is no normal ground.' So this LEA loses a large proportion of its population to fee-paying schools, and another 44 per cent leave the borough to attend faith-based and foundation schools elsewhere. Thus, the LEA has a very large proportion of FSM in its schools, and very little LEA-level segregation – equality of poverty. The head of an inner-London school pointed out: 'You have got everything from one million pound houses to refugee accommodation in the hotels, to council property to charity property all within yards'.

Where the population is not bifurcated, segregation can still be lower because of the uniformity of the population. For example, the head of a community school in Swansea pointed out that locally: 'Fifty per cent of households have no income other than state benefits . . . and the number of people with university degrees is zero'. And, in this LEA, where schools drop substantially below their PAN they are merged, and this process mixes the intakes up again.

However, where the population is varied then the segregated role of residence can be crucial, either if catchment areas are enforced through the use of distance criteria (see Chapter 9), or because of travel difficulties in rural areas. One rural LEA contains both Cheltenham with its large companies and technology-based industry, and the Forest of Dean with one of the lowest economic activity rates in England. It has shown little change in labour market or unemployment figures since 1988. Therefore the role of residence is crucial in keeping levels of segregation relatively high (see below).

Another factor related to levels of socio-economic segregation in schools is the degree of ethnic diversity in each LEA. Figures for the ethnic composition of children attending schools and the proportion for whom English is an additional language show that LEAs with greater diversity of residents have lower levels of socio-economic segregation. Although this is clearly related to the overall levels of poverty and the population density, as discussed above, it still accounts for some of the further variation in segregation. The head of an unpopular inner-London LEA school reported that its FSM figures dropped from 50 per cent overall to 37 per cent some years ago, but have now risen again to 50 per cent, but:

> It's not just the FSM, it's the gender and the culture as well. If it was 60 per cent [FSM] white girls you would get very different levels to Muslim girls, would get very different levels with mixed genders, different if it was boys, 60 per cent white boys God help you. . . . Well there's two girls' schools . . . in this neck of the woods therefore I'm always going to have more boys.

An officer from a London LEA near Heathrow airport explains:

> We've had a huge influx of refugees over the last 5 or more years from Somalia, Kosovo, Albania, and also way back this was a huge area for new Commonwealth settlements. . . . We had a huge rising population in [LEA] and we are looking at having to build another school in the north.

Due to population changes this LEA has ended up with parts where there are plenty of nearby school places, but not enough residents to use them, and other areas where there are enough nearby residents but the local schools are seen as undesirable.

The role of residence

Schools and residential segregation

The largest single factor determining the level of segregation in schools is the pattern of local housing, since even in a system of choice most children attend a school near their home. As one of our rural LEA respondents puts it – whatever system of allocation is used: 'it has always been preferable to live closer rather than further, even before the 1988 Education Reform Act.' The irony of this, as one commentator notes, is that 'in Britain, the dominant view . . . is still that selection of students by ability . . . is an insidious route back to elitism . . ., yet selection by residence is acceptable even if it is leading to the concentration of privilege among better-off families living close to more-desired schools' (Hirsch, 1997: 163).

Apart from the fee-paying boarding sector, schools typically serve local areas (Gorard 1997b; Taylor 2002). Such areas vary in size. Fee-paying day schools, foundation schools, voluntary-aided church schools, specialist schools, and Ysgolion Cymraeg often take students from a larger 'catchment' than community schools – but access to day schools is ultimately controlled by distance from home. Consequently, schools tend to educate particular communities based around their location, and their intakes largely reflect the variety, nature and cost of local housing. This is most obvious where schools have formal catchment areas from which they draw students – a very typical situation in the UK between 1960 and 1988 (Dore and Flowerdew, 1981), and increasingly again since 1998. The same occurs in instances where schools are oversubscribed and 'distance' criteria are applied to allocate places. As a result the composition of intakes are and always have been, even from 1988 to 1997, highly related to the residential characteristics of their locale. There has been a pro-gressive rise in the use of schools further away from home since 1980 (Stillman, 1990), presumably partly as a result of choice policies. And, as was also indicated (but not reported) by the Smithfield study in New Zealand (Waslander and Thrupp, 1995), out-of-catchment schools are now more frequently used by children who live in 'struggling' rather than in 'prosperous' neighbourhoods (Parsons *et al.*, 2000).

The geography of residential development in the UK has a particular history which makes it distinct to that of other European countries or even the US. The urban landscape has grown and changed via a blend of public and private residential development, resulting in a mosaic of housing markets within towns and cities varying in terms of cost and the nature of tenure. Even within social housing there is a specifically British pattern of polarisation, so that the policies of public landlords have a noticeable effect on the nature of local schools (especially with regard to a small number of particularly disruptive children, Clark *et al.*, 1999). Urban growth over the last 150 years in the UK has coincided with major developments in the education system. State investment in both areas has also tended to lead to developments at similar times meaning that their histories over the period are intertwined. Therefore, differentiation in the urban geography of towns and cities is related to differentiation in the composition of school intakes (Wilson, 1959; Robson, 1969).

British cities represent a distinct ecological structure, largely as a result of the large public housing sector (Herbert and Thomas, 1990). They are typically characterised by distinct neighbourhoods, each with their own socio-spatial dialectic. This is largely a product of the relationship between housing submarkets and social class. As Dennis and Clout (1980) have argued, different social groups live in distinct areas of the city and variations between neighbourhoods cannot be ignored (Reynolds, 1986). Residential differentiation can influence more than variations in housing since, 'the social geography of the city is itself likely to generate or reinforce differences in values from one neighbourhood to another, for the socio-demographic composition of different neighbourhoods creates distinctive local reference groups which contribute significantly to people's attitudes to life' (Knox, 1995: 62). The role of schools and education in urban, and even rural, life plays its own part in generating and reinforcing these different values between neighbourhoods. Indeed, many schools have been part of creating neighbourhoods, as they provide significant points of community contact (Davies and Herbert, 1993). As Robson (1969) discovered in a study in Sunderland, parental attitudes towards education were strongly affected by the character of their residential neighbourhood. Wilson (1959: 845) has also stressed the link between residential differentiation and schooling, 'the *de facto* segregation brought about by concentration of social classes in cities results in schools with unequal moral climates which likewise affect the motivation of the child, not necessarily by inculcating a sense of inferiority, but rather by providing a different ethos in which to perceive values'.

The introduction of comprehensive schools after 1960 produced the most recent major increase in the number of schools. The growth of comprehensive schools is illustrated in Figure 7.5, which shows their impact on the education landscape during the 1960s. A survey by Benn and Simon (1970) suggests that by 1968, 27 per cent of comprehensive schools were purpose-built, but this varied across the country, such that in London 46 per cent of comprehensive schools were purpose-built.

As these new schools were being built the state was having to create large-scale public sector housing estates on the periphery of cities or the development of new towns in order to meet the growing demand for housing. This led to a two-fold pressure on school segregation. First, new comprehensive schools were needed most in New Towns and the large peripheral council estates. Second, as cities became larger it was more difficult for schools to draw students from other areas. As Benn and Simon (1970) reported, the most severe obstacle to the notion of the 'community school' was the inequality and class segregation of large urban areas, as this prevented a balanced community mix. The situation was not helped by the fact that during the first stages of comprehensive schooling new schools were discouraged in areas which already

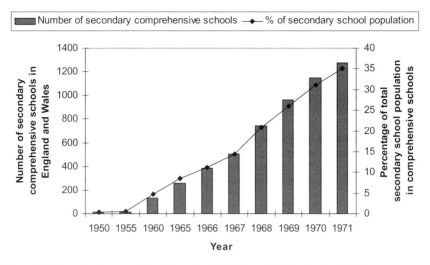

Figure 7.5 Growth of comprehensive schools 1950 to 1971, England and Wales.

contained grammar schools – the inner cities and wealthy suburbs (HMSO 1958). Even when, in the latter stages of this reorganisation of schooling, grammar schools were converted to comprehensive status many retained their grammar ethos and reputation. An obvious example of this was in the greater likelihood that ex-grammar schools would have sixth forms (Kerkchoff *et al.*, 1997).

This parallel development of residential areas and school reforms mean that segregation between schools has always existed (Taylor and Gorard, 2001). Benn and Chitty (1996) report that at the peak of the comprehensive process (1968 perhaps) 62 per cent of comprehensive schools mainly drew children from council housing estates or areas of mixed housing with a substandard element. By 1994 this had fallen back to 31 per cent of comprehensive schools. What this figure does not show is whether this is because comprehensive schools simply had more socially mixed intakes by 1994, or whether residential differentiation itself had fallen. Leech and Campos (2000) illustrated the impact that the relationship between residence and schools has had on the housing market, and in particular on house prices. They report that in Coventry there is an estimated price premium of 15 per cent to 19 per cent for neighbourhoods surrounding popular schools. This is more significant given that Coventry LEA operated a 'designated' area policy for over-subscribed schools, as recommended in the 1999 Code of Practice on School Admissions. In general, the rising cost of property in desirable catchment areas is leading to 'selection by postcode' and educational 'ghettoisation' (Association of Teachers and Lecturers, 2000).

Most cities feature residential segregation by class and ethnicity which affects residential access to public services. It is a key determinant of institutional segregation (Willms and Paterson, 1995). The structure of the housing market is such that there is differential access to housing for particular groups in society, further compounding the unequal access to 'better' schools (Tomlinson, 1997b). Given the serious inequities that already exist in the residential-based system, many parents choose new houses with local schools in mind, both in the UK and the US (Goldring and Hausman, 1999; Holme, 2002). One of our interviewed heads in London said: 'You often get it with divorced families where the parents are actually trying to make up their mind . . . who the child lives with on the basis of which one lives nearest the best school.'

If this catchment area link was weakened, even slightly, during the 1990s by a programme of school choice, then perhaps residential segregation has also declined over time by creating a circle of integrating forces? This is what Taeuber *et al.* (1981) describe as the 'Belfast' model. Using a proportionate index of dissimilarity equivalent to the segregation index used in our own work, Taeuber *et al.* found some evidence that residential segregation by ethnicity declined in Kentucky following the increasing integration of schools. Patterns of housing and of schooling can be mutually determining (e.g. the price of local houses affects school intakes, and the perceived desirability of schools can also affect the price of nearby houses). Some developments are attempting to overcome this using the 'Poundbury' mixed housing model. As the head of a foundation school in a new unitary authority explains: 'They are going to put 95 houses here . . . they have had to agree to a certain proportion of it being social housing or starter homes and not entirely five-bedroom luxury at £300,000 plus which is what most of the houses round here are.'

Preference for policies to produce mixed housing schemes providing enough affordable houses in each area are popular with those, such as Demos and IPPR, who wish to extend choice to the socially excluded (Sutcliffe, 2000). A similar phenomenon was hypothesised by Goldhaber (2000) who suggested that, paradoxically, by increasing choice in urban areas one can actually reduce white flight (residential segregation) as parents no longer need to move away from city centres in order to use suburban schools. It is certainly the case for a variety of reasons (the nature of travel etc.) that geographical location is the key to understanding the impact of choice on the school system (Herbert, 2000).

Residential differentiation and school segregation (inter-LEA)

Actually, the direct relationship between levels of residential differentiation (unemployment) and school segregation (FSM) is modest (using the imperfect measures described in Chapter 3). Figure 7.6 illustrates the two measures for each LEA. There are some LEAs which either have high residential differentiation but low school segregation, or low residential differentiation but high school segregation. At the two extremes are Buckinghamshire and Knowsley LEAs. In Buckinghamshire the distribution of unemployed adults by enumeration district produced a segregation index score of 0.22. Based on the line of best fit for Figure 7.6 the segregation index score for FSM in schools should be around 0.23. However, the levels of school segregation are much higher, producing a score of 0.47. Knowsley, on the other hand, has greater residential differentiation than Buckinghamshire (segregation index=0.28), which in turn would suggest that school segregation would be greater than that in Buckinghamshire (estimated segregation index=0.30). However, the actual level of school segregation was significantly lower (segregation index=0.08).

The overall levels of segregation between schools contrast quite markedly between the two LEAs. For example, some of the schools in Buckinghamshire have six times more students eligible for free school meals than the LEA average. One feature that distinguishes them is the greater number of grammar schools in Buckinghamshire. Since places in grammar schools are allocated on students' academic abilities, and research has consistently shown that grammar schools tend to over-represent children from middle-class families, it is perhaps not surprising

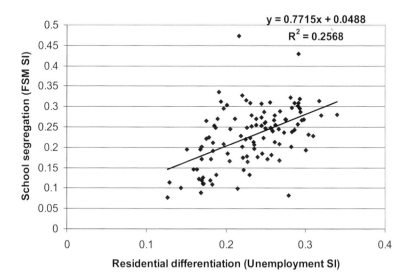

Figure 7.6 Scatterplot of LEA measures of school segregation and residential differentiation.

that segregation is much higher in Buckinghamshire than in Knowsley despite their respective levels of residential differentiation. This is confirmed by the finding that taking into account the effects of residential segregation and the presence of grammar schools leads to a greatly improved prediction of socio-economic segregation between schools (compared with Figure 7.6). The model is further enhanced when it accounts for urban-rural differences between LEAs ($R=0.71$). The addition of this variable allows us to focus more clearly on the relationship between school segregation and residential differentiation in urban areas, where it has been shown that there is greater movement of students between schools (Taylor, 2002). In this way, a substantial proportion of the variance in school segregation can be accounted for by local levels of residential differentiation in each LEA.

School locations and their intakes (intra-LEA)

Figure 7.7 shows the correlation for each LEA between the proportion of schools intakes who were eligible for free school meals in 1993 and the levels of residential deprivation in the respective locale of each school (as measured by the Townsend index of deprivation). The method used here to determine the levels of residential poverty for a school locale is to use the indices of poverty for the ward that the school was located in. For the whole sample of schools there is a strong correlation between Townsend's index of deprivation for their respective ward and the proportion of each school's intake eligible for free school meals ($R=0.70$).

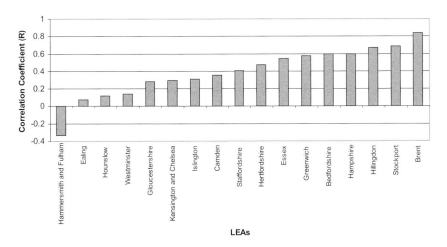

Figure 7.7 Relationship between school segregation and levels of deprivation of school locale, for a sub-sample of LEAs.

There can, however, be varying degrees of correlation between school segregation and levels of deprivation for the respective school locales. This is best illustrated in Figures 7.8 and 7.9. These maps show the Townsend index of deprivation by enumeration district and the levels of school segregation (1993 segregation ratio) for two LEAs: Brent, and Hammersmith and Fulham. In Brent there was a strong correlation between school composition and locale, but in Hammersmith and Fulham there was a small negative relationship between the two. In Brent, the northwest to southeast residential change in deprivation mirrors the levels of segregation in schools (in the figure, the larger school circles are in the heavily shaded residential areas). The schools in the north of the borough have very low proportions of students eligible for FSM, whereas those in the south clearly have very high proportions of students eligible for FSM. The example of Brent contrasts quite markedly with Hammersmith and Fulham, where, once again, there is a north–south residential poverty divide. However, in this instance the levels of school segregation are more evenly spread across the LEA

The differences between these LEAs point to further potential explanations for school segregation. First, over a quarter of students in

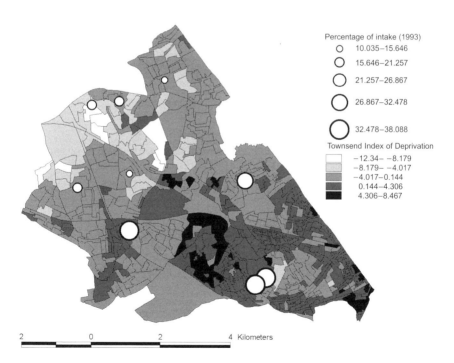

Figure 7.8 Proportion of school intakes eligible for free school meals and residential poverty, Brent LEA.

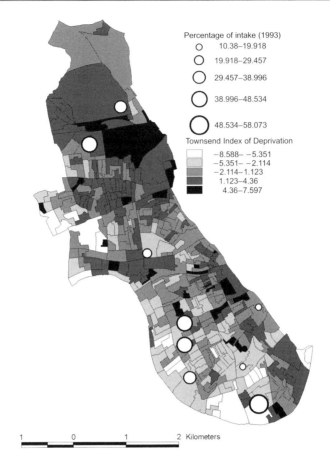

Figure 7.9 Proportion of school intakes eligible for free school meals and residential poverty, Hammersmith and Fulham LEA.

Hammersmith and Fulham attend fee-paying independent schools (28 per cent in 1997) compared to only 2.3 per cent in Brent for the same year. The match between the socio-economic characteristics of the residential base and the state-funded school population will therefore differ in each area. Second, LEAs exhibiting lower correlations between school and residential characteristics tend to have proportionally more schools with a large number of surplus places in (over 25 per cent surplus). For example, in 1998 a quarter of secondary schools in Hammersmith and Fulham had 25 per cent or more surplus places. This contrasts quite markedly with only 8 per cent of schools with similar surplus places in Brent. Greater surplus capacity in schools gives parents greater opportunity to obtain a school place of their choice, thereby breaking the link between residence and school composition (see also Chapter 10). In Brent, nearly all the schools became grant maintained, giving them greater autonomy in their management. It has been argued, by others, that such schools were likely to find ways to select students indirectly so as to give themselves a market advantage in terms of school outcomes, and this has led to very little success in breaking the link between residence and school mix.

Of course, catchment areas could be amended to counter the problems created by residential segregation, most notably for unpopular schools, as observed by the head of one of these in a new unitary authority: 'But since they shifted some of the boundaries around . . . there were very few if any problems like that this year. The change to catchment areas that affected this current year group has actually smoothed things over slightly.'

However, it is generally very hard to change catchment boundaries because of public resistance and, ironically, the possibility of damage to the unpopular school (according to an LEA representative):

> We are often pushed to change the catchment area particularly by the school and we have found that can be very counter-productive because any changes . . . generate quite a high level of emotion, but what it usually ends up in is a lot of negative press for that school. So therefore you start off with doing something to support the school . . . and you actually just drag it through the dirt.

Historical catchment areas therefore generally remain as they were even though residential and economic changes make them inappropriate (and LEAs try to help unpopular schools with image building and extra funding instead). For example, an officer in a rural LEA said:

> Some of the housing development has happened within their catchment area which has meant people are getting into the school from there, so those traditionally over the years that might be expected to have got a place . . . are suddenly finding that there is no more room at the inn for them.

Another said: 'There's a . . . school in a village called [name] that has increased its numbers tremendously because the number of houses in the area has grown a heck of a lot over recent years.'

This helps explain why some catchment area LEAs move towards a more segregated local school system, and the situation is worsened when a rigid catchment system exists alongside schools with the ability to set their own geographical boundaries, as we show in the next chapter.

Conclusion

We are now moving some way towards understanding the impact, or perhaps lack of impact, of the introduction of open enrolment to the education system in England and Wales. In terms of children from families in poverty, England and Wales has a socially divided secondary education system. These divisions tend to be lowest in urban areas with good transport, and low residential segregation. Divisions are highest in mixed rural/urban authorities with poor public transport, or with high residential segregation. The first type has tended to decrease segregation still further since the Education Reform Act 1988, while the second has tended to remain static. Therefore, as we noted at the beginning of this chapter, it would be incredibly difficult to say with great accuracy that open enrolment in itself, giving parents the opportunity to choose the school for their child, actually increases or decreases segregation. Structural factors that exist, whether open enrolment was introduced or not, are dominant in determining the levels of segregation. Some of these structural factors are outside the education arena and controlled by changes to the national and local economy, the housing market and residential development. Within the education system there may be a number of other secondary factors that determine levels of segregation between schools. These include the type of schooling provided, and the process of allocating school places; which are the subject of the next two chapters.

Chapter 8

The impact of school organisation

Introduction

The previous chapter examined subnational (Wales–England), regional and local variations in levels of segregation and it demonstrated how local socio-economic conditions can be seen to regulate levels of socio-economic segregation between schools. In this chapter we move to the second set of factors in our model, relating to school organisation. By school organisation we mean the number and mix of different kinds of secondary schools that can be found in any administrative area, such as LEAs. The mix is defined by curriculum objectives, the student intakes, forms of governance and admissions policies. In the maintained sector post-1944, four kinds of schools made up the majority of secondary provision: selective grammar schools, secondary modern schools for the academically less able, church or voluntary schools and all-ability comprehensives, which gradually replaced the former selective and secondary modern schools.

A key feature of educational policy since 1980 has been the trend to grant schools more autonomy over their operations at the expense of LEA control and this policy has been embraced by both Conservative and Labour administrations. At the time of writing, this trend looks set to continue. The claim is that 'diversifying' the system via the introduction of new kinds of schools, and creating 'specialist' colleges, academies and schools will contribute to raising standards. Thus, city technology colleges, introduced in 1986, and grant-maintained (GM) schools established in 1988 were intended to diversify educational provision and provide parents with a choice of school outside the control of LEAs. Local secondary school systems in England may now include any or all of the following kinds of schools; LEA all-ability comprehensive schools or 'community' schools, selective grammar schools, 'voluntary' or faith-based schools, specialist schools, technology schools, 'foundation' (formerly grant-maintained) schools and fee-paying schools. In Wales there is less diversity and most schools are community schools, but an increasing proportion of these are designated Welsh-medium schools (ysgolion

Cymraeg) which share some of the characteristics of non-standard schools, including preferential funding, and enlarged catchments.

The trend towards greater school autonomy has meant that an increasing number of schools also exercise some measure of control over their admissions policies. From the introduction of GM schools there have been concerns that schools would employ their powers to recruit the most able and least troublesome students (Fitz *et al.*, 1993). As the number of autonomous schools has increased there has also been a concern that in seeking out the most able and motivated students they might contribute towards the development of a two-tier, socially polarised system. So, have these changes in school organisation given rise to changes in the social stratification of schools? That is a question that we attempt to answer in this chapter. Given the present government's commitment to increasing the proportion of specialist schools in the comprehensive secondary sector, it is a question of considerable interest to policy-makers and practitioners.

For that reason much of the chapter is devoted to schools that have control over their admissions policies and to the examination of the impact of the growing number of specialist schools. We turn first, however, to one hitherto little explored factor that has a considerable influence on patterns of segregation, namely the actual number of secondary schools in national and local systems.

School numbers

One of the key variables that relates to school organisation is change in the simple number of schools in an area. This is closely related to another variable that is affected by school reorganisation – surplus places which were reduced with the number of schools in the early 1990s, and have continued to reduce from 12 per cent of all places in 1995/1996 to 8 per cent in 1999/2000 (Audit Commission, 2002). Our model suggests that changes to the number of available schools are closely related to the rates of change in between-school segregation (and the number of surplus places is related to the number of appeals, see Chapter 10). The level of socio-economic segregation between schools tends to fall when LEAs rationalise their education provision by closing schools. When LEAs have been able to close struggling schools then their intakes are notionally allocated to alternative schools. This means that parents have to send their children elsewhere without taking the initiative themselves. The ensuing movement of pupils redistributes those living in poverty to a number of alternative schools, indirectly reducing the levels of segregation between schools.

What is the process by which this redistribution occurs and what are its consequences? Where schools are oversubscribed, most schools and

LEAs get around the problem of making decisions by simply expanding, and this means ignoring the planned admission numbers (PAN). A popular school in our study faced new housing development and the merger of other local schools, yet even so they reported: 'Because we were continually increasing our standard number, I would say that until four years ago everyone who applied got in.'

In Wales, the Popular Schools Initiative has allowed a few schools to expand to meet local demand. In England the same thing happens, but less publicly and less formally. Whether they agreed with this 'policy' or not, most LEAs and all school interviews reported popular schools expanding to meet demand. One rural LEA we visited had a school with a PAN of 370 which is now taking 490 per year. A popular community school in a new unitary authority regularly negotiated an increase every year:

> With [pre-unitary authority] the phone call would have been – this is the number and can you take an extra thirty, no we need two new classrooms – and it would be done. . . . With [new unitary authority] so we applied to increase our number and the LEA opposed it. After that we went to the Secretary of State and . . . they caved in at the end. We then changed our admission number to 227. . . . Because we were continually increasing our standard number, I would say that . . . everyone who applied got in.

Other schools enjoyed the same flexibility. One foundation school reported: 'We have been expanding a lot . . . we have just had a basic need bid that is extra funding from the DfEE to expand the school still further.'

While a rural county LEA admitted:

> It is very difficult if you have got a 1233 school to say you can't take 1234 or 5, so unless we have strong case i.e. health and safety . . . we don't go to appeal because the school down the road has got places . . . We don't necessarily publish admission numbers at the standard number. We consult with the governors each year . . . if we have exceeded it we have exceeded it. We are now trying to get a PAN which reflects reality.

The same kind of thing happens in London LEAs: 'The members wanted to respond to this public feeling . . . and what they wanted for their children . . . and they expanded [school] just like that – 25 extra places.'

An unpopular 11–16 school in a new unitary authority had to merge with a similar school as it was losing numbers, and took the opportunity to add a sixth form:

> Many parents of the brighter children in particular were taking the decision at the end of year six – let's go straight to schools with a sixth form – which is why eventually the decision was made to close the two schools and open up . . . . as an 11–18 school.

Far from leading to increased segregation, as some commentators feared (see Chapter 2), it can be argued that this process alleviates somewhat the problem of segregation by residence.

Diversity of schools

We noted in earlier chapters that school segregation declined from 1989 to 1995. We also noted above that this period featured an expansion of school autonomy including greater school level control over admissions policies. It was a period where parents could choose between a growing number of categories of secondary school, a growth in out-of-catchment placements, and a large growth in appeals. In regions such as Wales with little diversity of secondary schools (grant-maintained, fee-paying, selective schools and city technology colleges) there has been a markedly lower level of segregation than the national average for England. Is it the case then that choice without diversity tends to lead to lower levels of segregation than simple allocation of school places by area of residence, whereas choice with diversity prevents this? We consider this question below.

As we have seen, local levels of segregation of disadvantaged students (chiefly those from families living poverty) are largely determined by noneducational factors, such as the geography of each area. Once these wider factors are accounted for, then areas in which there is little diversity in the nature of local schooling (where all schools are LEA-controlled comprehensives, for example) have generally lower levels of segregation, and have until recently tended to reduce those levels further. Areas with considerable diversity on the other hand (where school allocation by selection, faith, fees, or specialism appears) have higher levels of segregation, and have tended to maintain these levels over time. Where diversity increases, so too does segregation (in the main). This remains the case in the analysis of our national dataset whatever the publicised criteria of allocation to schools are (and the considerable range of these criteria can be seen in Chapter 9).

To be more precise, within LEAs, the relationship between school types and segregation is an ogival one. Areas with high levels of selective, voluntary-aided, grant-maintained or fee-paying schools had higher levels of segregation than their neighbours, and show little change in segregation over time (e.g. Bromley, Buckinghamshire, and Haringey). Areas with large changes in segregation (in either direction, see Gorard and

Fitz, 2000) or lower initial levels of segregation contained mostly LEA-controlled comprehensive schools.

In Shropshire, for example, a large proportion of the schools were foundation or fee-paying and the county retained its initial level of segregation over time (actually rising from 26 per cent in 1989 to 27 per cent in 1996). Hammersmith and Fulham contained one very famous and popular Foundation and many fee-paying schools, and increased its segregation from 16 to 24 per cent over the same period. It is now almost as segregated as a typical rural area. Knowsley contained one Foundation but no fee-paying schools, and its segregation decreased from 12 to 6 per cent. Trafford, with one of the highest proportion of selective schools had a massive 35 per cent segregation in 1989.

The implications of this for the current expansion of specialist and faith-based schools should be immediately apparent. Whatever merits these schemes have (and the evidence for these merits is far from conclusive, see Chapter 6), they also present a real danger of creating greater socio-economic division in the education system. The authors argue that we should, on the other hand, be aiming for less division, since school compositions are related to their performance. However, the same argument applies to areas with relatively high proportions of foundation (opted out) schools (and to Welsh-medium schools in Wales), even where these schools are not specialist, faith-based or selective. What all of these minority school types have in common is the ability to act as their own admission authorities, and perhaps it is this, rather than their 'marketing' identities, that is the chief determinant of increased segregation in their local areas.

The presence of fee-paying schools is also related to increasingly segregated LEAs. This may be related to their admission arrangements, such as the use of selection and the ability of some parents to express their commitment to a particular religion. Diversity drives segregation by giving people a reason other than perceived quality, rightly or wrongly, to use a school other than their nearest. The relationship between fee-paying and segregation by FSM may seem surprising to some, because the two groups are clearly disparate. But it must be recalled that the removal of non-FSM families from maintained schools would affect their composition in the same way as an increase in FSM families in the same schools (see Appendix). Although our segregation measures focus on the poorest 20 per cent of the population, the other 80 per cent *are* factored into the calculation.

It should be noted that many schools controlling their own intakes also have overlapping identities. For example, many grammar schools became grant-maintained in the fear that local authorities may prevent them from using selection in their admissions. Also, many of the current specialist schools are foundation or voluntary-aided schools, and this new status gives schools the further possibility to use some form of selection in their admissions. For example, the criteria that they employ if they are over-subscribed could differ from that stated by the LEA, giving them the opportunity, it is argued, to use criteria that may disadvantage those from less advantaged backgrounds.

Under the SSFA they are constituted as admissions authorities and, in effect, have equal status to LEAs because they can issue their own admissions documents, determine their admissions criteria, and process new entrants into the school. These school have created and/or main-tained lower levels of FSM students on their rolls and in consequence have benefited from higher levels of performance in public examinations. These types of school have in the past given little priority to the proximity of applicants in their admissions criteria. One effect of this has been to attract considerable numbers of out-of-borough students on their books. We found foundation and voluntary schools in inner London where more than 90 per cent of the intake came from outside the host LEA. In practice this means that local children are denied access to local schools and these LEAs register relatively high levels of social stratification in their schools. The problem here is not that schools recruit widely, but that they are competing with schools with very narrow catchments (i.e. the playing field is not level). One inner London LEA officer noted:

> All bar two of our secondary schools became grant-maintained . . . which meant that for admission purposes we had no control whatso-ever and still don't . . . I forgot to mention that there is quite an outflow into the grammar schools [in adjacent LEA] which is really upsetting for schools.

A rural LEA officer explains how Foundation schools using apparently the same admissions criteria as the community schools can lead to segregation:

> I picked three or four at random and they're all remarkably similar to [county admissions procedures]. I think where the problems arise is that they can for example annexe a larger bit of catchment that didn't belong to them before and we have no power to say they can't do that.

The same thing happens with faith-based schools, according to the officer at another London LEA: 'Because we've got predominantly voluntary-aided schools so they take from the diocese rather than locally . . . across Central London.'

Thus, only around 50 per cent of local children attend a state school in this borough. The remainder go to nearby LEAs (usually faith-based schools) or to fee-paying schools, meaning that this wealthy borough has a very high proportion of children in poverty (and, of course, little LEA-level segregation). As with many LEAs, having multiple admission authorities within one LEA makes it almost impossible for officers to be certain about first preferences. This was seen in an adjacent LEA as a problem for particular schools:

> I think it [growth of faith-based schools] will polarise more if we're not very careful. . . . That was the issue with most of the other heads that the church schools were interviewing because they're looking at religious affiliation . . . but seem to be interviewing for other criteria as well.

Similar impacts on local levels of segregation, albeit for different reasons, occur when families have a choice of medium of instruction. The head of a rural English-medium community school in Wales pointed out how the traditionally 'privileged' Welsh speakers go to ysgolion Cymraeg in adjacent LEAs (and these schools like Foundation and faith-based ones do not have local catchments), and that even the English speaking 'incomers' cannot compensate for the relative poverty of those remaining:

> The Welsh families from this area go to [school] and you can imagine the converse, you have the English medium kids from [LEA] coming here. . . . They are basically very English people who have moved to the area and don't like the Welsh element . . . and you know the medium of communication here is mostly English. . . . The parents perhaps are a little bit more alternative than the usual . . . more towards the hippy end. It is not always professionals, some come down from [English city] and claim dole here basically.

A school in the same area pointed out the anomaly that pupils going to Welsh-medium schools get free transport, however far it is. Diversity in this context and its resulting segregation is the outcome of a nationally supported, LEA policy rather than market-driven. Although unintentional, these seemingly progressive policies can and do give rise to socially stratified schools. The local Welsh-medium school with which the above school competes has just received over £6 million additional funding. A growing number of parents are using WM, as a kind of grammar school, and then moving their children on just before GCSEs. Our informant claimed, 'They select quite rigorously; if your Welsh isn't up to it then they have the excuse academically – a vicious circle – as the WM results improve they are perceived as more desirable'.

One London LEA officer was quite clear about the similar impacts of different forms of diversity:

> I forgot to mention that there is quite an outflow into the grammar schools [in adjacent LEA] which is really upsetting for schools . . . [On the growth of faith-base schools] I think it will polarise more if we're not very careful. That was the issue with most of the other heads that the church schools were interviewing because they're looking at religious affiliation . . . but seem to be interviewing for other criteria as well . . . [On specialist schools] One is a language college and therefore highly sought after because if you're doing languages you're going to be bright and if you're bright it's going to be a good school and if it's a good school you're going to go there.

The schools themselves seem to agree. The head of a London Catholic girls school serving the same area:

> We are right on the borders of [three other LEAs]. . . . The interview has changed over the years and we now ask them to bring in their books and we look at their reports and . . . we focus very much on their learning and their progress rather than much about their actual preference for us . . . In September last year we took in . . . between 90 and 100 Catholics and that was the total amount . . . that applied so the other 120 . . . you can cream off from the other.

The head of a specialist school acknowledged:

> Because we're very wealthy it's resented . . . if you see around the school it's like a university campus. We've got everything, there's money everywhere. I've got £3 or 4 million tucked away in the money markets. . . . The teacher contact ratio is 72 per cent for this school, but 84 per cent in the LEA.

Even schools in educational action zones can use the same basic strategy of appearing to improve by receiving more money and greater control over admissions. One EAZ head said that he had the full support of the DfEE (as it then was) to refuse entry to children with educational problems. He simply 'pretends' that the school is full so that there is no need to take all comers.

Specialist schools

One route to meet targets for increased diversity is through increasing the number of specialisms from four to seven, to include engineering, science and business and enterprise. A parallel development is to establish 'a new category of advanced specialist school which would be open to high-performing schools after 5 years in the specialist school programme' (DfEE, 2001b: 48). The policy-makers are keen to point out that this will not lead to 'a free-for all between schools' nor to 'dismantling all local education services', since the 'freedom must be earned, not conferred at whim without regard to the interests of children or the needs of the local community' (p. 6).

Critics of the specialist school programme are concerned that the establishment of these new forms of schools will lead to the advancement of a two-tier education system (Thornton, 2001) and further vertical differentiation. A specialist school can expect to receive an additional £100,000 of matched funding towards capital expenditure. This money must be spent on enhancing the facilities that are required for the school's particular specialism. Specialist schools can also expect to receive a recurrent budget of £123 per pupil per year for the first 4 years to implement their specialist programme. Approximately a third of this should be targeted to assist in sharing innovative and best practice with other local nonspecialist schools. However, both of these additional resources can also have effects on the rest of the school. For example, capital investment improves teacher and pupil morale and can lead, on occasions, to greater pupil performance (PriceWaterhouseCoopers, 2001). It also means that the standard capital and recurrent resources available to all schools can be diverted elsewhere to other departments.

Any school must identify £50,000 from private sources in order to be eligible for specialist school status. It could be argued that the potential for schools from all neighbourhoods to raise this amount of private finance is not evenly distributed. For example, it may be very difficult for a school located in a poor neighbourhood of a deindustrialising city to find private partners who would be willing to donate up to £50,000. This major obstacle could perhaps prevent schools in the lower tier from ever moving into the upper tier of a two-tier system. However, again according to the Technology Colleges Trust nearly a third of specialist schools are located in inner city areas. Whether these are actually located in challenging areas is considered below.

A second mechanism of the specialist school programme that could advance a two-tier system is the opportunity for schools on the programme to select up to 10 per cent (or perhaps 15 per cent) of their pupils on the basis of aptitude in their specialism. A debate has emerged surrounding the difference between selection by aptitude and selection by ability, the latter appearing to refer to selection by the general ability of a child rather than the specific ability of the child within the specialism. In either form, however, any kind of selection must enhance the school's ability to generate relatively higher examination results – at least in one subject. Given that opportunity it is interesting that only a small proportion of schools actually implement this. According to the Technology Colleges Trust, only 7 per cent of specialist schools do so, and a number of these had partial selection before joining the specialist school programme.

When schools (or LEAs) allocate places to pupils they can follow their published criteria in fact, but not in spirit. For example, a selective specialist school might allocate 10 per cent of places on aptitude in one year, and whatever the argument for exceptional talents in one curriculum area it remains the case that all academic aptitudes tend to correlate with each other. Thus, selecting (for that is what it amounts to) some students tends to improve raw score examination scores. In subsequent years the school could use its published criterion of favouring the brothers and sisters of those at the school before allocating the 10 per cent specialist places. As general aptitude also tends to 'run' in families this approach is likely to raise scores even further. Such 'covert' selection could repeatedly happen year-on-year. However, on the basis of our work on admissions more generally, we would argue that it is also possible for schools to have a 'select' intake without applying any selective criteria. Indirect consequences of both the improved funding and/or the ability to select on aptitude may appear in open enrolment and per-pupil funding. The general popularity of a school on the specialist school programme may be enhanced by improvements in its infrastructure and examination results. A full and expanding school will benefit from per-pupil funding. Factors such as these may be partly why specialist schools appear successful to naive observers, but even this tactic may, of course, leave overall LEA and national indicators unaffected. The school may be simply 'robbing Peter to pay Paul', and not contributing to any overall improvement in educational standards.

Specialism, or reputation for a curriculum subject, is anyway a negligible factor for families choosing a new school (Gorard, 1999a), both in the state-funded and fee-paying sectors (Gorard, 1997b). Ironically, market forces in the UK appear to push schools towards a rather 'dull uniformity' rather than diversity. Most of the diversity in the school system is pre-existing and long-term (e.g. voluntary-aided) or else 'artificially' created (e.g. CTCs). In whichever direction the theoretical arguments surrounding diversity and choice go (Hargreaves, 1996a, 1996b; Walford, 1996a, 1996b) it is still the case anyway that the specialisms themselves are somewhat specious – it is not clear for example why a particular suburb should be especially concerned with, or blessed with talent for, a specific curriculum area. It is already the situation that the cost of travel borne by families and LEAs limits the number and range of schools that they are able to consider.

The rise of the specialist school

The number of schools awarded specialist school status in England increased almost year-on-year after they were first introduced in 1994 (Figure 8.1). There was a slight fall in the number of schools entering the

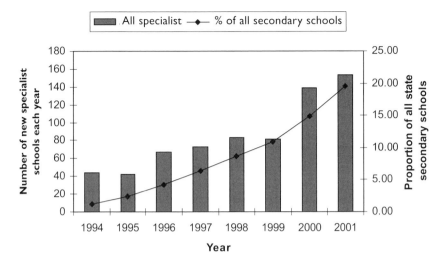

Figure 8.1 The rise of specialist schools by year, England 1994–2001.

programme between 1998 and 1999, however, between September 1999 and September 2000 there were 134 new specialist schools raising the total number of schools on the programme to 529. By March 2001 there were already 73 schools designated as specialist schools that year, well on the way to equalling the take-up for 2000.

By September 2000 just less than 15 per cent of all state secondary schools were on the programme. According to the Government's targets specialist schools will account for an estimated 28 per cent of all secondary schools by the year 2003, and a total of 1,500 (40 per cent of the total) by 2006. This proportion should be considered against the fact that the heavily-researched foundation and voluntary-aided schools, two key elements of school diversity, already account for 14 and 15 per cent of secondary schools, respectively. However, within the specialist school programme there is considerable overlap between these two types of schools. The early specialist schools were either foundation or voluntary-controlled schools. Community schools now provide the largest share of specialist schools, followed by foundation schools, voluntary aided schools and voluntary-controlled schools. But these are, of course, not proportionally representative of the overall composition of secondary schools in England. Only 15 per cent of community schools are currently on the specialist school programme compared with around 26 per cent of all foundation schools. Community schools remain under-represented.

The origins of the policy go back to 1993 with the introduction of the technology colleges programme for the purpose of enabling selected schools to specialise in technology, science and mathematics (Noden and West, 2001). The current pattern of specialisms that schools have is largely a product of the earlier introduction of first technology college status, followed by language college status, and then arts and sports college status. In 2000 technology colleges still accounted for the greatest share of new specialist schools. Meanwhile, the other forms of specialisms were being introduced at an equal rate. By September 2000, the majority (58 per cent) of schools on the specialist school programme had technology college status. This was in comparison to language colleges (19 per cent), sports colleges (12 per cent) and arts colleges (11 per cent).

By March 2001 there were still 14 LEAs in England that did not have any schools on the programme. This contrasts with Wandsworth where more than half of the schools were on the programme, encompassing 64 per cent of the secondary school age population. Similar proportions could be found in Hackney, West Berkshire and North Somerset. In Birmingham there were a total of 21 secondary schools on the programme, the highest in England. This is closely followed by 18 in another large LEA, Essex. Generally it is urban LEAs that have the highest proportion of schools on the programme. But there are a number of key exceptions to this, including Cornwall (35 per cent of schools), Durham (33 per cent of schools), and Gloucestershire (29 per cent of schools).

In the education quasi-market, the specialist school programme is seen as contributing to horizontal diversity, a condition deemed necessary for an efficient market to operate (Higham *et al.*, 2000). However, unlike the apparent 'failure' of two other supply-side programmes, city technology colleges and sponsored grant-maintained schools (Walford, 2000), the specialist school programme is unfolding rapidly as a feature of the education landscape.

Segregation and specialist schools

Overall, 29 per cent of secondary schools in England became more 'privileged' in their intake between 1994/1995 and 1999/2000. In this instance, more 'privileged' means that these schools already had less than their local 'fair share' of children from families in poverty, as measured by their entitlement to free school meals, and that this proportion declined further (i.e. their segregation ratio was less than one, and moved away from one over time). It is, in essence, these 29 per cent that are driving the move towards greater overall segregation in the system since 1997 – although there are, as ever, regional variations in this from 24 per cent of schools segregating in the north west to 35 per cent in the eastern economic region. This trend towards segregation is considerably worse in grammar (69 per cent) and upper-age 14–18 comprehensive (67 per cent) schools than among secondary-modern (17 per cent) or 11–16 comprehensive (16 per cent) schools. It is also worse among all specialist schools combined (37 per cent), particularly those for languages (43 per cent), and foundation (43 per cent), and voluntary-aided CE (57 per cent) specialist schools. The latter is particularly interesting showing that, however neutral the school admissions policies are except with respect to religion, religious schools are attracting or 'selecting' an increasingly privileged intake and this has implications for the proposal to expand this sector as well.

While the pattern is complicated by age range, gender mix, and local authority, those schools taking an increasingly privileged intake tend to be specialist, or selective, or their own admission authorities (e.g. GM or VA). Where more than one of these is the case the tendency is significantly enhanced. While 16.5 per cent of the total school intake was eligible for free school meals in 2000, in specialist schools this was only 14.4 per cent. However, this overall figure hides the variation within the specialist school programme. Specialist schools for sport and arts have similar compositions to all schools, and the difference lies in the technology and especially the language schools (10.2 per cent FSM). There is also variation by type with community specialist schools being more similar in composition to their non specialist counterparts, while all other school types are more privileged, especially voluntary-aided Catholic specialist schools (only 7.1 per cent FSM) and selective schools (2.1 per cent). This raises the question of whether it is the specialism, the prior school type, or the interaction between the two that is driving the segregation?

To recall, there are different forms of specialisms, different types of schools on the programme, different admission policies, different lengths of time on the programme, and some schools allocate places based on selection by aptitude. Because of these complexities the following discussion examining the impact of specialist school status on admissions focuses on more detailed case studies. Of the LEA sample only nine had existing specialist schools (28 schools in total). These 28 specialist schools represent all forms of specialism that a school can currently have, and represent all types of state-funded school (e.g. community, foundation and VA). We use the term 'designated specialist school' to convey the confusion over the concept. It could be argued that there is no such thing a 'bog standard' school, since all have a distinct ethos and a distinctive skills portfolio among their staff (see Thornton, 2001). In addition, there are several schools that have a clear, acknowledged and publicised specialism which are not specialist schools in current policy terms. An example is the former ILEA centre for music, which has specialist facilities and teachers, and selects 10 per cent of students on the basis of musical aptitude. This is not a 'specialist' school.

Of these 28 schools, 10 had increasingly privileged intakes over time, as determined by their segregation ratios. Only five schools increased the relative proportion of children eligible for free school meals between 1994, the first year of the programme, and 2000. The intakes of two of these were still under-represented with such children relative to other schools in their particular LEAs. The remaining 13 schools saw no significant change to the composition of their school intakes, although 'no change' includes having maintained an already privileged intake.

The most notable feature of the 10 polarising schools was that these were all their own admission authority, i.e. they had autonomy in their admissions arrangements from their respective LEA. This meant that they were able to apply their own oversubscription criteria, and in the order they preferred. The relationship between the autonomy in admissions and their specialist school status can impact on their intake in two stages. First, since specialist school status increases the popularity of a school (West *et al.*, 2000) these schools are simply more likely to apply their oversubscription criteria, whatever these are, than other schools. Second, their oversubscription criteria could be applied, even inadvertently, to ensure they get the most able and the most socially 'advantaged' children. The three most-used criteria were: selection by aptitude, interviews for religious affiliation, and the use of the family rule.

Few specialist schools report using selection by aptitude in their admissions (West *et al.*, 2000). Of our 28 schools only four selected a proportion (10 per cent in all cases) of their intakes based on aptitude in the relevant specialist subject. Three of these were VA (religious) schools and, consequently, also required parents to show their religious affiliation. One of these schools distinguished admission places allocated by selection and admission places allocated on religious grounds. In the other two VA schools, both Roman Catholic, 10 per cent of places were reserved for children that could prove their aptitude in the specialism and whose parents had demonstrated their commitment to the Roman Catholic faith. This could be seen as 'selection within selection', almost guaranteeing that these schools admit the most academically able children.

It is perhaps not surprising, therefore, that the selective specialist schools, including the selective foundation school, have admitted an increasingly socio-economically 'advantaged' set of children (Figure 8.2). Children eligible for free school meals were increasingly under-represented in these schools relative to other schools in their LEA (where a segregation ratio of one represents a school perfectly in proportion with its LEA).

Of the remaining 24 specialist schools in the detailed sample, another six had significant falls in their segregation ratios, again indicating that they became increasingly segregated from other schools in their LEA (Figure 8.3). Even though none of these schools applied the selection by aptitude criteria in allocating places they still had autonomy in their admission arrangements. Typically they required parents to show their

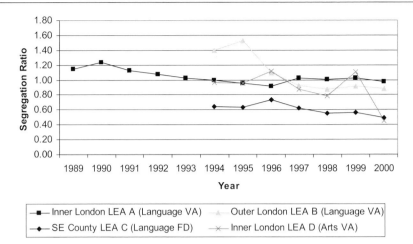

Figure 8.2 Selective specialist schools: change in composition of school intakes.

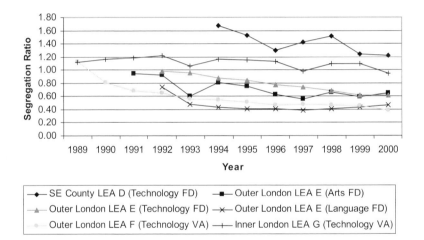

Figure 8.3 Non-selective specialist schools: increasingly socio-economically advantaged intakes.

commitment to a religious faith (see above) or applied oversubscription criteria, such as the family rule, to provide 'selection by proxy', i.e. where parents are more likely to be given a place because of allocative procedures applied before the programme was instigated and before the 1998 Schools Standards and Framework Act attempted to make oversubscription criteria more fair and transparent.

In one LEA (Outer London LEA E) all three specialist schools there have always had less than their fair share – around half – of local poor students.

And, since becoming specialist schools these have seen their share fall further. Thus, although not selective at all, these three ex-grammar foundation schools were managing to recruit an increasingly privileged intake, and were therefore more likely to be successful in examination terms and so gain further in market appeal. One reason for this may be the family rule, whereby priority is given to those whose family members had previously attended or worked at the school. Another may be glimpsed in the views of the admissions officer in the LEA:

> I think we've got two at the moment. One's a language college and therefore highly sought after because if you're doing languages you're going to be bright and if you're bright it's going to be a good school, and if it's a good school you're going to go there. There is another one . . . but I think they're looking at that way to increase the ability levels of their intake, although of course it's only allowed to be a small percentage. But the knock-on effects.

However, in the sample there were three other specialist schools which had autonomy for their admissions yet did not show any indication of having more socially 'advantaged' intakes over time. Indeed these three schools took more children eligible for free school meals over time, relative to other schools in their LEA (Figure 8.4). Their stories may explain this apparent contradiction. First, the two specialist schools in outer London LEA B typically have unfilled places each year. In other words these schools would appear to be unpopular, even given their new status. Consequently these schools have not generally over the period been in a position to employ their own oversubscription criteria, irrespective of whether they have the particular criteria that would cream-skim their applicants. The third school is located in a south-east LEA H, and, uniquely it could be said for foundation schools, uses the same oversubscription criteria promoted by the LEA in all other schools. Hence this school, it could be argued, is in no 'better' position to cream-skim its applicants than any other school. In addition the particular oversubscription criteria used in this LEA is 'designated areas'. As long as the applicant lives in the designated area of a school they are almost guaranteed a place in that school.

This discussion has tended to focus on foundation or VA specialist schools. However, this has been data-driven, as these are the schools whose intakes have changed significantly over time. These types of schools are more likely to use selection by aptitude in their admissions, or have benefited via their oversubscription criteria from the potential increase in popularity arising from their new status. Where there have been exceptions to this the unique situations of such schools has helped explain their non-conformity.

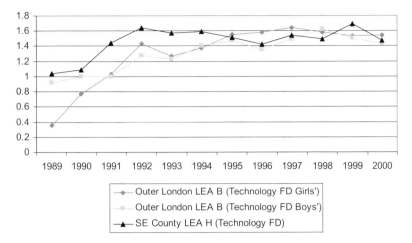

Figure 8.4 Non-selective specialist schools with autonomy for admissions: increasingly socio-economically advantaged intakes.

Conclusion

If a policy of increased diversity is deemed desirable in the UK, and that is present government policy (Smithers, 2001), then our analysis argues that it should be organised fairly. If advocates of diversity and specialisation are convinced that this is the best route to raising standards then in all fairness, to test whether their policy options are the right ones, specialist and the anachronistic faith-based schools should not receive preferential funding. Nor should they be allowed to select, or to use a different admissions process to the schools with which they are in competition. Then we will be able to see the strength of their advocates' arguments. That would go some way to permitting a 'level playing field' comparison between different kinds of secondary schools. Two LEAs in our subsample have specialist schools that are based on catchment areas just like the remaining schools in the LEA (Gorard and Taylor, 2001). These specialist schools take approximately their 'fair share' of disadvantaged students, but they do not have superior public examination results.

Our first conclusion would have to be that it is difficult to assess the likely drawbacks and advantages of increasing the proportion of specialist schools in England. For, in addition to the standard difficulties of establishing a causal model, we face a very large number of confounds. The definition of specialism has changed over time, and the current definition is so recent that appropriate longitudinal data are scarce and volatile. The prior and continuing nature of each school – whether VA, GM, selective, modern, or community – may alter the impact of specialisation. The local method of allocating places at schools, the possibilities for travel, differential funding, and the actual subject specialism of the school are additional inter-weaving influences. The analytical importance of place, time, proportion, and hierarchies of implementation that we have encountered elsewhere in our study are confirmed. Our second conclusion therefore is that the relative cost-benefits of specialist schools need to take these factors into account. Without this analytical complexity, comparisons between them and ordinary community schools are unlikely to be of much value, other than in politically rhetorical terms.

In answer to the question posed at the beginning of this chapter, our study has suggested that schools that are selective, or are their own admissions authorities, or are specialist tend to increase the socio-economic segregation of school intakes (or retain higher levels in an era when segregation is decreasing more generally). When schools have two or more of these characteristics together – foundation specialist or selective specialist, for example – this tendency is far stronger. In this, we are in agreement with a number of other commentators. A study at the Open University suggested that opted-out schools tended to reduce their proportion of FSM during the 1990s (in Dean, 1999), another that faith-based schools increased racial segregation (in Passmore and Barnard 2001). In fact a review of relevant research concluded that 'greater diversity and specialisation between schools leads to greater social inequality and larger differences in attainment between schools' (Croxford, 2001: 68). This is far removed from Hargreaves' (1996a) notion of diversity that retains the antiselective comprehensive principle.

Clearly the accounts of specialist schools and colleges with superior facilities, 'magic' white boards in every room, higher salaries, 4-day working weeks for staff, home-grown curricula, etc., are impressive, and worthy of emulation and improvement. To achieve this for all schools it would be necessary, although not necessarily sufficient, for taxpayers (and perhaps other 'investors') to approve increased per capita resources across the board, and for a revision of existing legislation to release schools from government and local government control of their curriculum and day-to-day activities. Simply allowing more schools to become specialist, and perhaps allocate a proportion of their places to students on the basis of that specialism, cannot bring such changes about. Rather, specialisation could lead to several clear disadvantages without any obvious compensation for most families. Many governors and school managers support this position (although on what evidence-base is unclear), seeing specialist schools as divisive and 'likely to increase the gap between advantaged and disadvantaged areas' (Thornton, 2001). Policy-makers need to weigh up the purported advantages of specialist schools – in urban areas with preferential funding – against the potential disadvantages in terms of overall equity.

Chapter 9

The role of the LEA

Introduction

The final set of determinants of change, and the last (in sequence) to play a role in the distribution of students to schools, relates to the admission arrangements employed by the LEAs. Our analysis has already been able to account for all of the variation in levels of socio-economic segregation between schools. Similarly, it has also been able to account for nearly all of the variation in the rates of change in segregation across LEAs. In other words, with a few contextual variables we could say with almost complete certainty whether schools in an LEA are likely to have become increasingly more segregated or less so, and by how much. It may seem surprising that this can be achieved even without knowing anything about the nature of parental choice and competition at the local level. This is not to say that the local education market and the way parents choose schools do not play a part in determining levels of segregation. For example, population density has a bearing upon the amount of school choice parents have. However, the impact of choice alone appears to be negligible in predicting segregation at the LEA level. But from another perspective, this conclusion is not surprising. The choice policy is after all a national one, and so any variation must, by definition, be locally induced.

The range of variation between LEAs in terms of levels of and changes in school-based segregation is large (see Chapter 4). However, most of these differences can be explained in terms of differences in the local population (levels of poverty and so on), in local geography (population density, nature of housing, etc.) and in the range and mix of local schools (foundation, faith-based and so on). There is little variation left to be explained in terms of other aspects of allocating students to school places, such as those usually associated with markets and choice (the factors in preceding chapters lead to a model with $R^2=0.98$). This, in itself, is an important finding and a valuable corrective to many previous accounts of the impact of marketisation (see Appendix). West and Pennell (2002: 208), for example, claim of the variation in segregation between LEAs, that 'on a priori grounds this is likely to be, at least in part, the result of the way in which quasi-markets are structured and operate in different parts of the country'. A posteriori, this suggestion looks much weaker. This variation in segregation between LEAs was already present before the introduction of explicit market forces, and was not therefore even partly the result of the way quasi-markets operate. Factors such as geography precede school allocation procedures, both in terms of statistical importance in our model but also historically. For example, the population density of inner London is largely determined by factors unrelated to the market in schools, so that it makes more sense to consider the impact of population density on the operation of local markets (see Chapter 7). Nevertheless, what we do in this chapter is consider the variation in LEA admission policies and school allocation procedures – through a typology of all LEA responses to national policy, and then through a more detailed consideration of three contrasting LEAs.

Significant variations have been identified in the ways in which LEAs and schools allocate places when there are more applicants than there are places available (Fitz *et al.*, 2002a). As discussed earlier, LEAs that use catchment or designated areas tend to have greater levels of segregation and are likely to see increases in the level of segregation over time (Gorard and Fitz, 2000; Gorard *et al.*, 2001a). LEAs have reduced the number of surplus places considerably over the last 10 years through a programme of school reorganisation and rationalisation alongside a population bulge in the number of children of secondary school age. This means that schools are increasingly more likely to become oversubscribed. Consequently, the use of particular oversubscription criteria, such as religious commitment (see last chapter) or designated areas has increased.

LEAs are important because it is they who are responsible for the organisation of schooling at the local level, including the mix of selective and nonselective comprehensive schools, single sex schools and voluntary (mainly faith-based) schools. Historically, they have had a major part also in school admissions arrangements, that is devising the principles and policies that regulate which students have the right to attend what school and the basis upon which schools admit students. Some LEAs moved ahead with comprehensive schooling earlier and faster than others, while some retained selection and, alongside admissions policies, these activities in turn shaped and reproduced the extent to which local schools were already socially segregated by 1989. Nevertheless, the pre-eminence of LEAs has been a source of frustration to successive governments seeking to shape and influence who gets what and where in the education system. LEA capacity to shape the local school system has always been constrained by the existence of the faith-based 'voluntary' schools sector and it was further diminished, post-1988, by self-governing grant-maintained (GM) schools.

The 1998 Schools Standards and Framework brought LEAs back into the admissions arena in a modified form. The importance of a role for the LEA comes from their claim to be holders of essential local knowledge (Beecham, 2000), a claim they use to defend themselves against abolition or integration with other services (Slater, 2000). This 'managerial' side to the education market has been further reinforced by the Code of Practice on School Admissions, outlining guidelines on the allocation of places in cases of oversubscribed schools. Typically this has led to a return to a policy of 'local schools for local children', either through the use of designated or catchment areas, or by the allocation of places based on travel or proximity between a school and a student's home. What this has done is tighten the link between the socio-economic characteristics of the local residential neighbourhood and the socio-economic characteristics of the schools' intakes.

Application procedures

Although the criteria for allocating school places, set down by admissions authorities, are the most obvious focus for the attention of researchers (e.g. Mayet, 1997), they only represent one aspect of the admissions process. Arguably as important are the standard procedures which parents must go through to complete the transition from primary to secondary school. These procedures dictate the minimum level of involvement for parents, and also the level and type of activity required to apply to more than one prospective destination institution. There is less variation in these procedures than is found when examining the allocation criteria (see below), and the different procedure types that we have discerned can be usefully grouped into five categories.

Catchment areas and designated schools

This category of application procedure includes all those LEA admissions authorities which specified a 'default' school preference which would automatically be acted on if no further action was taken by a parent. This is similar to the kind of procedure which commonly operated in many LEAs before the 1988 ERA. Individual LEAs sometimes use the term 'catchment areas' which refer to traditional methods of allocation, and so for admissions purposes are as arbitrary as any other geographical area defined by an admissions authority, such as the area which a school 'traditionally serves'. For example, the guidelines for parents with children in schools under the control of Caerphilly LEA state that:

> Headteachers of primary schools will be able to inform parents of the secondary school which their children should normally attend. If

parents wish their child to attend a secondary school which does not serve their locality, they should contact the Education Department for advice.

(Caerphilly, 1999/2000: 3)

This procedure is clearly directed at maintaining a 'catchment area' system of allocating secondary school places. The language used is prescriptive in tone as parents are informed of the school which their children 'should normally attend'. The additional fact that, should they want their child to attend a different school, they must 'contact the Education Department for advice' suggests that such a request is exceptional and can only be dealt with at a higher administrative level. The process is further 'mystified' by the lack of information about the procedures which would follow such action. A similar example, but couched in a more accessible way perhaps, is that of Wiltshire LEA, who state that:

Naturally you will want your child to attend a school where you believe he or she will be happy and receive a good education. Most parents are satisfied that their designated area school can provide this. You may, however, prefer your child to attend another school. . . . If you wish your child to attend a school, other than the one designated to serve your area, you will need to complete the relevant parental preference form.

(Wiltshire, 1998/1999: 8)

Although, in this case, the language is less prescriptive and presents the choice of an alternative school as a less deviant action than does the previous example, parents wishing to select another school are still required to take action which is not required by those whose children will attend the 'designated' institution. A related procedure presents parents with a form and notification of their catchment school, and allows them the option to express a preference for an alternative. Five of the LEA admissions authorities employed applications procedures which approximately corresponded to this model, and five to the previous model.

Enclosed with the LEA's letter confirming your child's entitlement area school will be a form on which you can (i) accept the entitlement place and/or (ii) request alternative places at different middle or high schools. For parents wishing to ask for a different middle or high school there is space on the application form to express a preference for either one or two schools.

(Isle of Wight, 1999/2000: 8)

Admissions policies which are structured around a principle of placing children in 'default' institutions based on residential criteria do nothing to encourage the free choice of secondary schools by their supposed 'consumers'. It would appear that these kinds of policies are not very far removed from the previously existing 'catchment area' system. Making alternative choices in the 'new' system requires parents to make efforts above and beyond the standard application procedures (whether these be automatic or not) and therefore hinder rather than facilitate making any kind of active choice. The most obvious outcome of this would be a kind of stasis in which little 'market activity' takes place, except amongst the most confident families, and especially in light of the 1997 Rotherham judgement (DfEE, 1999a: 21). The head of one foundation school in our sample complained of the LEA:

> As an authority they are bureaucratic and overbearing. . . . In admissions, for example, they are extraordinarily difficult. As an authority they are corrupt . . . there is a massive amount of collusion [in appeals] and parents are denied their rights. . . . The enrolment is not open at all. I mean, [LEA], as I mentioned earlier have just clung onto the same old catchment area – the control model. There's a complicated machinery there to make it appear . . . different, but it's not different at all . . . it's exactly the same now as it was 17 years ago when I first came.

Single form applications

This type of application procedure is the most common amongst the LEA admissions authorities in the sample. It is also, arguably, the procedure which is most empowering to the choosers, as it presents the opportunity for them to select a number of alternative schools and, in most cases, place them in order of preference. This is done via a single application form sent home from a child's current primary school.

> If your child attends a West Berkshire primary school you will receive a personalised application form along with this booklet. If your name is not on the West Berkshire LEA student list database at the end of July, or your child attends a school outside West Berkshire or an independent school, you must complete a 'non-personalised' form . . . It is also important that you state three preferences in order to increase your chances of obtaining an alternative preference if we are unable to meet your first preference.
>
> (West Berkshire, 1999/2000: 10)

Although this example is taken from the West Berkshire LEA admissions literature, almost identically worded examples can be found in the

Reading LEA and Bracknell Forest LEA guidelines (there is clearly some regional 'policy-borrowing' taking place after the break-up into unitary authorities). This approach to organising admissions applications is arguably the most enabling and also the fairest, as all parents must go through the same procedure regardless of their preferred institution. Only one application is needed (assuming that the child is placed in a school on the list) and, except for any appeal hearings, this is the only administration in which parents must participate. Application forms are distributed through primary schools and allowances are made for parents with children in schools outside LEA jurisdiction. This policy seems designed to maximise the ease with which parents can exercise choice and might therefore maximise any potential market activity.

Single preference applications

This is perhaps the simplest of the applications procedures which do not automatically offer a 'default' choice of institution. Parents wishing their child to be considered for secondary schooling within these LEAs may only state one preference. This is a policy used by five of the LEAs in the sample. For example, Cardiff's policy states that:

> If your child is attending a county or a Church in Wales primary school and is due to transfer to a secondary school next September you will receive a letter from the council which will ask which school you would like your child to attend. You will also be advised of the school which your child would normally attend by reference to the primary school he/she is attending.
>
> (Cardiff, 1999/2000: 7)

This procedure is less restrictive than the 'catchment' procedure as it does allow parents to make one choice, whether that be the school their child would 'normally attend' or another institution. It does not, then, make the assumption that the child will attend a default secondary school but, again, the tone of the language suggests that this might be the most appropriate action to take.

Multiple form applications

In our sample, three authorities required parents to make separate applications for each school they wished to be considered for entry to:

> You must obtain a separate application from for each school of your choice. Please contact the schools direct for application forms.
>
> (Hillingdon, 1999/2000: 4)

In addition to Hillingdon, Gloucestershire and Swansea follow a similar practice – the first because of its size and diversity and the second for reasons of financial stringency. However, in most LEAs there are a number of secondary schools which act as their own admission authorities. These may be foundation schools, voluntary-aided schools or city technology colleges, but because their admissions are not managed by the LEA parents must typically make a separate application to each institution. Some schools operating outside of the LEA admissions system require parents to make an individual, dedicated application. It is true that some LEAs co-ordinate the admissions of all state secondary schools in their area, whether under their control or not, but this is by no means universal practice. It is important to recognise the very different applications procedures required by these institutions (West *et al.*, 1998; West and Pennell, 1997a).

School allocation procedures

The sample shows a considerable diversity, both in the types of criteria used by admission authorities to select students when an institution is oversubscribed, and in the order of priority in which these criteria are applied (as also noted by Mayet, 1997). Unless otherwise specified these criteria relate to those schools remaining under LEA control (i.e. community schools). Obviously, most LEAs have a number of allocation criteria, and the order in which these are applied and the number of cases they are likely to affect are also important (see White *et al.*, 2001).

Parental or sibling connection

One of the most common criteria used by admissions authorities to prioritise students in cases of oversubscription is that of sibling or parental connection. Several variations appeared in the sample of admissions policies, more frequently relating to sibling than parental links. Of those relating to 'sibling links', the most common variations were similar to the following example :

> Applicants who will have a brother or sister at the school who will still be on the roll when they join; (For this criterion, 'brother or sister' includes any whole- or half-brother or sister by blood or adoption, and any step or foster brother or sister who lives with the child for whom the application is made at the date of application);
>
> (Camden LEA, 1999/2000: 7)

The rationale underlying this particular criterion is obviously practical, relating not only to issues such as travel to school, but also to considerations of students' well-being and security in a new environment. Parents with children already in attendance will presumably also be more familiar with a particular school staff, organisation and curriculum. These benefits are, however, less clear in the second variation in this group. For example, The Green School for Girls in Hounslow prioritises:

> An applicant with an older daughter who is *or has been* at the School.
> (Hounslow, 1999/2000: 17; emphasis added)

This variation is apparently much less common than the first and is more usually found in single-sex or religious foundation schools. The practical implications of a sibling having attended the school previously are less obvious than having a sibling currently attending but, as argued above, there may be some advantages of familiarity for parents. Formulating the criterion along these lines opens up institutions to criticism regarding the equity of such policies, a case which is strengthened by the existence of other policies which extend this idea further. The clearest example of an LEA-wide policy which extended privilege to those students who had 'parental links' with a school was in Reading Borough Council's allocation criteria, where priority is given to:

> (E) Children who have family connections with the school. (These are limited to father, mother or older sibling(s) who attended or are parent governors or existing staff members at the school.)
> (Reading, 1998/1999)

It is also important to note that such criteria are sometimes amalgamated with others. Sibling-links often appear as subcriteria, such as in the case of Gumley House Convent School, above, where they are used to differentiate between students who satisfy other criteria in equal measure. Another variation is provided in the general guidelines set down in Greenwich. They state that priority will generally be given to:

> b. children who are the siblings (brothers and sisters) of, or who live at the same address as, students already at the school.
>
> *However*, absolute priority may not always be given to such children who live some distance from the school (for example, if the family has moved away from the local area);
> (Greenwich, 1999/2000: 7)

This case reverses the previous one, instead using 'proximity' as a qualifying criterion which can be used in cases primarily relating to sibling links. The use of such 'qualifications' is commonly found in admissions arrangements, but there is little consensus between LEAs regarding the primacy of some criteria over others. Allocation criteria which at first examination are very similar can thus be seen to have quite different implications for parents and their children when applying to over-subscribed schools. Such variation in definitions can occur even within one LEA, if it contains more than one admissions authority (when, for example, foundation schools are present in that LEA).

Proximity

The last example in the above section, from Greenwich, relates to an issue which featured in almost all oversubscription selection criteria – proximity. Whilst this concept, like 'sibling links', may at first sight appear to be straightforward, in fact several different definitions and measures were found within the sampled documents. The simplest calculation of proximity used by admissions authorities is the actual distance between the home of the child and the chosen school, measured in a straight line. For example, Camden LEA gives

> priority to those living closest to the school measured in a straight line 'as the crow flies', between the home and the main entrance of the school;
>
> (Camden, 1999/2000: 7)

And Essex County Council similarly measures:

> Straight line distance from home to school, the closest to the school being given the highest priority.
>
> (Essex, 1999/2000: 11)

A more sophisticated measure is employed by some others, which takes into consideration the walking distance between the child's home and the school:

> Priority 5
> This gives priority to students living nearest the school based on the distance from home to school measured along the shortest walking distance by public highway and lighted footpath. The distance will be measured from the front door of the home address to the school entrance nearest to the home.
>
> (Bexley, 1999/2000: 9)

One measure of proximity, which only appears in the admissions arrange-ments published by Hertfordshire County Council, takes a completely different approach. Priority is given to:

Children who would have the longest extra journey to get to an alternative school with places available.

(Hertfordshire, 2000/2001: 8)

This 'relative proximity' represents an innovative approach to measurement as it aims to minimise the overall distance students have to travel to school. However, it is not without its problems as it could be very difficult to ascertain which alternative schools have places available at a time when all schools are in the process of allocating places. There are also considerable difficulties for suburban schools when using this method to deal with those wishing to travel out from urban areas, and those wishing to travel a much greater distance from rural ones. It may therefore allow schools considerable discretion in practice.

Catchment areas and 'feeder' or 'linked' primary schools

There are two further variations on the theme of 'proximity', which are closely linked to historical factors as well as practical issues. Either in conjunction with, or instead of, other measures of proximity, some admissions authorities give priority to students living in 'catchment areas' or attending 'feeder' primary schools. These two concepts were more generally associated with admissions arrangements which operated before the 1988 Education Reform Act, and the system of open enrolment which that legislation gave rise to. But they were still employed by over half of the admissions authorities as selection criteria in the event of a school's oversubscription. The following extracts outline which children will be given priority according to this principle.

Children who live in the school's defined area.

(Bristol, 2000/2001: 3)

Children living within the school's Joint or Consortium Area will be given priority when places are allocated using geographical considerations.

(Bristol, 1999/2000: 10)

Those children who live in the school's traditional local area will be offered places first.

(Bridgend, 1999/2000: 8)

Those children who live in the school's traditional catchment area will be offered places first.

(Carmarthenshire, 1999–2000: 8)

The first two extracts use similar criteria, which are defined imprecisely or refer to a defined area which is unlikely to be immediately recognisable to parents (i.e. the school's Joint or Consortium Area). The two extracts from the most recent admissions publications from Bristol LEA are included to show that changes do take place from year to year, and that such changes may not be immediately understandable to parents (or researchers), but could presumably have very real implications for some applicants.

The last two extracts, both from South Wales, are included for two reasons. First, the Carmarthenshire admissions arrangements are one of the few policies within the sample LEAs which actually contained a reference to the then out-dated concept of 'catchment areas'. Reasons for this can, at this stage of the research, only be speculative. It may be either that the term is now simply unfashionable, or perhaps that omitting it provides admissions authorities flexibility to redefine these traditionally designated areas as they wish. Second, the similarity in their wording is notable and is also repeated verbatim in the admissions arrangements of seven other LEAs in South Wales (out of a sample of eight). This criterion is also applied first in seven of these LEAs. This points to a collaborative approach to policy-making, due to certain regional or national considerations specific to the area.

The prioritising of students from 'linked' or 'feeder' primary schools is also commonly found in admissions policies. This is sometimes used in conjunction with catchment area criteria, but is also sometimes used as a surrogate for the latter, with traditional links between schools established before 1988 still being used as a template for admissions arrangements following the Education Reform Act. For example, priority may be given to:

(a) children who attend a nearby primary school included in an approved linking arrangement with the secondary school concerned.
(Greenwich, 1999/2000: 7)

Students who attend the family nursery/infant/junior schools and who live in the 'catchment' area.
(Conwy, 1999/2000: 3)

Some admissions authorities actually deny the existence of such an area in the documentation they produce:

No catchment area or zone has been laid down for any school. Any student living in any part of the Borough has the right to a place at any of the 10 schools for which the Authority controls admissions *provided that the demand does not exceed the admissions number listed against the school.*
(Bolton 1999/2000: 3, original emphasis)

However, this statement is followed by two qualifications:

> It should be stressed that the proximity criteria does ensure that students resident in the local community associated with a particular secondary school (and expressing a preference) will normally have a higher priority than children living further away. It has always been recognised that Turton High School serves the Turton community and therefore all students living within the Urban District of Turton will initially be considered for places in this school *provided it is their first preference*.
>
> (Bolton, 1999/2000: 3, original emphasis)

It appears that while mention of catchment areas is absent from much recent education legislation, and this is recognised by admissions authorities, in some cases their presence has been substituted by allocation criteria which operate according to very similar principles and have the same effect in practice.

First choice or strong request

Some admissions authorities specify that, in the event of oversubscription, priority will be given to students who specified the school as their first preference (and even where this is not stated it may be an underlying assumption).

> In the event of over-subscription, all first preference applications will be considered prior to all second preferences, all second preferences to all third preferences and so on.
>
> (Camden, 1999/2000: 7)

A related criterion has been summarised here under the term 'strong request'. This is more commonly used by the admissions authorities of foundation schools (usually those which were single-sex or with a religious character), but can also be found in the admissions arrangements published by LEAs.

> (iv) children whose parents have given reasons which the governors consider to be 'compelling' for admission to the school.
>
> (Hampshire, 2000/2001: 9)

This criterion is similar, but not identical, to those relating to a school's 'ethos' (see below). It allows parents to present a case for the admission of their particular child to a particular school. It could be due to a preference for the distinctive 'ethos' of a school, its curriculum or organisation, or may relate to particular social or medical considerations which are not covered elsewhere in the allocation criteria. The danger is that it lies open to the charge of favouring the more literate and educated families in the area.

Age

Age is perhaps the simplest and least ambiguous criterion used. Priority is generally given to older children. It only appears twice in the general admissions arrangements for LEAs, where it is be used as a tie-breaker, but is more commonly used by foundation schools.

> (i) Chronological order of date of birth.
>
> (Carmarthenshire, 1999/2000: 8)

> (ii) Children who will be 11 years old on or before 31st August 2000.
>
> (Cornwall, 2000/2001: 3)

The reasoning behind Carmarthenshire's policy is not clear in the case of secondary schooling (as it would be, perhaps, in the case of entry to an infant school) whereas Cornwall clearly intends to prioritise students who, for whatever reason, are in the school year below the rest of their age group.

Single-sex, religion or ethos

These criteria are grouped together as they all relate to particular characteristics of the school and the suitability of potential students for the reproduction of the school's character. Single-sex schools, by definition, only allow entry to students of one sex. Foundation schools operating on the basis of attachment to one particular faith frequently devote many of their allocation criteria to screening potential entrants for evidence of religious commitment. For example, Catholic schools specified criteria such as 'priestly support', attendance of a Catholic primary school, church attendance and parents' faith. A criterion of this kind was only found in one of the admissions policies of an LEA, and relating to non-foundation schools.

> (ii) for Church of England controlled schools only – children from families who are active members of the Church of England and whose parents request admission on denominational grounds (you will need to provide a certificate from the vicar, or other competent church authority, as evidence of regular church attendance).
>
> (Hampshire, 2000/2001: 9)

The inclusion of such a criterion in general admissions policies is unusual. This could be partly because most schools with a strong religious tradition have opted to become foundation schools, or it may be that in some areas such a criterion would be seen as controversial or politically insensitive.

Medical, social or special educational needs

This category covers all of the other criteria that mentioned any kind of special consideration which should be taken into account for a particular child's education or welfare. Although the point was not explicitly made in many of the documents, it is assumed that this does not include any children with special educational needs (SEN) 'statements', as schools are legally obliged to admit a child if that institution is specified on his or her statement. The emphasis is usually on medical rather than social circumstances. This is also qualified (as are SEN statements) by a need to demonstrate why the child should attend that particular school. Written confirmation from a medical practitioner or social worker is often required. For example:

> The LEA will give priority to applicants who have a medical or social need (this must be supported by a letter from a doctor or social worker).
>
> (Hammersmith and Fulham, 1997/1998: 8)

For most LEAs, a 'social' need must be identified by (noneducational) professionals in order to be considered valid. Of the six admissions authorities that specifically mention 'social need', only one outlines circumstances in which 'professional' advice would not be sought. The others require evidence to be presented by medical professionals or social workers. The definition of 'social' need here appears very similar to that of medical necessity. However, the admissions arrangements formulated by Bexley County Council provide an exception to this. The document differentiates between children with SEN statements, children with 'medical conditions', and 'social and domestic grounds' which can be taken into consideration. The guidance given for the identification of relevant 'social and domestic grounds', only to be applied in 'exceptional cases', are detailed below. Cases may be considered when:

> the disability or medical condition of a parent or sibling is such that it would result in significant hardship if the child did not attend the school nearest to home, nearest to the place of work of the parent not suffering the condition, or nearest the home of the family's child member;

a single parent working full time would suffer hardship if the child did not attend the school near his/her workplace or convenient to the travel to work arrangements; or

a child is identified by Social Services as 'in need', and the Director of Social Services and Housing Services recommends that the need is best met by the child's attendance at a particular school.

(Bexley, 1999/2000: 9)

This is one of the few cases where the definition of 'social' need is extended beyond the official diagnoses of medical professionals or social workers. Another example of this appears in the admissions policies of Hertfordshire County Council:

where a family break-up has made relationships very difficult at the only possible alternative school; or
where there is recorded evidence of severe bullying which makes a fresh start necessary at a particular school.

(Hertfordshire, 1999/2000: 9)

Other criteria

There is one element of admissions policy which warrants special mention. Greenwich LEA uses the results of the London reading test to allocate students to particular schools:

The main purpose of the test is to make sure that each secondary school has, as far as possible, an even balance of students in different reading ability ranges and is therefore a truly 'comprehensive' school – the aim of the school is to ensure a balanced intake for each school and not to give preference to children who perform better.

(Greenwich, 1999/2000: 6)

This is a 'banding' strategy and was a common practice within the former Inner London Education Authority (ILEA) of which Greenwich was a part. Greenwich is one of the few admissions policies which contain any elements directly originating from the main principles of comprehensive education. The importance of this can be seen in the lower than expected segregation in Greenwich. Although the sample contains other former members of ILEA, no similar policies appeared in their published admissions policies.

Another interesting criterion which we found in only two LEAs (both formerly making up one single authority) appears in the documentation as 'educational reasons'.

(d) Educational Reasons

Valid educational reasons include the provision of subjects or extra curricular activities at the preferred school not available at the designated area school or other schools closer to home, the overall size of the preferred school, its layout and classroom organisation, the sizes of its individual classes, or, in the Salisbury area, whether or not it is a single sex school.

(Wiltshire, 1999/2000)

The Swindon documentation for the same year is almost identically worded. Although such a criterion could have easily been incorporated into the 'strong request' or 'sex, religion or ethos' categories, it has been highlighted here simply because it defines these needs as 'educational', rather than as anything else. References to education are noticeably absent from most of the other criteria.

Three contrasting LEAs

A key strategy of LEAs to affect the enrolment patterns of schools in the new education market is in the way they manage the admissions system. There are a number of different ways in which LEAs do this. For example, LEAs encourage cooperation between schools (e.g. Pembrokeshire) and provide extra resources to schools that are adjacent to other schools that are allowed to expand as a result of being popular with parents (e.g. Staffordshire). LEAs manage the admissions system by discouraging or preventing schools from exceeding their published admission number, thus ensuring that potentially unpopular schools cannot lose any more student admissions (e.g. Hampshire). Another significant way in which LEAs manage the admissions system is by modifying the admissions criteria that they use to allocate places. For example, this could be by changing the feeder school network to create new channels of student transfer to less popular secondary schools (e.g. Cardiff), or by redrawing the catchment or designated areas (e.g. West Berkshire), or by introducing 'relative distance' criteria to ensure that rural LEA students get priority over students from a neighbouring urban LEA (e.g. Staffordshire). The three case study LEAs presented in this section, Cardiff, Brent, and Hertfordshire, offer significantly different market scenarios, that begin to help us interpret and explain potential changes to school intakes since the introduction of the 1988 Education Reform Act.

In some of our study areas, such as Gloucestershire, Essex and Hillingdon where the majority of secondary schools 'opted out', LEAs were in effect left 'minding the store' through the task of monitoring, as they were still required to do, whether new intakes of children had acquired secondary school places. As one official told us, because of the large number of GM and voluntary schools in the area, his LEA was composed of 192 admissions authorities. Not only did multiple admissions authorities diminish LEA capacity to match students to places, the 1989 Greenwich judgement enabled parents to express a preference for schools outside their own LEA, and thereby made admissions policy more complex to administer. Key beneficiaries of the judgement were the GM and voluntary-aided schools, who were given an unrestricted capacity to expand their catchments.

While most LEAs persisted with catchment areas as a primary means of allocation, there were visible hot spots, notably in Bexley, Bromley, Barnet, and Hammersmith and Fulham (among others) where local children were not obtaining entry into local schools as places were now going to out-of-borough families. These cases occurred most frequently in the London area where the LEA size and population density meant that boundary-crossing was relatively straightforward and cost-effective. They also occurred in areas which still have selective schools, and in areas where GM schools operated rigorous selection procedures.

This admissions loophole was addressed in the School Standards and Framework Act 1998 (Sections 84 and 85). The Act placed a duty on the secretary of state to issue a code of practice on school admissions. The subsequent codes published in England and Wales contained measures to design to ease the admissions confusion (see Chapter 1). In terms of admissions policies, LEAs remain the meso-level institutions of the kind created in 1944. They have a key role in the interpretation and 'recontextualisation' (Bernstein, 1996) of national policy frameworks at the local level. For this reason there is considerable variation in how local educational arenas of choice are constructed and there is significant variation in the way in which 'choice' is framed. To carry this idea forward we discuss three case study LEAs in detail.

Cardiff: local schools for local children

The first strategy is for LEAs to ensure that schools provide for the needs of their local children, and hence encourage parents to choose their local school. This tries to reduce the movement of students between schools and thus prevents school rolls from falling other than due to natural demographic changes in the local population. In many Welsh LEAs there is an active policy towards this:

> The overall policy of the County Council has become local schools for local children so the key proposal that is going through at the moment is suggesting that we move from link schools or feeder schools to going to catchment areas.
>
> (Cardiff LEA)

Some LEAs go further and print the name of the local catchment school on the admissions forms that parents complete when transferring their children from primary to secondary school to encourage parents to apply to that local school (e.g. Wrexham LEA). In Caerphilly LEA there is, and never has been, a real market. There are 1,500 surplus places in 12,000 but none of the council members is prepared to countenance losing places in their area. Everyone gets their first choice. There are no open days and no school visits. Parents are presented with a form with the neighbourhood school printed on it, and nearly all are happy with this as their attitude is reportedly 'my grandfather and father went to this school'.

What is striking about Cardiff is that its secondary schools are highly socially stratified (for Wales) and have been over the last decade or so, the period of our study. Now, and in the past, over one third of secondary school students would have to move before each school had an equal share of socially disadvantaged children as measured by proportions of free school meals (FSM). The figures for special educational need and first language students follow a similar pattern.

Social segregation is further reflected in the steep differences in examination performance as measured by the percentages of children obtaining GCSE A*–C. For example, in 1999, in Glan Ely High School (then in special measures) 9 per cent of students achieved 5 GCSE A*–C, while Cardiff High School recorded 76 per cent. These results reflected the proportion of children on FSM in each school. Of Cardiff's 20 maintained secondary schools, five are voluntary faith based (two Church in Wales, three Roman Catholic), and the others are community schools. Two of these are Welsh medium schools, where the language of instruction is Welsh. There are only four admissions authorities in Cardiff, a very low number compared with some other authorities in our sample. There are no foundation, specialist or technology schools or city technology colleges (CTCs) in the LEA, but a significant proportion of the fee-paying schools in Wales are located within it.

The relatively stable pattern of school stratification reflects an initial pattern produced by residential and socio-economic segregation that has been maintained and reproduced by Cardiff's admissions policies. Two key elements can be identified. The first is the feeder primary school arrangement that operates across the city. The second is the administration of the admissions policy, including the information supplied to parents, which effectively frames the kind of choices available to them. We discuss each in turn.

Link primary schools

Cardiff's admissions policies featured feeder or 'link' primary schools attached to designated high schools. The default position is that the LEA wrote to parents at each of the primary schools to indicate the secondary school to which their child had been allocated. Parents were able to indicate their preferences for other schools and could ask to be considered elsewhere, but they were, in effect, treated as applicants from other catchment areas and oversubscription rules were applied where this was necessary. Clearly, these arrangements have interacted with the housing market, and this relationship is reflected in the elevated house prices in the areas around the primary schools that feed Cardiff High School, for example. This 'selection by mortgage' has continued the pre-1988 situation, of using residence to secure primary school places and so gain entry into popular and oversubscribed secondary schools. This system is being replaced by a more conventional catchment area system based on geographical proximity rather than primary school attendance. The reasons for this are complex.

The LEA is faced with four broad problems. The first is oversubscription in a quarter of schools in the primary and secondary sectors, with the primary sector being most affected. A larger number of schools are undersubscribed. The second is that it has 'a surplus . . . in the region of 800 spare places in primary and 2,500 in secondary' (Cardiff LEA interview). Third, there is a northward and eastward drift of students. This is the growth area of the city. Students leaving the schools that served the peripheral estates to the west also take school places in the north east. Fourth, is the problem of meeting central government policy on the reduction of infant class sizes. Some of these problems could be overcome by the LEA asking the National Assembly for Wales to reduce the Standard Admission Numbers (SAN) in primary schools. While this is seen as reducing the number of surplus places and will contribute to the reduction of infant class sizes it also reinforces 'the overall policy of the County Council [which is] local schools for local children'. However, in reducing the size of primary schools the catchment area is also reduced and residential segregation is likely to be increased.

In its School Organisation Plan 2000–2005 (Cardiff County Council, 2000a) the LEA admits that this will not have the desired effect of redistributing secondary school places across its schools. It proposes that:

> Eligibility for admission to a secondary school would therefore depend upon residence within a catchment area boundary *and the primary school attended would not be amongst the eligibility criteria* (our emphasis). This would ensure that the policy of local school for local children is carried through into the secondary sector.
>
> (Ibid.: 19)

The document goes on to note that:

> . . . it may be necessary to revise primary and secondary catchment area boundaries to ensure that local populations are appropriate to the SAN of secondary schools.
>
> (Ibid.)

These changes are set within a manipulation of the SANs which would reduce student numbers in some schools and increase them in others, although it is not clear from the plan in which directions theses changes would work. Such adjustments are seen primarily as the basis for the efficient use of resources and the possible transfer of support to those schools who most need it. The proposals do not specifically address the socio-economic and academically stratified character of the system. An indication of how tightly the 'link schools' catchment policy works in relation to community schools admissions patterns, however, was revealed in our interview where one respondent reported:

> I would say that there is virtually nil free transport in the community schools, Radyr being the exception because it covers a rural area. Otherwise all our [free] transport is all Church and Welsh medium.
>
> (Cardiff LEA interview)

And this is the problem. Families are entitled to free travel if they live more than two miles from a primary or three miles from a secondary school. The Church and Welsh Medium schools with free transport provision contain student populations with lower proportions of disadvantaged students. So, paradoxically, the free transport policy benefits most the socially advantaged schools and the families with resources to use schools outside their LEA-designated catchment area; definitely not a 'local school for local children' policy here. So while Cardiff's approach maintains and reproduces the connection between residential and school segregation, past advantages enjoyed by the voluntary schools have been secured by more open enrolment policies and now via the SSF Act recognition of their status as stand-alone admissions authorities.

We asked our interviewees directly how they saw LEA admissions policies in light of the stratified nature of the system. They were clearly aware of the difficulty, but had limited means to address the problem:

> The broad answer under the last government of course the capacity of the LEA to try and tackle that problem has whittled away and away and away until basically the last government seemed to have a policy of let the market rule and in which case the ability of the LEA to actually do anything about situations was extremely limited. This government announced that it seemed to me that it did want to have

a slightly different approach but really still the measures we have to tackle this situation are rather limited but we do see that the need to have a role in this for economic [reasons] if for no other reason actually . . .

I mean in my personal view at the end of the day if there isn't a clear government national policy that councils can if you like make social policies to equalise the effects of socio-economic conditions I think in one sense you are always going to be struggling against bigger trends, you know, bigger authorities so that is the key really and I don't know if your project can lend weight to the notion at the end of the day that if actually the government is really serious about maximizing the potential of all children then it has to tackle this issue. I mean there isn't any doubt about it in my mind that what happens in schools is this notion you need a *critical mass of students* (our emphasis) who are you know well disposed towards education and if you do get into a situation where a school is struggling against high numbers of students with special educational needs particularly in an emotional area, difficulties you know the school is having to contend with a whole range of social factors as well as teaching very effectively and that range of problems reaches a certain proportion it then becomes distracted from its main function and really there can be no comparison at the end of the day between a school that simply doesn't have to deal with those problems or of a different order of a different magnitude and one which is constantly with them day in day out. It just seems to me that there are two different kettles of fish . . .

The last government line was basically and I suppose in a sense the last government line is we sort of recognise that and the answer we have well what we are going to do is we are going to let this business of critical mass sort itself out by the market and it will sort itself out by the market because those schools that don't attract enough students will simply be on a white line which means that the kids from those schools will have to mixed in with other schools and I don't know whether that was practical but at least you can see it was at least a possible solution but I don't actually see what and quite where this current line is leading in terms of real policy attack on the issue but it has been around for years hasn't it.

(Cardiff LEA interview)

While the officers see the creation of 'critical masses' of school-focused students in schools across the city as a key to raising standards in the school most under pressure and surveillance (Glan Ely School has had 11 inspection visits in 6 years), there is little, in their view, they can do to bring that about. Moving from link schools to catchment areas addresses issues of efficiency, not equality or equity.

Framing choice

LEAs have a statutory obligation to supply parents with information about schools available to them, their characteristics, availability, application procedures and criteria for deciding entrance to oversubscribed schools. Cardiff's version is a brochure titled Admission to Schools (Cardiff County Council, 2000b) with a subtitle, 'Information for Parents 2000/2001' and subtitled 'Where schools are part of the family'.

Following the feeder school principle, parents are notified of the school their child has been allocated. The link schools and their designated high schools are clearly set out in the admissions brochure. Also recorded in the brochure is a table from which popular schools, and schools where preferences exceed places, can be identified. Parents wishing to select an alternative must complete a form. The pro forma clearly conveys the accepted grounds for seeking an alternative. Parents are required to set out (a) compelling medical grounds, (b) compelling social grounds or (c) attendance of siblings. There is also nearly a page available to give additional information in support of the request. No curricular or pedagogic preferences can be expressed, for example. The only 'get out of jail card' for most parents in these circumstances is to go to appeal if the request for an alternative schools fails, and the grounds can then be widened. For families with limited English/literary skills, however, the procedures might well be a considerable deterrent.

The 'local schools for local children' principle is stated and it is also embedded in the criteria employed in deciding admissions to oversubscribed schools. In Cardiff highest priority in applications for school places in secondary school are to 'students who are within the defined catchment area of the school' (Cardiff County Council, 2000b: 1) and within that those who are closest as measured by the shortest practicable walking route. The other criteria then applied are: students moving into the catchment area of their preferred school; compelling social or medical grounds; and older siblings at the preferred school.

Requests to attend an alternative school go to the School Decisions Committee, composed of three or four elected members advised by LEA officers. Their task has been eased however by the Rotherham judgement. This requires parents to state a preference for a particular school otherwise lose any priority that the LEA automatically gave them in allocating students to their designated local school. Similarly, LEAs have pointed out to parents that by not stating a preference for their local school they are not guaranteed a place there. That has forced parents to consider more carefully an application to an oversubscribed alternate school. According to our interviewees:

> in doing that last year the actual number of alternative requests plummeted. We get a high percentage of say Whitchurch, or Radyr

people saying I can go to Cardiff, now they thought well hang that school we won't be able to go up there so the actual number of requests went down. So much so that with . . . statutory appeals last year we put them later on in the year than we had previously and the Rotherham one we didn't actually hold any secondary appeals for transfer last year. The first year ever, the year before, we had had 18 but last year we didn't actually hold any appeals we were able to accommodate because of movement again because numbers go down every year but previous to that the Rotherham ruling and people accepted and not going for it then and as you can actually see we actually avoided having any secondary appeals last year, it was quite amazing.

(Cardiff LEA interview)

Brent: co-ordinating a complex system

Brent LEA has something of a north–south divide: the north is generally London suburban, while the south east corner is inner urban. It has a complex social mix that our respondent described in these terms:

> Brent is either the most ethnically diverse Borough in Europe or the second most ethnically diverse Borough in London. It is also one of the most deprived or seventh most deprived or something like that and the thirteenth/twentieth most deprived borough in the country. Most people would argue that there is a sort of a north/south divide in the borough. You have some sort of relatively inner city areas, you know, Harlsden and Kilburn, certainly South Kilburn and places like that in the south of the borough. And then you have got Kenton and Kingsbury, Queensbury, sort of fairly affluent suburbs in the north but at the same time there are areas of affluence in the south as well. . . . You have got schools that are in an affluent ward but right on their doorstep are estates where you know a lot of refugees and asylum seekers are housed, so I think there is great mixture in most school catchment areas.

(Brent LEA inteview)

There are 13 secondary schools in Brent of which only two are community schools. It has been Conservative-controlled in the post-1988 period, and secondary schools were actively encouraged to become grant-maintained. Of the remaining secondary schools, eight are foundation and three are voluntary schools. In all, there are 12 secondary admissions authorities. Parents apply directly to the schools for admission. The LEA acts as little more than a clearing house for students without a school place in the summer prior to transfer to secondary education. The

LEA's OFSTED Report (OFSTED, 1999: 14) notes that the 'LEA manages the supply of school places effectively' and that 'Admissions arrangements are complex but they are well handled'.

Brent falls into the category of LEAs that were desegregating, or, in other words, there is a more even spread of entitled children across the borough's secondary schools. In 1989, just under one third of all students on FSM would need to be redistributed across the secondary sector from each school to have an equal share. By 1999 however only about 16 per cent of students on FSM would have to change schools for there to be an equal share amongst schools. Three narratives provide an account of this desegregating trend. The first relates to grant-maintained (GM) schools in the LEA, the second concerns admissions to the two remaining LEA-controlled community schools and the third is the persistence of the north–south divide.

Grant-maintained schools

Brent LEA has maintained a long-standing amicable and working relationship with GM schools in its administrative boundaries. Even under Labour control, when only a minority of its schools had opted out, the then Chief Education Officer invited GM headteachers to his briefing meetings along with other LEA heads (Fitz et al., 1993). In subsequent years, Conservative administrations proactively encouraged secondary schools to seek GM status. Schools, such as Preston Manor, Kingsbury, and Claremont, all in the north, which sought and obtained GM status maintained their popularity and the character of their intakes. They typically have about half the share of children on FSM that they would have under 'ideal' conditions where those children were distributed equally. That pattern has remained stable over the last 10 years. Other schools appear to have changed their intakes dramatically once they became GM.

Two schools, Copland (formerly GM, now Copland Community and Technology School) and Cardinal Hinsley RC High School for Boys, had large proportions of FSM students in their populations in 1989. These fell dramatically in the period 1989–1993, although they still retained more socially disadvantaged children in their intake than the northern schools. These changes could account for much of the desegregation we see in Brent. Although Copland now has increasing numbers of FSM again, it and other schools seem to have employed their admissions policies to change the character of their recruits.

Copland selects students on the basis of a standardized national test, from which students are banded and ranked within each band. Fifty-five places are then offered to band A (high performing) students, 110 places to the middle band B and a further 55 places go to band C applicants.

Copland has an idiosyncratic admissions policy in that it has consistently recruited 20 students above its standard number. The LEA reports that this strategy is permissible within existing legislation. Two other schools, Queens Park and Cardinal Hinsley have a similar trajectory to Copland. These schools give priority to applicants who have siblings already in the school, and as these schools have been repositioned in the market it is likely that their catchment areas have also reduced in size.

LEA community schools

Two community schools, Wembley High School and Willesden High School may well have paid a price in terms of their market location by remaining LEA community schools. Since 1989, the proportion of FSM children in these schools has steadily increased. They began the period of this study with less than their share of FSM, have steadily desegregated but they have now moved to a situation where these schools have slightly more than their share of socially disadvantaged students. Willesden is also in 'special measures'. A similar trajectory applies to John Kelly Boys Technology School, and to a lesser extent, John Kelly Girls Technology School.

The John Kelly Schools, Willesden and Wembley High Schools generally have unfilled places in the summer of each year. LEA officials suggest that unsuccessful applicants from oversubscribed schools apply to them. In a total population of 33,000 applicants, however, the LEA reports that about 600 families are looking for places just prior to the new school year. In that sense, the system 'clears' relatively well, given the number of admissions authorities and the diversity of admissions criteria that apply across the borough. However, the LEA admissions criteria that apply to community schools are likely to contribute to the increasing proportion of children in poverty that are entering those schools. At Wembley and Willesden the first admissions criterion is, 'Children looked after by the local authority' (Brent Education Services, 2000). While this certainly guarantees admission for children who conventionally might be thought difficult to place, this criterion can be read in terms of creating and maintaining 'sink' schools.

The north–south divide is evident in the percentages of 5 GCSE grades A*–C achieved by secondary schools. Preston Manor, Kingsbury, Claremont and St Gregory's Boys Schools achieved 56, 54, 54 and 57 per cent respectively. These figures are well below the private, faith-based Al-Sadiq and Al Zahara Schools (91 per cent), the Islamia Girl's School (86 per cent) and the Swaminarayan School (88 per cent), although these also feature low numbers of examinees. Willesden achieved 13 per cent A*–C grades, and other schools in the southern group in the range 30–40 per cent.

It is the schools in the north which are heavily oversubscribed and which attract numbers of applicants from other LEAs, such as Harrow, Barnet, and Ealing. This is not surprising given their location close to LEA borders in the north. Our interview data suggest that Preston Manor, Kingsbury and Claremont generate about 50–100 appeals each per year, most of which are unsuccessful, and that they compete with each other in a local market. Preston Manor and Kingsbury also select about 15 per cent of their students and in the past have been known to hold their entrance examinations on different Saturdays so ensuring that students face serial testing and that some finish up holding multiple places. The LEA has tried to encourage more standardization in the admissions procedures but admits it has little power to force compliance.

Brent is an example of an LEA that has few powers to 'smooth' any segregation that arises within the borough because nearly all of its schools act as their own admissions authorities. It has a role in advising parents where there are places available for children in the summer prior to entry. It also assists in the composition of appeals panels and via the admissions forum has made some headway in standardizing admissions practices. Certainly the schools have been successfully encouraged to report to the LEA which students have been offered places where, and the LEA monitors the match between students and places. In these circumstances, the notion of the catchment area, unlike Cardiff, does not mean very much.

In its statutory duty to provide parents with information about schools in the LEA and about their admissions policy, the principle of transparency works towards framing 'choice'. In the admissions brochure, Finding a Place for Your Child in the Year 2000 (Brent Education Services, 2000), for example, all maintained secondary schools are listed. Under each school there is also information about the number of appeals for admission and the number that were successful. From this parents can determine the over- and undersubscribed schools, and where application, therefore, carries high and low risk.

While the north–south divide between schools measured on a number of dimensions has remained stable some schools have experienced considerable increases in the number of children on FSM in their students populations, while others, most notably GM schools, can be seen to have falling proportions of FSM. The overall pattern is one of reducing segregation, and despite all of the above it is probably the availability of places in some schools (see also Chapter 7), coupled with elements of banding, that has led Brent to desegregate since 1989.

Hertfordshire: equalising access

Hertfordshire maintains 77 secondary schools and 17 middle, deemed secondary, schools. Its administrative area is composed of a number of medium-sized towns and a large number of villages. The south is best regarded as an extension of the greater London conurbation while the north is much more rural. Unemployment is low and this is reflected in the proportion of secondary school students on free school meals, about 7 per cent, less than half the national average. Just over 7 per cent of students are of ethnic minority origin and the proportion of children with SEN statements is 3.7 per cent, which is in line with the national average. Between 10 and 15 per cent of the student population enters fee-paying schools. Recent downturn in the fortunes of the aerospace and associated manufacturing industries has resulted in some of the students returning to the state sector and to a slight rise in the number of students eligible for free school meals. Those trends may well account for the decline in the pattern of school segregation over the last few years. Overall, school segregation is high. About 30 per cent of students would have to change places for schools to have an equal share of FSM students.

In the case of community schools, families in Hertfordshire are required to complete the secondary transfer form (STF) and name three preferred schools. Published admissions criteria for all schools give parents a clear indication of which schools they are most likely to gain admission. These arrangements, put into place in 1999 replace earlier allocation procedures in which parents could express a preference for an alternative by letter. 'Moving On', the LEA admission brochure (Hertfordshire, 2000), provides parents with considerable information about the number of applicants to all secondary schools, postcode data of successful applicants to schools, vignettes of families choosing schools, and fairly straightforward advice on maximising chances of obtaining a place at a preferred school. It explicitly advises them to list their local school amongst their preferences.

The current admissions rules, which apply to oversubscribed LEA community and voluntary schools, prioritise children with statements of special educational needs, children with medical or social reasons for attending a particular school, siblings in the school at the time of application, and geographical proximity, determined by the shortest designated route. In the case of single-sex schools, priority for secondary schools is determined by postcode and by what is called the 'traditional area', identified by proportions of families who have in the past selected that school as their first choice.

There are four administrative units in the county with local area education offices, but the sharpest contrast is between the north and the south areas and the narrative of the LEA admissions arrangements can be told in its handling of admissions for these areas. The schools in the north area are all LEA community schools, and LEA admission rules apply. There are relatively few out-of-county applicants and over 90 per cent of families obtain places in their preferred schools. The south area is a different matter. According to our informant only about 80 per cent of

local children obtain places in local schools, many of which are foundation and voluntary schools operating as their own admissions authorities,
and some of which are academically selective.

Hertfordshire is distinctive in its proactive employment of the School
Standards and Framework Act. This arose from the legacy of the former
grant maintained schools and voluntary schools creating their own
admissions policies, and recruiting out-of-county students. The result of
this was that local families were unable to obtain secondary school places
in local schools. OFSTED noted in its inspection report, for example, that
in 1998 nearly 1,000 children had not secured a place by February for the
coming academic year. As a result of its new co-ordinated admissions
arrangements this figure had fallen to just over 100 in the following year,
and most of these were in the south (OFSTED, 2000). Under the new
arrangements, foundation schools feed back to the LEA which applicants
they have admitted to their schools and this allows the LEA to inform the
parents of unsuccessful applicants about any remaining places.

Hertfordshire has also vigorously challenged foundation and voluntary
schools admissions' policies before the schools adjudicator. It has applied
to the adjudicator on 26 occasions to seek changes to the admissions
policies of foundation schools. It succeeded in forcing them to add
geographical proximity to their admissions criteria, and, in some selective
schools, forced those schools to admit fewer children by academic
selection than had previously been the case. The LEA has employed two
main arguments in these applications. First, it pointed out that local
children had been denied places in nearby schools. Second, it argued that
selective schools had operated in ways inimical to the LEA's responsibilities to raise standards of attainment in its county schools.

As a result, applicants from other LEAs entering Hertfordshire schools
fell from 18.3 per cent in 1999 to 15.9 per cent in 2000, a pattern that is
geographically uneven. In the south of the county there has been a slight
increase in the number of out-of-county applicants gaining places. In the
north area, applicants from other LEAs have declined from 14 to 12 per
cent over the same period. Countywide, about 92 per cent of students
achieved a place at their preferred schools. Generally, the county has
managed to bring out-of-county applicants to foundation voluntary
schools into line with the countywide figures, reducing the proportion
from 17 to 15 per cent. There are still schools which draw heavily from
other LEAs, most notably Dame Alice Owen, which still recruits 66 per
cent of its intake from outside the county.

In combination, the county's publication of standard criteria, co-
ordination of admissions across the county, and its vigorous pursuit of
changes to the admissions policies of former grant maintained and
voluntary schools, has brought about something resembling a 'local
schools for local children' admissions policy in the majority of areas. It

also reduced its levels of segregation, by a small amount in the same period.

Conclusion

We have shown that recent national education policy, be it the 1988 Education Reform Act or the 1998 Schools Standards and Framework Act, has not been evenly implemented across the LEAs of England and Wales. School choice opportunities in Cardiff, Brent and Hertfordshire are structured very differently. A combination of organisational, structural and demographic factors have, on balance, muted many potential impacts of the reforms on school intakes. Normative patterns of school use are similar today to 1989, and have not been substantially affected either by the market reforms or by the administrative actions of LEAs. Popular schools, those schools which have had many more applicants than there were places available, have remained popular over the last decade. These schools have generally had the largest catchment areas, the best examination performances and relatively small proportions of students entitled to free school meals. Likewise, the least popular schools, those with fewer students than the schools' standard numbers, relatively poor public examination performances, and relatively high proportions of children on free school meals, have not changed their character in the same period. There is little evidence to suggest that social class patterns of choosing have intensified since the introduction of market-driven policies.

Whatever the national legislation in force, admission authorities appear to have considerable leeway in the formulation and operation of their admissions procedures. LEAs have shown relatively little variation of practice over time since 1979, finding ways of accommodating their existing processes within the changing national framework. For example, the sample LEAs in Wales have all been consistently under Labour political control since 1979, and as late as 1997, 10 years after the ERA 1988, their literature still spoke of 'catchment areas' which they all retain today (although Cardiff used linked feeder schools as first criterion, and catchment area as second). Given that diversification via GM schools and CTCs was never successful in Wales, one interpretation that could be drawn is that little except terminology has changed in terms of school admissions in Wales in the past 20 years.

Greater variation between LEAs is shown in the sample from England, perhaps partly due to a more varied picture of local political control, and therefore partly to local policies of selection or encouraging the move to GM status. In fact, given that all are working within the law, the scale of differences in policy is remarkable. Variation between LEAs is unlikely to decrease as a result of the 1998 School Standards and Framework Act, and is perhaps more likely to increase as more individual schools become the key admission authorities. As was the case during the 'tripartite' era of selection, when some LEAs allowed parents unrestricted choice, so today some areas, while apparently working within a policy of limited market forces, are actually exercising their relative freedom and creating subtly alternative models. LEAs that have retained some element of banding (mostly ex-ILEA such as Greenwich, Hackney, Lewisham, and Tower Hamlets; see West and Pennell, 1997b) have levels of segregation in their schools running at half what would be expected ceteris paribus. LEAs that use catchment areas as their main method of allocating places have levels of segregation around 20 per cent higher than would be expected otherwise, and, as explained above, LEAs where a large proportion of schools are their own admissions authorities also have above average segregation.

Chapter 10

Market frustration for families and schools?

Introduction

We now know a considerable amount about how and why families choose particular schools, and we do not intend to repeat that here (see Gorard, 1997d, 1998d). The key findings are that families generally do not report choosing schools according to classical economic theory. They do not consider many alternatives, and they select schools largely on the basis of the safety of their 10-year-old child rather than exclusively for academic reasons. Most parents are happy to use their local school. Most of the others would not have been happy to do so whether the ERA88 was in force or not. We have also, perforce, had to consider the role of schools in relation to that of school organisation (Chapter 8) and the LEA (Chapter 9). The main focus of this chapter, therefore, is on the final piece of the school allocation process – appeals by parents against unsuccessful school preference.

The vast proportion of variation in levels of segregation and changes over time is accounted for by structural factors. Given that geography and school organisation anyway precede school allocation procedures in historical terms, this means that the impact of increased market forces, if there is any, is likely to be confined to the margins of change. Policy changes at the Westminster parliament, the action of the adjudicator, and even the growing number of appeals are not related to substantial changes in socio-economic segregation in schools. This interpretation of our statistical results is confirmed by our interviews. Most families get their first preference school (as expressed), and most of these use a nearby traditional or catchment school. Most of the remaining families would probably not have used these schools even if the policy had been different. Increasing parental choice has not reduced the proportion of students in fee-paying or in faith-based schools, which have never used their LEA school allocation procedures. Oversubscription criteria are anyway only relevant to schools with more applicants than places, but it is important to recall that several schools are: 'just taking what we can get. We are fighting for as many as we can.'

Although choice policies do not appear to have either the full benefits their advocates had hoped or the dangers of segregation their opponents feared, it is clear that they are generally popular with parents, and also with many LEAs and schools. But in many areas there is considerable doubt that they have made any difference, except symbolically, at all. A rural LEA officer reported that choice has been minimal because of travel limitations, that nearly everyone gets their expressed preference, and that it has become increasingly used by families from a wider range of socio-economic backgrounds:

> Unless you live in an urban area maybe with two or three schools in your general community you don't particularly have a choice . . . because we haven't extended our transport policy . . . I come at that from the opposite end which is the number of parents who don't win an appeal is probably 1 per cent and by definition 99 per cent are not totally unhappy about it. A majority of parents certainly get their first choice . . . I think parental preference initially was something which was taken advantage of by relatively few people, more informed maybe. There is greater awareness now I would say.

An officer from another rural LEA agreed with all of these points (which also confirm our notion of a starting-gun effect, Chapter 4). Families do not have much choice in reality, and since 95 per cent or more choose their traditional catchment schools it is relatively easy to accommodate everyone, but the remaining 5 per cent represent a range of backgrounds:

> When the government started talking about parental choice . . . I think parents got misled into thinking they'd got choice when in fact there's very little. . . . This only led to more appeals, with no chance of them winning unless we have made a mistake . . . I would have to say that a lot of our appeals are from people who are not particularly articulate. We get terribly scrappy notes with bad punctuation, not very well written, so it's not necessarily the most articulate middle class who are submitting appeals.

Her counterpart in a London LEA has been in post for a long time and also sees no real change since 1988:

> I am not sure if there was any difference in the admittance to schools. I think the schools that are popular have always been popular and vice versa . . . [On the other hand] when it changed in 1976 . . . those schools remained over-subscribed because they were ex-grammar schools and that's continued [and had an effect on local house prices].

Appeals as exit with voice

In the United Kingdom, parents have been given the opportunity to 'vote with their feet' by not sending their children to schools that they believe are not satisfactory. This was a key element proposed by advocates of the market (Friedman and Friedman, 1980; Chubb and Moe, 1988) to force schools to be more responsive to the needs and desires of their consumers. However, in the context of the UK, parents have only been given the opportunity to express a preference for an alternative school, and since there are limits to the number of students a school can admit (the planned admission number) published criteria are used to prioritise students to school places. This mix of open enrolment and bureaucratic rules has created a quasi-market form of admissions (Le Grand and Bartlett, 1993). Consequently some parents do not get a school of their choosing, but the 1988 Education Reform Act did give such parents the opportunity to appeal against their allocated placement.

The introduction of open enrolment in schooling has generated a radically new component to how schools and public bureaucracies (i.e. the providers) should respond to the changing needs and wants of parents (i.e. the consumers). According to Hirschman (1970) this is a form of 'exit' (expressing a preference by voting with your feet) that, it is believed, will make schools and bureaucracies more responsive than they were when 'voice' (expressing a preference by arguing a case) was really the only means to change the production of education. Admission appeals in the UK education market are unique in that they provide a formal, more sophisticated, example of a process where 'voice' is being used to argue for exit. The presence of such appeals in the education market highlights an important limit that would not generally occur in a free market for goods, for example. The presence of appeals in the admissions process can be seen as having two purposes. First, it provides a mechanism for ensuring that whichever institution allocates school places does so with the notion of parental preference in mind. Second, it provides parents with the means to be given a full justification for the original decision and to present further evidence that they believe may reverse this decision.

Some commentators on the impact of markets in education have suggested that open enrolment advantages the middle classes (Jeynes, 2000) because they possess greater levels of social and cultural capital (Bourdieu and Passeron, 1992). Consequently, it could be argued that parents going to the appeal stage of the admissions process, and preparing successful appeal cases, are also likely to have relatively greater social and cultural capital. Therefore, our interest in the pattern of admission appeals is whether it is such middle-class parents being prompted to 'voice' their frustration with the new education market. Previous chapters have shown that parents from both ends of the socio-economic spectrum are actively participating in the simple process of open enrolment. However, there may still be a distinction between 'alert' and 'inert' parents (Willms and Echols, 1992) when it comes to appealing against their school placement.

The appeals process currently operates in the following way. Once the decision about allocating school places has been made, parents are entitled to appeal against this decision. If a parent lodges an appeal they are then invited to present their case to an appeals panel, specifying the choice of school to which they wish to send their child. At the appeals hearing the admission authority defends their decision to refuse a place to that particular child. The final decision of the appeals panel is binding for the admission authority (whether LEA or school, as in the case of foundation and some faith-based schools).

Growing level of appeals

Appeals over school places have risen dramatically since they were first introduced (Table 10.1). In the 6 years between 1993 and 1999 the number of appeals lodged by parents for secondary school places more than doubled from 24,581 (4.21 per cent of all admissions) to 60,454 (9.62 per cent of all admissions). By 1999/2000 this amounted to nearly one in 10 parents of that year's admissions appealing against the decision in allocating them a school place. This is quite significant since in a recent survey (Flatley *et al.*, 2001), and in reports to us by LEAs, over 90 per cent of parents generally get their first preference of school (see also DfES, 2001a). Therefore, it could be argued that the number of parents appealing equals those not getting the school of their choice. There have even been reports that parents are 'cheating' in their appeals, by providing a false address, or renting a second home, within the school's catchment area (Luck, 2000). The proportion of 'alert' clients has therefore grown significantly since 1988. Those snapshot studies made soon after the Education Reform Act 1988 will not have realised this, and may quite validly produce quite different findings from those of studies made some time later.

The head of one popular school complained that there were now so many appeals (and even illegal re-appeals) on medical grounds that 'I

Table 10.1 Secondary appeals as a percentage of admissions (DfES, 2001)

	1995/1996	1996/1997	1997/1998	1998/1999	1999/00
% Appeals	5.99	6.65	7.63	8.70	9.62
% Heard	4.33	4.89	5.49	6.31	6.44
% In favour	1.36	1.53	1.78	2.05	2.08

did ring my colleague at [unitary authority] and asked if I could have an ambulance for the first day of term!' One explanation for this rise is a growing awareness by parents of their rights to express a preference of school and of their rights to appeal:

> The number of appeals has increased significantly. Parents have become much more aware of their rights or what they perceive as their rights [. . .] Perhaps the political emphasis on parent power has raised people's awareness so people are more inclined nowadays to appeal that they would have been five or six years ago.
>
> (Large southern county LEA, admissions officer)

Given the suggestion that parents are perhaps becoming more aware of their rights to appeal, some admission authorities, notably foundation or voluntary-aided schools, are reluctant to encourage parents to appeal. This tension is perhaps inevitable since these schools are their own admission authorities and it is they that have refused admission:

> I worry about this, but I think although a lot had the right to, I think very few do [appeal]. I do have evidence but I'm not going to state the schools where the parents are telling us that the schools are refusing appeals on the grounds that you're number 300 on the waiting list and they're only going to do [appeals for] the first 50. Which is illegal.
>
> (Outer London LEA, admissions officer)

In such cases local education authorities (LEAs) often act as 'enforcers' by making it their responsibility to make parents aware of their rights to appeal and to make the process as transparent as possible:

> We have certainly take a great step to ensure that parents are aware that when they raise issues with us we do inform them of their rights and we would defend them to the utmost to ensure that parental preference is taken on board.
>
> (Small southern county LEA, admissions officer)

Even where parents lodge an appeal against the decision to allocate a school place for their child not all of these go to the next stage of the appeals process, to present their case in front of an appeals panel. The proportion of appeals actually heard against the number of appeals lodged was around 70 per cent over the period (second row in Table 10.1), despite slight fluctuations year-on-year, with the remainder not going any further. It is considerably easier to lodge an appeal than it is to actually go to the next stage and prepare a written argument that is then presented in front of a group of appeals panellists. It is perhaps not surprising that a number of parents drop out of the process at this stage. In some cases this could have been because the original decision had already been reversed, but, according to the LEA admissions officers, this was rare. Instances where this may occur are where parents are very high up on a school waiting list and while waiting to appeal a place becomes available in a desirable school and is offered to them. Some parents who have lodged an appeal are discouraged to continue with their appeal by the LEA. In a number of situations LEAs held their own preliminary stage to the appeals process:

> One of the interesting things that we have in [LEA] of, decisions were made by [LEA admission] officers, all the applications would come in and all the rest of it, and decisions would go out to parents and before parents – they have a right to get a statutory appeal – but if they were not happy with that decision at that stage then we would have a further process by which we could ask that their appeal be reviewed by the authority and at that point that review was undertaken by a panel of elected members . . . and if they still didn't get their place then they could go on to the statutory appeal – it was an additional stage.
>
> (Large eastern county LEA, deputy director)

However, even though this appears to give parents a chance to have an appeal reviewed before going to the statutory appeal panel, the process was criticised. When asked if this extra stage to the appeal was still operational they responded:

> We got criticised by the Ombudsman who suggested that it was actually a confusing stage for parents who thought it was an appeal when in fact what it was was just a further stage before the final, final, LEA decision and the Ombudsman didn't like the idea that you had a LEA decision but then there was a further review of that decision. It also started to prolong the time-scale and so after considering it the view was that we took that stage out.
>
> One of the interesting things, and the jury's still out on this, is there is a suggestion that that is actually increasing the number of appeals or statutory appeals because that actually filtered out some parents who at that stage felt OK we didn't like the decision but we've had a chance to make representations about it and get it reviewed, we've still not got out place but we'll settle, as it were, at that stage.
>
> (Large eastern county LEA, deputy director)

While LEAs had removed the formal stage, it is still apparent that some LEAs felt they had a role in justifying their decision to parents before the appeals were heard. This probably discourages a significant minority of parents from going to the next stage of the appeal. Approximately one quarter of parents who lodge an appeal, or 32 per cent of parents who get their appeal heard, are successful in their appeal, i.e. they get a place in the preferred school (third row in Table 10.1). Between 1993 and 1998 this figure fell gradually but began to rise thereafter.

Of the secondary admissions in each year, the proportion of parents who have their appeal upheld has risen from 1 to 2 per cent over the period. This figure remains very low but does mean that proportionally twice as many parents were successful in their appeal by 1998/1999 than they were in 1993/1994. This should give parents encouragement. However, LEAs do not necessarily see it that way. Instead they see it as a reflection of their own ability to arrange the new form of admissions arrangements well:

> We might go along with a case that we think is a 'winner' for the authority and we lost it and you think, well what went wrong there? . . . Last year we did quite well – I think on the whole I think the number of appeals that were approved were slightly less, and don't know whether these figures balance that up, but we did work very hard.
>
> (Eastern county LEA, admissions officer)

The appeals process has two stages. In the first stage the admission authority has to convince the admissions panel that the school in question cannot accommodate any more children. If successful in defending the original decision the second stage will examine the individual circumstances of the parents. Even if the parents' appeals were upheld LEAs would still know if their own case, and their original decision, were correct. Of course the danger of the LEA not being able to present their case well in stage one becomes apparent:

> The panel at the end of that stage has to decide whether or not we've produced and made a case. If they say no there is no case, you're not presenting the facts as they really are, then all the children who are appealing [for a place at that particular school] get in.
>
> (Large southern county LEA, admissions officer)

The responsibility placed on a particular admissions authority to get their original decisions right often leads to a sense of personal victory, perhaps detracting from the real purpose of the appeals process:

> In the past the decisions have been taken by the admissions team but someone else presented the case: people who have experience in schools but didn't deal with the issue of decision-making arrangements. . . . I'm sure we work a lot harder [now] than our previous colleagues, because part of it was that you didn't want to let yourself down, or you didn't want to let your decision down by losing the appeal. . . . One year where we had a new person in doing the appeals . . . and they've been relegated! And it was just not understanding the system, she was getting conned by headteachers.
>
> (Eastern county LEA, admissions officer)

This situation puts LEAs, in particular, in a difficult situation. On the one hand they have a responsibility to the parents to inform them of their rights to appeal, yet on the other hand it is they that have to defend their case to the appeals panel when a parent does appeal. This difficulty does not apply to all admissions authorities however. As discussed earlier the voluntary-aided or foundation schools, who have independence in the admissions process, do not always fulfil their responsibility to inform parents of their rights with as much enthusiasm as the LEAs.

Another issue that emerges from reviewing the appeals process is the confusion that appears over the attempt by LEAs and the government to make the admissions process as objective as possible. If the allocation of places in oversubscribed schools was, as is encouraged in the 1999 School Admissions Code of Practice, as transparent and fair as possible then, theoretically, there should be few appeals. They certainly should not be rising. This tension is particularly felt by community schools who have no real responsibility in the admission arrangements yet are often the ones who have to deal with the outcomes of any appeal:

> Lots of heads do not, and governing bodies do not, accept the appeals system, and they say to me that – if we have got an agreed plan how can anybody be admitted above that, that is ridiculous. . . . They just don't accept that somebody can get into their school above the agreed number on appeal. When I say they don't accept it of course they have to accept it. They question it and regard it as being illogical and ridiculous.
>
> (South Wales urban LEA, admissions officer)

In the Audit Commission's report, 'Trading places: the supply and allocation of school places', one of their key recommendations was to, '10. Manage demand for places by . . . pursuing strategies aimed at controlling the overall levels of appeals' (Audit Commission, 1996: 59). However, practical solutions to this while encouraging parental choice and maintaining efficient provision appear to be limited:

[The Audit Commission survey] seemed to think that we should do more to try and reduce [appeals] or to try and settle them, but then if more people decide to appeal I don't quite know what you can do about that. You can reduce the number of appeals to nil and let them [parents] go to any school they want, but then you can't manage the situation properly.

(Eastern county LEA, admission officer)

Given these concerns it appears that the level of frustration in the admissions arrangements is rising. However, the overall level of market frustration is not equally distributed across England.

The nature of appeals

It has already been suggested elsewhere that the 'starting-gun' effect is the result of slowly increasing awareness of consumer rights among poorer families, resulting in an enormous increase in appeals against allocation of a nonchoice secondary school. If this were so, one might expect the pattern of changes in segregation in any area to be related to the proportion of parents prepared to appeal. Appeals are being used here as an indicator of competitiveness in the local market in which they occur, and of the proportion of 'alert' families willing and able to appeal (Willms and Echols, 1992). If the changes noted in Chapter 4 are related to market forces, then the changes should perhaps be greater in areas where a higher proportion of parents go to appeal.

In fact, this is not so. There is no significant relationship between appeals per LEA in 1994/1995 and desegregation. One of the LEAs with the largest decline in segregation had zero appeals (Knowsley), while the LEA with the largest proportion of appeals had an increase in segregation close to zero (Enfield). All of this suggests that there is no positive (linear) relationship between the observed changes in segregation and the level of competition for places in schools. It is also noteworthy, that despite the overall lack of relationship between appeals and desegregation, appeals are slightly more common in areas with higher proportions of FSM ($R=0.25$). This is contrary to preconceptions that areas with higher levels of poverty would have fewer families prepared to appeal. Another way of reading the same data would be that areas with highly polarised family incomes are generating more appeals in a system of choice based on league table indicators. All of this suggests that there is no positive relationship between the observed changes in segregation and the actual level of competition for places in schools.

The local level of appeals is inversely related to the number of surplus places. It is not clear whether appeals are a natural and expected outcome of market forces, or whether they are a symptom of the failure of the market (Taylor *et al.*, 2002). What is clear is that any area can elect to spend local tax income on funding surplus places, or on holding an increasing number of appeals.

There are considerable variations in the number of appeals lodged by LEA in England. For example, in Enfield 56 per cent of parents seeking a secondary school place for their children in 1998/1999 lodged an appeal against the decisions made. This had increased from 38 per cent in the previous year of admissions. At the other extreme in North Tyneside, similar in population size to Enfield, less than 2 per cent of their parents went on to appeal against their school placement. The LEAs with a high occurrence of appeals were typically urban/metropolitan authorities. However, this did not hold for all urban authorities, as illustrated by the examples of Enfield and North Tyneside. Similarly, there were a few rural LEAs with a high proportion of appeals being lodged, such as Lancashire, Hertfordshire and Buckinghamshire. What, then, are the causes of both the year-on-year increases of, and the unequal spatial distribution of, parental frustration with their school placement? Using the figures in Table 10.1 as our explained variable, multiple regression suggested four key drivers of variation, which we then considered in our interviews with senior LEA officers.

Greater 'consumer' behaviour of parents

One of the most significant variables to emerge from the regression analysis was the density of each LEA. More urban, and highly populated, authorities tend to have more appeals lodged. It has already been suggested that parents have become more aware of their rights to appeal, and, as more parents appeal over the decision, more parents are encouraged to appeal due to the increasing number of appeals upheld in the parents' favour:

> I think perhaps sometimes it depends on . . . you might get one school where there is a lot of success one year, so people will think – oh, they're very successful, it's not such a losing battle after all.
>
> (Eastern county LEA, admissions officer)

LEAs have appeared to become increasingly active in giving parents the opportunity to appeal, even in areas where many schools operate their own admissions arrangements:

> One of the standardised documents we are trying to produce is a standardised rejection letter, all schools are supposed to, in their rejection letter, say, 'I am sorry you have been rejected for your place because the school is full', or whatever it might be, 'If you want to

appeal against this decision contact . . .'. So the schools inform the parents at that stage and because as I have said we have now got a standard wording for them to use in that respect so they will tell the parents, parents will get information about what to do next.

(Outer London LEA, admissions officer)

Underlying parents' greater awareness of their right to appeal is their growing awareness of their right to make a preference for any school they wish to send their child to:

What has changed is an increasing number of parents are not choosing the school that they would traditionally have been their local school.

(Large eastern county LEA, deputy director)

As more parents seek alternatives to their local school there will be more parents who will want to lodge an appeal over their school placement. Similarly, the spatial variations in appeals lodged may be related to varying levels of activity by parents in the market place. Indeed the greater propensity of appeals to be lodged in urban/metropolitan LEAs reflects the greater opportunities that parents have in urban areas to choose alternatives to their local school. Further evidence of this relationship between greater parental activity in the market place and the levels of appeals can be seen in Figure 10.1. Using students' home postcodes in a geographical information system, the proportion of students not

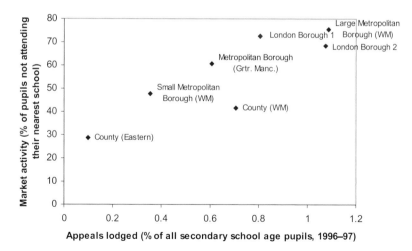

Figure 10.1 Relationship between market activity and appeals lodged for seven LEAs in England.

attending their nearest school was calculated for 1995/1996 in seven
LEAs. These LEAs represented different areas of England, north and
south, urban and rural. Using the proportion of students not attending
their nearest school as a proxy for parental activity in the market place
it can be seen that there is a relatively strong relationship with the
number of appeals lodged (but not, we repeat, with changes over time
in segregation). This also illustrates that there is not necessarily always
a direct relationship between student density and market activity of
parents in the education market place. For example, there was little
difference in the degree of parental activity in one metropolitan
borough and a county LEA. This would suggest that other factors are
also of importance.

However, it is easy to exaggerate this growth of consumer behaviour.
Appeals have gone on since 1946, and not only on religious grounds
before 1980 (West and Pennell, 1997b). The number of appeals grew in
the 1970s, which led to some embarrassment since appeals were then
held centrally over what were essentially local issues, such as what was
reasonable expenditure on transport. According to the head of a London
specialist school:

> It [shenanigans] has always gone on. Even before choice [the
> primary] head encouraged the parents of clever kids to buy a school
> uniform, and be photographed by the press outside the gates, barred
> from their 'choice' school by the LEA.

Pressure on school places

Another factor that is related to the level of market frustration in
England is the number of surplus places in the schools. The fewer the
surplus places in any LEA the less chance parents will have in getting
their choice of school. Indeed, some LEA admission officers reported
that the pressure for places played a crucial role in determining market
frustration:

> I think a lot of it is to do with pressure on places. I think that is a
> particular problem that we have in [LEA] at the moment. We are very
> short of places in some areas. . . . There are no places for extra
> children, so where are they going to go? It's miles and miles, they
> can't come down here to the south because that's full, there's
> nowhere to go.
>
> (Large southern county LEA, admissions officer)

The local incidence of appeals is likely to reflect the degree of popularity of the schools. If, in one authority, there are a few schools that are

heavily oversubscribed then there may be a greater number of parents wishing to appeal over the admission decision. 'Hotspots' of appeals (Audit Commission, 1996) can, and do, occur. Schools that had the highest preference ratio, i.e. those that were relatively most over-subscribed, tended to also have the highest appeals ratio, i.e. the relative number of appeals lodged. Consequently, it may be areas where there are few 'good' alternatives for parents to choose from which prompt more appeals.

Diversity of schooling

At a more general level, the appeal hotspots may also be related to the presence of school diversity in the market place. The regression analysis showed those LEAs with a high proportion of selective schools tended to have a high number of appeals lodged. This suggests that where the admission of students goes beyond the use of typical oversubscription criteria, applied to the majority of maintained schools, there is greater frustration for parents. A similar relationship can be seen when com-paring the number of appeals lodged across all of England by the types of maintained schools there are (Figure 10.2). Foundation schools, formally grant-maintained schools and which the majority of grammar schools became, had the highest proportion of appeals lodged. Com-munity schools, formally county schools, generally had fewer appeals lodged against them than the other types of schools found in the education market. Only in the last 2 years has the incidence of appeals for such schools reached the same levels as for voluntary-aided, or denominational schools.

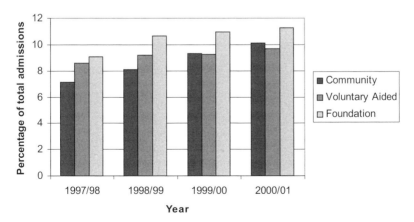

Figure 10.2 Appeals lodged by type of school, England 1997/1998 to 2000/2001.

The social advantage of parents

The final variable that was significant in accounting for the incidence of appeals was the additional educational needs (AEN) Index. This is an index calculated by the DfES to measure the local levels of social disadvantage, used in the allocation of resources; the higher the index the more educationally and socially deprived the LEA. This index had an inverse relationship with the number of appeals lodged, i.e. the more socially and educationally advantaged the LEA the greater the incidence of appeals being lodged. This would support the claim that parents with greater social and cultural capital are more likely to appeal during the admissions process. This was sometimes supported by the LEA admissions officers:

> Poor families, or families where language is a problem, were struggling with the form, so they weren't making an appeal.
>
> (Eastern county LEA, admissions officer)

Even where parents were having their appeal heard there were apparent differences in who was going to be more successful:

> The difficulty is going to be that particular people might still get their way as opposed to non- . . . Because they'll be able to put down better their reasons for wanting a school and will be better able to explain it.
>
> (Eastern county LEA, admissions officer)

However, not all LEA officers agreed with this:

> What I see sitting in these appeals is that there is a wide diversity of people, and basically what it boils down to is that everybody has an idea of which school they want for their child and they want to fight for that. So you get a wide cross-section. What you notice is that you may be getting different types of arguments used in an appeal.
>
> (Small southern county LEA, admissions officer)

There is evidence that as time passes more parents become aware of their rights, both to express a preference for a school, and to lodge an appeal. Therefore, parents from more socially disadvantaged backgrounds are likely to participate. One informant expressed it in the following terms:

> I think probably 10 years ago for want of a better term it was more middle-class parents who were involved in that sort of activity and that is definitely not the case now. One might also say the reverse,

that there is a very large percentage of parents who end up at the appeal stage that you will by no means describe as middle class.

(North-west urban LEA, admissions officer)

However, a commentator from a rural LEA points out that appeals ought not to happen, by their very nature, and when they do they should seldom be won: 'The only way they can win an appeal is if we have done it wrong, and to raise parental expectations. . . . I think it is disgusting.'

Conclusion

A key component in determining the extent of market frustration is the level of overall market activity taking place within a particular area. The level of market activity in turn is closely related to the geography of each LEA. For example, urban education markets have greater access to schools leading to greater parental activity in the market (Taylor, 2002) and subsequently to a greater number of appeals. Ironically, even though such areas provide a greater choice of schools to parents than more rural LEAs, consumer expectation and hence frustration is still more prevalent. However, this study also highlights a number of other features, both structural and behavioural, that are related to the degree of admission appeals within each local education market.

Structural explanations are generally related to the provision of schooling in an area, in particular the level of school diversity and the number of surplus places across the authority. Diversity of schooling in the UK is generally related to varying levels of private/public governance, ownership and funding (Bradford, 1993). A high level of autonomy enjoyed by schools in particular LEAs tends to lead to greater levels of market frustration. The level of frustration is also related to the occurrence of 'hotspots' of popular schools, where the supply of school places is well short of demand irrespective of the number of school places available across an entire LEA or school system. The traditional form of diversity in the UK system of schooling is based on elements of exclusion/ inclusion, such as religious membership, academic ability, and proximity and accessibility. Such diversity, based on forms of exclusion/inclusion rather than consumer demand, appears to be of some significance in generating frustration with the quasi-market provision in the UK.

Appeals have received little attention from academics and policymakers alike. Consequently, it is not clear whether the cause of appeals in the education market is due to the 'market' or the role of bureaucracy in its operation, nor whether their occurrence is an integral part of market forces at work or a sign of growing frustration among families (as suggested by MacLeod, 2001). The significant number of appeals being lodged in recent years highlights how market reforms in education admissions are now at a cross-roads. The reforms have prompted many LEAs to rationalise their provision, reducing the number of surplus places in their schools and closing schools that tend to be the least popular. While the former lessens the opportunity for parents' preferences to be met, therefore leading to a rise in the number of appeals, the latter (as we have seen) can lead to less segregation. Appeals will also rise considerably in the coming years as parents are allowed to lodge more than one appeal, one for each school place refused. There will be a greater financial cost as a result of the increased number of appeals being made. Schools themselves will have to 'pay' for every appeal made against them. This would imply that it is the schools' responsibility for not finding a place for a child rather than the bureaucracy of the market. Perhaps these are the healthy signs of a heated market in schools. However, it might be more sensible for this money to be spent in creating the required number of places, thereby reducing the number of dissatisfied parents and appeals.

Chapter 11

Re-appraising the impact of markets

Introduction

One theme that emerges from this body of work is that who goes to which school and who gets what in secondary education is largely determined by the wider social and economic structure within which the education system is located. Thus far, educational policies rooted in social welfare or market-orientated principles have had a minimal impact on that basic social ordering. We should not be surprised, for that has been the unyielding message of many social commentators such as Marx, Durkheim, Bourdieu, Bernstein and Halsey.

In this study, the key factors that regulate levels of segregation are outside the education arena, namely the national and local economy, the housing market and residential development. Within the education system there are, however, a number of policy-based factors that determine levels of segregation between schools. These include the provision of school places and the form of schooling provided. Our analysis suggests it is only after all of these factors have contributed to the unequal distribution of particular children to schools that the way in which school places are allocated and the market behaviour of families has any effect. These further factors suggest that a return to catchment areas, based on residence, may lead to further socio-economic segregation in schools.

That being said there is a positive aspect to the recent history of educational performance and achievement. There have been considerable improvements in social inclusion and opportunities by gender, ethnicity and class, and these improvements apply to education as much as any other social phenomenon. It would be inappropriate to deny, or downplay, the extent to which the education system has opened up since 1944 and provided opportunities to social classes and to social groups previously denied access to education and its credentials. Kelsall and Kelsall (1974) for example, present evidence that the gap between the top and bottom of the social scale in economic, power and status terms was being reduced by the 1970s. Although inequality and injustice for the socially disadvantaged has a long history (MacKay, 1999: 344), in fact, 'if you take a long-term historical perspective of the provision of education in the UK throughout its entire statutory period . . . you could say that a constant move towards greater justice and equity has been the hallmark of the whole process'. Whatever our complaints may be in retrospect, the 1944 Education Act, the comprehensivisation of schools, the 1988 Education Reform Act and a host of other initiatives, have all attempted to produce greater social justice in our education system, and to some extent they have all succeeded. To admit these improvements is not to deny the existence of the remaining problems, and they are considerable, but to help describe the current situation more precisely and so define those problems more closely.

Summary of results

Our study is the most extensive exploration of the impacts of market-orientated policies on a national system of education. A fresh picture emerges about a stratified British schooling system in 1989, that has been changed but not transformed by the introduction of choice and competition policies (Gorard *et al.*, 2001b, 2002b). This runs counter to more conventional narratives of increasing 'polarisation' and 'stratification' that emerged from small-scale, snapshot studies of education markets. It also tempers somewhat the social justice arguments of market-policy advocates. Building on our political arithmetic approach to policy-relevant research, this project has demonstrated the continuing importance of viewing policy impacts over long time intervals and in a variety of localities. By these means we have been able to derive a broader and more complex account of the impact of policies in general, and education markets in school systems in particular.

The purpose of our research was to examine the extent to which the introduction of educational markets gave rise to changes in the social composition of secondary schools in England and Wales. Using official statistics for this purpose, from the introduction of the Education Reform Act 1988 (ERA88) onwards, we measured changes over time in the tendency for pupils with particular socio-economic characteristics to cluster in particular schools (termed segregation). We considered a variety of reasons for the changes and regional differences in segregation that we encountered, and also began to relate these to changes in school output figures (i.e. public examination results). The project therefore moved from description and measurement to exploration and explanation. It also raised unforeseen methodological and research-capacity issues. The key findings are as follows.

From January 1989 to 1995, we found the degree of segregation by poverty in all secondary schools in England declined annually from a high of 35 per cent to around 30 per cent (meaning that 30 per cent of children from poor families would have to exchange schools for there to be no segregation by poverty). The turning point, 1995/1996, was the first year in which all students in compulsory years at secondary schools had enrolled since ERA88. This figure for segregation has subsequently risen annually to nearly 33 per cent by 2001. The pattern of reduced segregation was repeated when we employed other commonly used measures of the socio-economic composition of school populations, such as statements of special educational need, first language use and ethnicity. It also applied to Wales and all primary schools in England, and to all of the indices of segregation we employed. The decline and recent rise in segregation between schools iterates at national, regional and most local education authority (LEA) and school district levels. Analysed at any level of aggregation, schools have generally converged over time in terms of the socio-economic characteristics of their 'disadvantaged' students.

In so far as it is possible to ascertain, school examination results have risen since 1989 both in absolute terms, and in relation to the fee-paying sector. This has had the side-effect of reducing differential attainment in terms of social groups, such as those defined by geography, poverty and ethnicity. However, the strength of the statistical link between socio-background of students and examination results has not weakened since 1989, and the scale of the difference between the top and bottom per-forming pupils remains very large (dwarfing the more commonly cited difference between boys and girls, for example). Our measures suggest that 90 per cent of the variation in school performance can be explained by the background characteristics of students and the nature of their schools, and that this has not changed since ERA88. One notable outcome of this aspect of our research is that we have been able to use our composition-based indices to defend the performance of comprehensive schools against other sectors, and to defend regions such as Wales against the charge of underperformance.

Using a combination of data, we have gone a considerable way towards explaining the different local levels of absolute segregation, and local variations where LEAs, against the grain, showed increases in the segregation of schools. We have developed a satisfactory explanation of the variation in both phenomena. A key feature here is that non-educational factors play the largest part in the determination of patterns of school segregation, and these have been largely undisturbed by the reform of education over the last decade. In general terms our model has three elements – local geography, school organisation and admission arrangements – and these are listed in descending order of importance, and in temporal order as determinants of segregation.

What we have shown is that the determinants of school segregation are various. The most important ones are geographical, including population density, the nature of local housing, the diversity of the local population, and local levels of residential segregation (see also Coleman, 1992; Willms and Paterson, 1995; Performance and Innovation Unit, 2001). Once geographical and economic determinants are accounted for there is little variance left unaccounted for in our model, and most that remains is accounted for by school organisation factors, such as the nature and number of local schools. There is almost nothing left for marketisation to explain. What choice policies may do is change the rules by which segregation takes place, but without markedly increasing or eliminating levels of segregation that are largely shaped by structural factors. Nevertheless, the educational history of the twentieth century was largely one of a slow decline in educational inequalities by social class, gender and ethnicity (Heath, 2000; Paterson, 2001; Bynner and Joshi, 2002).

There are recent signs of stratification increasing again in English schools. The trend towards school autonomy, which includes granting schools further powers to control their own admissions policies, has enabled these schools to maintain, reproduce and sometimes increase their 'privileged' intakes and segregate away from adjacent community comprehensives. This occurred before in social welfare systems (via selective systems and faith-based schools) and marketised systems (via grant-maintained schools, CTCs and specialist colleges). The change since 1997 has been largely in the scale of this diversification. Nevertheless, schools are still significantly more socially mixed than in 1988 in the sense that the intake to each school is generally a better reflection of the wider society from which it recruits (at least in terms of the most disadvantaged sections of each community). Their measurable outcomes are now significantly greater than in 1988, and differential attainment between identifiable socio-economic groups has been reduced. Taking a long-term view, education in the UK would appear to be moving in the right direction (despite the view of what we have termed the 'crisis' commentators, see Gorard, 2000b). We suggest a variety of complementary explanations for these findings, and these include that:

- Changes in the social composition of schools are a small part of a much larger trend dating back to 1944 and before, and largely unrelated to specific market policies. The history of UK schooling has generally been one of continuous improvement and 'comprehensivisation' through the provision of more and longer education. School segregation in Britain as assessed by the proportion of all social class variation at the school level has dropped for the most elevated social class from 13 per cent in 1980 to 6 per cent (Paterson, 2001). For the least elevated classes, segregation was 5 per cent in 1980, 7 per cent in 1988 (pre-ERA88) and 3 per cent in 1997. The improvements are similar for segregation by gender and ethnicity. Paterson suggests that other researchers claiming to finding an increase are simply looking at too short a period of time.

- School stratification is largely determined by residential stratification (which explains around half of the variance in school admissions). The policy of open enrolment broke the rigid link between area of residence and school assignment, and residential stratification declined over the same period.

- Market reforms have worked, in the sense of allowing poor families to use schools in areas they cannot afford to live in, and encouraging schools to concentrate on improving examinations scores. Out-of-catchment (out-of-neighbourhood) enrolment has increased among poor families. Where school choice is unsuccessful, legal appeals against unwanted assignment are now almost universal.

- Although our analytical tools are strongly composition-invariant, it is notable that the period 1989–1996 involved a growth in indicators of poverty, while 1997–1999 reveals a decline. What we are seeing, therefore, is partly greater 'equality of poverty'.

- School reorganisations, especially closures, have contributed to decreases in segregation by mixing up previous school intakes in new ways.

- The relatively muted impact of choice policies can be explained through the way in which local school admission authorities have interpreted the policy changes. LEAs have worked to protect schools by managing the admissions system, chiefly in terms of numbers and budget-share, in some cases by not adhering to the national legislation (and in one LEA by not apparently being aware of the relevant legislation).

Therefore, even such an apparently simple social scientific question as 'do markets cause segregation?' has complex answers. Our first answer is that the school system in England and Wales is certainly fairer now than it was in 1989, but the most recent trend, long after the maturation of the school choice process, is towards unfairness again. It is quite misleading to claim, as others have done, that either of these trends was the sole outcome of government policies of increasing parental choice. Such a claim would ignore the important role of changes in population characteristics and residential segregation, for example. However, our second conclusion is that market forces in education clearly do not lead, necessarily, to the kind of increased stratification that we had feared. The local variation in the implementation of national policy, and the lack of diversity or even of alternative schools in some regions, show the simple market-outcomes model to be invalid (see also Narodowski and Nores, 2002).

This leads to our third conclusion. The stratifying effect of market forces in schools depends, to a large extent, on the status ante. While we acknowledge that choice policies may well work against families not well endowed with finance and cultural capital they are no worse in their effects, and probably a great deal better, than simply assigning children to their nearest school to be educated with similar children living in similar housing conditions. In another scenario, were choice to be imposed on a system of random assignment to school, on the other hand, then the trend would arguably be towards the levels of stratification that we encounter now. In addition, the regional and local variation we found both in the practice of school assignment and in school-based trends show that localised, small-scale research (based only in inner London, for example) is inappropriate in isolation as a basis for generalisation. Finally, we have shown that there is no worsening crisis in the compulsory phases of UK education. More students are staying on longer, and more are gaining the qualifications recognised by employers and higher education institutions. That being said it is still working-class and some ethnic minority students who are likely to leave earliest, with fewer or no qualifications, and less likely to proceed on to post-compulsory education and training (Gorard and Rees, 2002). There is still the need therefore, to conduct the kind of rigorous large-scale mixed-method studies of the kind described in this book, in order to address the serious issues of social justice and differential attainment that remain.

Impact within the scholarly community

There has been a great deal of interest in our research in the US and the UK, although we detect some differences in its reception arising from differences in the research cultures and traditions on either side of the Atlantic. It is fair to say that UK researchers in the area of school choice have found the research challenging – not least because it has run against an established orthodoxy of suggested findings emanating from predominantly small-scale, fieldwork-intensive studies of the process of choosing schools. US researchers, and indeed researchers in other disciplines, have generally been more familiar with the scale of the research, the techniques and instruments employed and the means by which the conclusions have been drawn. Nevertheless, the need to explain and justify our findings to researchers whose finding are at odds with our own has had the positive effect of leading us to a wider consideration of the meaning and measurement of segregation, and of the most appropriate levels at which to examine it.

The importance and flexibility of our dataset has been shown in the way in which we were able to use it to address questions put to us by a variety of public bodies, such as The House of Commons Select Committee on Education and Skills, the National Union of Teachers, the

Campaign for State Education, and the Institute of Public and Policy Research who asked us, for instance, about the particular problems of schools in London, and about the trajectories of specialist and faith-based schools. These uses had not been specifically foreshadowed in the research. Similarly, we have been able to respond to requests by school governors and headteachers to provide useful contextual data for the performance of their school. At one point our data were being used by a consortium of headteachers in Rhondda Cynon Taff – one of the most disadvantaged unitary authorities in the UK – to defend their sector against the charge of underperformance. As well as this local significance, our work has proved to have considerable international policy relevance leading to invitations to speak worldwide, and also to an EU-wide study of indicators of equity in education, funded by the Socrates programme (see www.cf.ac.u/socsi/equity). It has also been used by both left- and right-wing pressure groups, to defend the record of community schools and justify neo-liberal policies, respectively.

We have contributed to a wider international debate within social science about the meaning and measurement of segregation, having developed a new method of measuring segregation in organisations. The key issue for us has been compositional invariance – the ability of a measure to handle simple changes of scale over time. While we have not solved the problem (no one index is ever likely to be the 'best' overall) our approach has generated considerable interest at the annual Cambridge Stratification Conference, in the pages of Sociology, and at the American Educational Research Association. We have also been part of an increased awareness and use of geographical techniques in educational research, which has enabled us to analyse and present our data in accordance with our underlying theoretical model of the importance of the 'local'. This work forms part of a new economic sociology of markets, which contradicts naïve universal explanations such as human capital theory and rational choice theory, and suggests instead that many of the determinants of complex social movements, such as changes in segregation, are historical and geographical.

There is no royal road to science . . .

We also feel that our methods and the findings form an important step towards the further development of a 'new' political arithmetic – a concept widely talked about, but little in evidence – in which complex situations can be examined by relatively simple mathematical techniques in combination with other forms of 'richer' data (Gorard and Rees, 2002; Gorard, 2002a). We have also successfully combined educational data with geographical information systems (GIS). But this again has led us into conflict, with those who would prefer more complex (but less appropriate) statistical approaches (Gorard, 2002b). At present the kind of research we have undertaken, here using complete national datasets, is well understood within the mainstream of social sciences, but is relatively new in the arena of educational policy analysis.

Our evidence has been the subject of some dispute (e.g. Lauder, 1999), sometimes on methodological grounds, but more often on inappropriate ideological ones (see Appendix). To some extent, though, the lack of the widely-expected changes as a result of introducing a policy of increased school choice is hardly surprising. Some observers had already suggested that this was a likely outcome (Levin and Riffel, 1997; Gorard, 1997b), and others in the US are discovering that competitive schemes such as the Cleveland voucher experiment (McGuinn and Hess, 2000) and the Milwaukee charter scheme (Hess, 2000) have produced no obvious reaction (other than symbolic ones by marketeers and teachers' unions) and little discernible change in the administration or leadership of publicly-funded schools. It is easy to exaggerate the actual significance of national policies in education (Bennett, 1999).

Where now with choice?

We are now in a position to be able to predict/explain, with some confidence, the levels of segregation across England and Wales, and this is a significant move forward in the debate. The benefits of this are two-fold. By accounting for other factors that may determine overall and changing levels of segregation it is possible to estimate the degree to which the process of school choice leads to social division. We can also begin to explain what properties within society and the education system are exacerbating, and limiting, socio-economic segregation between schools. This is useful for policy-makers, particularly those seeking ways of providing access to education that are fair and equitable. It is becoming apparent that the debate over the impact of the introduction of market principles to education may be distracting researchers and policy-makers from the real causes of unequal access and opportunities in education. These problems do not always have educational solutions.

Given that the genie is out of the bottle, it is very likely that some measure of parental choice of school will remain part of any future policy. The choice process can be reformed from the one described in this book, for example by co-ordinating the admissions process across and within LEAs (Sutcliffe, 2001). Using a single application form, and handling all responses on the same day nationally would help prevent multiple place allocation, wasted spaces, and would reduce bureaucracy. Given the

limitation of residential segregation, and its interac
segregation, incentives, such as council-tax exemption, c
for high-attaining primary pupils to attend designated se
in poorer areas (Schoon, 2001). Authorities should be enc
surplus places rather than an increasing number of appe
alise their school provision through closures where necessa
having a larger number of schools tied to rigidly defin
areas. The arrangements for free travel should be the same across LEAs
and between different school types. A return to all-school banding in
urban areas would help decrease socio-economic segregation further.

Choice does not lead, naturally, to diversity of provision. The pressure
to diversify school provision, and move away from the 'bog-standard'
comprehensive model, comes from policy-makers and their advocate-
advisers rather than popular demand. City technology colleges are few in
number. Many foundation schools changed to their current status to
avoid the threat of closure by their local authority. Specialist, faith-based,
and Welsh-speaking schools are not generally being driven to expand in
number by market forces.

However, the nature of local schools is, after residence, the main
determinant of the levels of social stratification in a local school system.
In summary, areas with high proportions of similar LEA-controlled
comprehensives tend to have low levels of between-school segregation
(by poverty, ethnicity, language and educational need). If this area is also
urban then the level of segregation has tended to decline further since
1989. Areas with a high proportion of nonstandard schools tend to have
the reverse characteristics. This is the danger (or cost) of having fee-
paying, specialist, faith-based, Welsh-speaking, or foundation schools.
The problem appears not to be the nature or desirability of the schools
themselves, nor even their funding arrangements, but their policies for
admission. What all of these types of school have in common is that they
routinely recruit students from a much wider area than the majority of
schools with which they are competing. On the other hand, where, for
example, specialist schools have a rigid catchment area just like nearby
comprehensives then their intakes more accurately reflect those of the
local inhabitants.

The implication for those wishing to see greater equity is that either all
schools should be allowed to recruit across larger areas (and appropriate
free travel should then be provided), or else all schools should be
restricted to nearby catchments. Most crucially, diversity of provision
should stem from demand, and should take place in a clear culture of
different but equal for all school types – with equal funding, and identical
procedures for application, allocation and appeals. Only then will we be
able to see whether it is the specialisation that makes specialist schools

ecial, or whether it is the religious ethos that leads VA/VC schools to better examination results, for example.

If school choice is to remain, our priority is to make it work as fairly as possible. Our final plea, therefore, is for greater understanding among children, parents and policy-makers of what school choice can and cannot do for them. We hope that this book will be part of that wider understanding.

The debate over measuring segregation

The issues discussed here, while seemingly esoteric, are important for a variety of reasons. Measures of inequality form the backdrop to a variety of sociological investigations, allowing the description of gaps in opportunity by occupational class, gender or ethnicity for example, and of trends in these differences over time and place. These preliminary descriptive patterns can then be explored in more detail to uncover their socio-economic determinants, leading to the amelioration of inequality. However, it has become clear from the 'index wars' dating back to at least the 1930s that measuring inequality is not a simple issue. Even measuring the strength of association in a simple two-by-two table gives rise to controversies that span generations, and still fascinate sociologists of science today (MacKenzie, 1999). Pioneers in statistics, such as Pearson and Yule, could not agree how to perform this (apparently) simplest of calculations. To some extent the results obtained in an investigation, and therefore the definition of further problems to be explored, are dependent on the precise nature of the measures used.

Comparing indices of segregation

We showed in Chapter 5 that additive methods such as the differences in percentage points are not appropriate, since we need to take account of changes over time in 'structural differences' (Marshall *et al.*, 1997). The more appropriate 'multiplicative' approaches to measuring segregation are generally based on standard indices. Given that the number of possible indices is large, we need to consider possible criteria for making judgements about their relative worth. James and Taeuber (1985), for example, suggested these three criteria, among others, for successful indices to satisfy:

- Composition invariance: The index should be unaffected by scaling of columns or rows, through increases in the 'raw' figures which leave the proportions otherwise unchanged.

- Organisational equivalence: The index should be unaffected by changes in the number of subareas, by combination for example of two subareas on the same 'side' of the line of no segregation.
- Principle of transfers: The index should be capable of being affected by the movement of one individual from one subarea to another.

As Taeuber and James (1982: 134) point out in relation to measuring racial segregation in schools, it 'does not depend upon the relative proportions of blacks and whites in the system, but only upon the relative distributions of students among schools'. However, this compositional invariance is not a simple concept (Kalter, 2000). Blackburn and Jarman (1997) suggest that all statistics of association are somewhat dependent on the absolute size of the marginal totals in any table. Some indices may have marginal independence with respect to one pair of marginal totals, but only in the unlikely real-life event of a row or column being multiplied by a constant. In addition, most measures of segregation, including matching marginals, tend to vary with the number of organisational units (Blackburn *et al.*, 1999). Thus, it is extremely difficult to find any indices at all which meet a strict version of these three criteria.

Nevertheless, we can begin to classify indices in terms of their closeness of match. For example, the sex ratio (or Hakim) index, once popular, is now generally seen as flawed on three main counts (Tzannatos, 1990). It is not easily interpretable, it is theoretically unbounded (never able to reach complete segregation, for example), and most importantly it is very sensitive to changes in population composition (leading to confusion between simple population changes and changes in the distribution of population elements between organisational units). Similar comments apply to the entropy or information [theory] index (H), and to the variance ratio. The Atkinson Index (A) is more complex to use than most indices, is difficult to interpret, and does not allow direct comparison between two or more studies (Massey and Denton, 1988). This is because A is really a family of indices (Kalter, 2000), whose use depends on the researcher's judgement in weighting of different parts of the segregation (Lorenz) curve. The complexity of several of these indices stems from their era of origin, where it was considered easier to square values to eliminate negatives than to use their modulus (despite the fact that the act of squaring may lead to some distortion of the results).

Isolation index

Noden (2000) and others recommend the use of the isolation index (I*) for measuring segregation, and it does have some advantages as a measure of exposure (see Gorard and Taylor, 2002a). For a table such as

A1, and a region with n subareas in which segregation may take place, and where i varies from 1 to n:

Isolation Index $=\sum (A_i/A) \cdot (A_i/C_i)$

However, it has a fatal flaw. Tables A2 and A3 produce the same value for I* even though there is clearly no segregation, injustice, inequality, or unevenness in the school system of Table A2 (since if all schools have the same proportion of disadvantaged children then there is no segregation, Taeuber and James, 1982), and there is equally clearly some segregation in Table A3. Whatever the isolation index (I*) is measuring, it is not segregation.

Dissimilarity index

The dissimilarity index (D) is the most commonly used for all types of areal social segregation (Taeuber *et al.*, 1981). While there was a period of what have been termed 'index wars' by Peach (1975) which started

Table A1   General table of segregation between schools

	Minority	Majority	Total
School 1	A1	B1	C1
School 2	A2	B2	C2
...			
School n	An	Bn	Cn
Total	A	B	C

Table A2   No segregation between schools

School	FSM	Non-FSM	Total	I*	D	S
A	20	80	100	0.08	0	0
B	20	80	100	0.08	0	0
C	20	80	100	0.08	0	0
Total	60	240	300	0.25	0	0

Table A3   Some segregation between schools

School	FSM	Non-FSM	Total	I*	D	S
A	0	100	100	0	0.36	0.33
B	0	100	100	0	0.36	0.33
C	20	80	100	0.25	0.73	0.67
Total	20	280	300	0.25	0.73	0.67

around the time of Wright (1937), the 'Pax Duncana' apparently crowned the dissimilarity index as the premier of all measures. Duncan and Duncan (1955a) presented a number of segregation indices and showed that they were all related to the segregation or Lorenz curve and, hence, to each other. Their paper showed that all other measures can be encapsulated by a judicious use of the population composition figures and D. However, it was another article by the same authors (Duncan and Duncan, 1955b), which made explicit use of D for their own research, that may have proved the catalyst for its current extensive use (see Lieberson, 1981).

Potentially D varies from 0 to 1, and represents 'the percentage of one group or the other which would have to move if there was to be no segregation between the groups' (Lieberson, 1981). Using the same table as for the isolation index, for a region with n sub-areas in which segregation may take place, and i varies from 1 to n, the index of dissimilarity may be defined as:

$$D = 0.5 * \sum |A_i/A - B_i/B|.$$

Its advantages are that it is considered independent of population composition (Taeuber *et al.*, 1981), that its widespread use allows comparability between studies, and that it is easy to comprehend while covering the same empirical ground as its 'competitors' (Massey and Denton, 1988). Unfortunately, it does not pick up all transfers (although it is capable of picking up some transfers), and the size of the minority population needs to be large in comparison to the number of units of organisation. More important perhaps is the doubt cast over its major claimed advantage of comparability over time and space by the work of Cortese *et al.* (1976). They claim that since D is not always organisationally invariant it is not reliable for use in comparing regions of different scale (for example).

Unlike the 'losers' in the war, D has long been considered as composition invariant, for even though Duncan and Duncan (1955a) acknowledge that the proportion of both subgroups is present in the calculation, they argue that D is unaffected by scaled changes in either group. Lieberson (1981: 63) agrees that D is not affected by population composition, and gives as an example 'if the number of whites in each subarea was divided by 10, then the index of dissimilarity would remain unchanged'. But by 1982, Lieberson and Carter concede that D is 'affected by group size under special circumstances . . . but the conditions under which a problem arises are quite extreme and are unlikely to occur in real-life circumstances'. What we have shown in our new work is that on a strong interpretation of composition invariance this is not, in fact, so. We agree with, and have developed, the critiques of Cortese *et al.* (1976), Taeuber and James (1982), and the later comments of Blackburn *et al.* (1995) that D is not entirely free of 'unwanted influence', and the conclusion of Wong *et al.* (1999) that D is sensitive to the effect of scale.

Segregation index

We describe the 'segregation index' (S) in Chapter 3. The major objection to S in principle is that it is not symmetric, so that if group A is the minority (or disadvantaged) then the formula gives a different answer for the majority group B. However, for some commentators, such as Lieberson (1981), asymmetry is not intrinsically problematic. The key issue with asymmetry is not having the two different values for the two groups but whether these give contradictory results, which for S they do not. In addition most definitions of segregation are primarily concerned with the distribution of one group only. For example, the definition of unevenness used by Massey and Denton (1988: 283) is where 'minority members may be distributed so that they are over-represented in some areas and underrepresented in others'. The definition is asymmetric since it is only concerned with the distribution of the minority group. This is what S encapsulates.

The key difference is in the base figure used to compare the distribution of any particular group. Hence, while D compares the proportion of two groups with each other by subarea, S compares the proportion of one group with the total for that subarea. This means that even if the proportion of students eligible for free school meals is substantially altered, S remains unchanged as long as they are distributed to each of the schools in the same proportions as the original figures. Since D is the proportion of all students who have to change schools for there to be no segregation, this will obviously be small if the ratio of disadvantaged students to the population is small, and vice versa. The size of D depends heavily on this ratio, which is completely unrelated to segregation. S, on the other hand, as the proportion of disadvantaged students who have to exchange schools, is unaffected by changes in the ratio of disadvantage to population. It is strongly composition invariant (Gorard and Taylor, 2002a).

Like D, S is already a very valuable and widely used measure of unevenness, but because it is termed differently in different fields, this has not previously been remarked. For example, a special case of S is used routinely to calculate gendered achievement gaps at school (Chapter 5). It is closely related to the Hoover coefficient of income inequality (Kluge, 1998), the women and employment (WE) Index used by the OECD (1980), the gender inequality index for disparities in subject choice (Brown, 2001), the WAVE or replacement index, and the 'relative citation index' which is the conventional bibliometric technique to compensate for differences between sizes of national academic communities (Research Fortnight, 2000). It is also related to the Hoover index of concentration (Massey and Denton, 1988), and the Concentration Index (Moir and Selby Smith, 1979; OECD, 1985). The method therefore has many of the same pragmatic advantages claimed by D. Being widely used allows numerous comparisons between time, areas, and even fields of research (Lieberson and Carter, 1982).

Other advantages claimed for D have been its ease of interpretation, and the fact that it limits the influence of population composition (Lieberson and Carter 1982). These same advantages are also true of S, which is as easy (perhaps easier) to interpret and, unlike D which now has questionable claims to composition invariance, it is 'strongly' composition invariant. In fact, S is perhaps the only measure of association usable for more than two cases which appears completely free of the influence of population changes. It is also, indirectly, advocated by Cortese *et al.* (1976) because it resolves an ambiguity over the meaning of D. Although reportedly easy to interpret there has been conflict over whether D represents the number of minority cases that would have to be moved or the number to be exchanged with majority members. Indeed D is often misunderstood as the proportion of one group or the other that would have to moved (Tzannatos, 1990). 'What is often desired is the proportion of minority population which would have to be exchanged while keeping the number of households per unit constant (Cortese *et al.*, 1976: 633). S represents precisely that strict 'exchange proportion'.

Critics of our study

A few UK-based commentators have disputed the findings described in this book, by citing at second hand what they claim are contrary studies. All of these 'contrary' studies we have examined show significant defects for the purposes for which they are being used. The most common defect is that they simply do not set out to test what we did. As with Gewirtz *et al.* (1995), they usually examined the process of choice at a very local and small scale (many in inner London only), and hypothesised a growth in polarisation as a result. They usually looked at only one year of entry, and therefore not only lacked a suitable comparator before the impact of choice, they actually lacked any comparator at all, and had no justification for making claims about changes over time. Willms and Echols (1992) used a sample size smaller even than our initial pilot study of six complete LEAs, and used data only from the first two years after relevant legislation became 'operational' (see Chapter 4 on the starting-gun effect). They showed that parents not using designated local schools in Scotland were, in general, better educated and of more elevated social class. What they did not show, nor even attempt to measure, was increasing segregation between schools.

Despite this, where our work has been cited by others in the UK, it has sometimes been written off in one sentence as having been suggested to be wrong by the writing of Noden (2000) or Gibson and Asthana (2000). For example, Adnett and Davies (2002: 196) claim that, 'Evidence produced by Gorard *et al.* (2001) suggesting that market-based reforms in England and Wales had initially been associated with reduced social polarisation has been challenged by Gibson and Asthana (2000) and Noden (2000)'. Similarly, West and Pennell (2002) contrast the finding of Gorard and Fitz (2000) that stratification was decreasing, with the work of Noden (2000) which purported to find the opposite (see below). Note that these authors make no attempt to take up the debate or show why they believe one side to be right or not.

In the same way, but informally, our work was previously written off as it was apparently contradicted by the study of choice in New Zealand known as the Smithfield study. In this final section, we therefore rehearse briefly our own commentaries on these three most influential studies.

The 'Noden' paper

The findings reported in a paper by Noden (2000) have been used to suggest problems with our own findings. Noden used figures from many schools in England 1995 to 1999 with an index of isolation to show that our results from all schools in Wales 1989 to 1997 with an index of segregation must be incorrect. This is a totally inappropriate comparison, using a different index in a different place at a different time, and it is unclear why this is not obvious to anyone who has actually read both studies. We have explained elsewhere (Gorard and Taylor, 2002a) that Noden's analysis of the England figures anyway has several problems. He committed the basic arithmetic error of deriving a national figure for segregation by finding the mean of the 149 LEA figures, irrespective of their size (see Gorard, 2001a). Noden did not acknowledge that we had already published the later figures for England anyway (Gorard and Fitz, 2000). He therefore presented our own results which had already been published in the media – that segregation was increasing in England from 1997 – as though they somehow gainsaid our approach.

We are glad that Noden has now publicly admitted the limitations of the isolation index he used in his earlier paper (Noden, 2002). He also now acknowledges the superiority of the one he previously criticised us for using (although his description of it is still incorrect, see Gorard, 2002c). It also means that Noden's paper 'Rediscovering the Impact of Marketisation' did not do what the title claimed. This is progress, but it may take a long time before other commentators, who have used the

Noden paper, without even superficial critique, will take on board its implications.

Noden does not like the conclusion that 'market forces in education clearly do not lead, necessarily, to the kind of increased stratification that we had feared' (Gorard *et al.*, 2001a). Unfortunately this is what the data say. So, other than making deliberate arithmetic errors in our analysis, there is little we can do to change the conclusions. The predictions made after the Education Reform Act 1988 (by Gewirtz *et al.*, 1995 for example) were quite clear that increased choice would lead to increased segregation by poverty. This did not happen. By the time that secondary schools contained only students who had entered in the era of choice, segregation was at its lowest recorded level. Of course, this does not mean that the reduction was due to choice – which is why our 1998 paper was called 'The Missing Impact of Marketisation'. But it certainly does not show an increase in segregation, due to choice or anything else.

The 'Gibson and Asthana' paper

The situation with the work of Gibson and Asthana (1999) is similar to that of Noden (Gorard, 2000d). They tried to to argue that their analysis of the GCSE scores in a sample of schools in England 1994 to 1998 contradicted our findings about the social composition of all schools 1989 to 1996. As with Noden it is the inappropriateness of the comparison that is most striking, and as with Noden, their calculations are in error. They based their calculations on absolute differences between proportions, which are very misleading since they confuse the genuine differences with changes in frequency (see Chapter 5). Coupled with the fact that Gibson and Asthana used this poor technique not on school composition data, but on a subsample of the school outcomes for a subsample of years, this shows how little attention their critique should have been accorded. If a standard method of expressing differences in scores over time is used, then their conclusions are reversed. Therefore, according to their own argument, as schools with poor results have been shown by their own data to be improving their performance relative to schools with good results, 'the polarisation thesis will have to be dismissed' (Gibson and Asthana, 1999).

Gibson and Asthana (2000) have also used the same approach as Noden, of quoting our own findings as if they were their own, and as if they somehow contradicted our findings. For example, we originally showed that a decrease in segregation could be associated with a growth in indicators of poverty – what we termed 'equality of poverty' (Gorard and Fitz, 2000). When Gibson and Asthana (2000) found the same phenomenon in their study, they reported it as showing that our findings are an artefact (and we know that they had read our paper before doing this since their own paper was an invited response to ours). Their chief point is that changes in the value of our segregation index (applied to FSM) are 'almost entirely consequent on the changing number of students on roll, and . . . the proportion eligible for free school meals'. It is interesting to speculate what they would have preferred, since a valid measure of segregation in terms of an indicator (like FSM) which took no account of the total number of students or the number of FSM students would be impossible to construct. To claim that the index is somehow defective because it is sensitive to changes in what it sets out to measure would be ridiculous were it not so serious.

It is somewhat confusing, but nevertheless pleasant, to discover that Gibson and Asthana (2000) later admit that there is nothing wrong with the method we use, since it has 'long been used by geographers and social scientists'. Their objection now is to the indicator we (and they) use. FSM is not a fixed characteristic of individuals, and therefore cannot be used with our method which, according to them, has been used 'always with respect to fixed categories such as race or ethnicity'. Three points should be sufficient to display how empty this 'criticism' is. First, their statement about previous usage of such methods is untrue. The method has been used in the past by highly respected social scientists to measure the relative mobility between social class categories, where the class of an individual is clearly not a fixed category. Second, we have also run our FSM analysis using only students in year 7 in secondary schools (Chapter 4). The results of overall de-segregation with local variations are the same as those using all compulsory school-age students, and since each year's cohort is unique, FSM is a fixed category at the time of the annual school census. Third, we have used fixed class categories in addition to FSM, such as first language and ethnicity and, as Gibson and Asthana already knew, the patterns of decreasing segregation over time apply to these indicators as well. Finally, it is important for readers to note that Gibson and Asthana (2000) actually confirmed that 'the state sector as a whole is becoming less socially stratified'.

The Smithfield study

Commentators have informally used the results of the Smithfield project looking at four schools in New Zealand from 1990 to 1994 to argue against acceptance of our findings from all schools in England and Wales from 1989 to 2001. This comparison is clearly invalid. The two studies are hugely different in scale, and took place in different countries, over different time periods.

In addition, we have shown elsewhere how the published results of the Smithfield project actually showed that there was decreased segregation after the abolition of zoning in 1991 (Gorard and Fitz, 1998a).

Despite their own figures contradicting them, Waslander and Thrupp (1995) claimed to have shown that segregation increased after dezoning in New Zealand. Interestingly, their figures for segregation no longer appear in the book emanating from the same project, which nevertheless continues to claim evidence that segregation has increased (Lauder *et al.*, 1999). The main impact of this change has therefore simply meant that the reader can no longer check their calculations, since there are no base figures for the four schools alone (Gorard, 2000a).

This is an important point, since the purported Smithfield results have had real impacts. Thrupp's (1999) book is based at least partly on this erroneous premise, as well as being described as sloppy, hypocritical and full of double standards (according to Stringfield, 2002). Fisk and Ladd (2000) have had considerable international attention, largely by citing the Smithfield study as the evidence for their claims. In amazing circularity, the Smithfield authors are now citing Fisk and Ladd as providing supporting evidence in their own defence, and there is a danger that readers will be misled into accepting this as some form of triangulation. As other writers in New Zealand have commented, it is becoming a major national scandal that the Smithfield authors have not sorted this muddle out.

In addition, we reject entirely the notion, represented by Thrupp (2001), that we should not publish our findings in case they are used by other commentators to advocate greater school choice (Gorard, 2002b). Our findings have been used by neoliberal commentators to try and justify choice schemes, as well as by left-of-centre organisations to defend local comprehensive schools, by Labour MPs to argue against their own party's policy on specialist schools, and by humanists to argue against increasing the number of faith-based schools. Our findings have been of considerable interest to local governors and overseas governments alike (as any Internet-based search will attest; see also Chapter 11). Our work is publicly funded and our responsibility is to disseminate it, while making as sure as we can that what we disseminate is rigorous and usable.

References

Abrams, F. (2001) Comprehensive exodus? *Times Educational Supplement* 20/4/01, 18–19.

Adnett, N. and Davies, P. (2002) Education as a positional good: Implications for market-based reforms of state schooling, *British Journal of Educational Studies*, 50(2): 189–205.

Adonis, A. and Pollard, S. (1998) *A Class Act*, Harmondsworth: Penguin.

Ambler, J. (1997) Who benefits from educational choice? Some evidence from Europe, in E. Cohn (ed.) *Market Approaches to Education*, Oxford: Elsevier Science.

Archbald, D. (1996) Measuring school choice using indicators, *Education Policy*, 10(1): 88–101.

Association of Teachers and Lecturers (2000) Social selection, *Report* 22: 5.

Astin, A. (1992) Educational 'choice': its appeal may be illusory, *Sociology of Education* 65(4): 255–260.

Atkin, M. and Black, P. (1997) Policy perils of international comparisons, the TIMSS case, *Phi Delta Kappa*, September 23–28.

Audit Commission (1996) *Trading Places: The Supply and Allocation of School Places*, London: Audit Commission.

Audit Commission (2002) *Trading Places: A Review of Progress on the Supply and Allocation of School Places*, London: Audit Commission.

Bagley, C. and Woods, P. (1998) Rejecting schools: towards a fuller understanding of the process of parental choice, presentation at the BERA Annual Conference, Belfast.

Baird, J., Cresswell, M. and Newton, P. (2000) Would the real gold standard please step forward?, *Research Papers in Education* 15(2): 213–229.

Ball, S. (1993) Education markets, choice and social class: the market as a class strategy in the UK and the USA, *British Journal of Sociology of Education* 14(1): 3–19.

Ball, S., Bowe, R. and Gewirtz, S. (1994) Schools in the market place: an analysis of local market relations, in W. Bartlett, C. Popper, D. Wilson and Le J. Grand (eds) *Quasi-markets in the Welfare State: The Emerging Findings*, Bristol: SAUS Publications.

Beecham, J. (2000) We need the middleman, *Times Educational Supplement*, 7/7/00, 15.

Benn, C. and Chitty, C. (1996) *Thiry Years On: Is Comprehensive Education Alive and Well or Struggling to Survive?* London: David Fulton Publishers.

Benn, C. and Simon, B. (1970) *Half Way There: Report on the British Comprehensive School Reform,* London: McGraw-Hill.

Bennett, N. (1999) *Product Differentiation and Parental Choice: the Workings of a Local Educational Market in an English Shire County*, Milton Keynes: Open University Business School Working Paper Series.

Berki, B. (1999) Parental choice in danger, *Times Educational Supplement* 23/4/99, 2.

Bernstein, B. (1996) *Pedagogy, Symbolic Control and Identity*, London: Taylor and Francis.

Blackburn, R. and Jarman, J. (1997) Occupational gender segregation, *Social Research Update* 16: 1–4.

Blackburn, R., Jarman, J. and Brooks, B. (1999) *The Relation Between Gender Inequality and Occupational Segregation in 32 Countries*, University of Cambridge: Cambridge Studies in Social Research, 2.

Blackburn, R., Siltanen, J. and Jarman, J. (1995) The measurement of occupational gender segregation: current problems and a new approach, *Journal of the Royal Statistical Society* 158(2): 319–31.

Blair, M. (1994) Black teachers, black students and education markets, *Cambridge Journal of Education* 24(2): 277–91.

Borland, M. and Howsen, R. (2000) Manipulable variables of policy importance: the case of education, *Education Economics* 8(3): 241–48.

Bourdieu, P. (1997) The forms of capital, in A. Halsey, H. Lauder, P. Brown and A. Wells (eds) *Education Culture, Economy, and Society*, Oxford: Oxford University Press.

Bourdieu, P. and Passeron, C. (1992) *Reproduction in Education, Society and Culture*, London: Sage.

Bowe, R., Ball, S. and Gerwirtz, S. (1994) Parental choice, consumption and social theory: the operation of micro-markets in education, *British Journal of Educational Studies* 42(1): 38–52.

Bradford, M. (1993) Population change and education, in T. Champion (ed.) *Population Matters: The Local Dimension*, London: Paul Chapman Publishing.

Bradley, S. and Taylor, J. (2002) *The Report Card on Competition in Schools*, London: Adam Smith Institute.

Bradley, S., Crouchley, R., Millington, J. and Taylor, J. (2000) Testing for quasi-market forces in secondary education, *Oxford Bulletin of Economics and Statistics* 62(3): 357–90.

Brent Educational Services (2000) *Finding a Place For Your Child in the Year 2000*, London: Brent County Council.

Brighouse, H. (2000) *School Choice and Social Justice*, Oxford: Oxford University Press.

Brown, C. (2001) Can legislation reduce gender differences in subject choice? A survey of GCSE and A level entries between 1970 and 1995, *Educational Studies* (27): 2, 173–86.

Brown, M. (1998) The tyranny of the international horse race, in R. Slee, G. Weiner and S. Tomlinson (eds) *School Effectiveness for Whom? Challenges to the School Effectiveness and School Improvement Movements*, London: Falmer Press.

Budge, D. (1999) Gulf separating weak and strong increases, *Times Educational Supplement* 30/4/99, 3.

Butel , J. (1988) Falling school rolls in one LEA, *Educational Studies* 14(2): 176–86.

Bynner, J. and Joshi H. (2002) Equality and opportunity in education: the evidence from the 1958 and the 1970 birth cohort surveys, *Oxford Review of Education* 28(4): 405–25.

Canovan, C. (2002) Minister adds vouchers to list of options, *Times Educational Supplement* 8/3/02, 2.

Cardiff County Council (2000a) *School Organisation Plan 2000–2005*, Cardiff: Cardiff County Council.

Cardiff County Council (2000b) *Admissions to School: Information to Parents 2000/2001*, Cardiff: Cardiff County Council.

Cassidy, S. (1999a) Pass mark 'fiddle' is strenuously denied, *Times Educational Supplement* 28/5/99, 2.

—— (1999b) Test scores did not add up, *Times Educational Supplement* 16/7/99, p. 5.

Cassidy, S., Mansell, W. and Hackett, G. (2000) Test marks queried by one in 7 primaries, *Times Educational Supplement* 23/6/00, 1.

CERI (1997) *Education at a Glance: OECD Indicators*, Paris: OECD.

—— (1998) *Education at a Glance: OECD Indicators*, Paris: OECD.

Chubb, J. and Moe, T. (1990) *Politics, Markets and America's Schools*, Washington: Brookings Institute.

Clark, J., Dyson, A. and Millward, A. (1999) *Housing and Schooling: A Case-Study in Joined-up Problems*, York: York Publishing Services.

Cobb, C., Glass, G. and Crockett, C. (2000) The US Charter School Movement and ethnic segregation, presentation at AERA, New Orleans, April .

Coleman, J. (1992) Some points on choice in education, *Sociology of Education* 65(4): 260–62.

Coleman, J., Campbell, E., Hobson, C., McPartland, J., Mood, A., Weinfield, F. and York, R. (1966) *Equality of Educational Opportunity*, Washington: US Government Printing Office.

Congdon, P. and McCallum, I. (1992) A demo-educational model for forecasting school rolls for localities, *The Statistician* 41: 573–90.

Conway, S. (1997) The reproduction of exclusion and disadvantage: symbolic violence and social class inequalities in parental choice of secondary schools, *Sociological Research On-line* 2: 4.

Cookson, P. (1994) *School Choice*, Yale: Yale University Press.

Coons, J. and Sugarman, S. (1978) *Education by Choice: The Case for Family Control*, Berkeley: University of California Press.

Cortese, C., Falk, F. and Cohen, J. (1976) Further considerations on the methodological analysis of segregation indices, *American Sociological Review* 41: 630–7.

CRE. (1983) *Secondary School Allocations in Reading*, London: Commission for Racial Equality.

Creemers, B. (1994) The history, value and purpose of school effectiveness studies, in D. Reynolds, B. Creemers, P. Nesselradt, E. Shaffer, S. Stringfield and C. Teddlie (eds) *Advances in School Effectiveness Research and Practice*, Oxford: Pergamon.

Croxford, L. (2001) School differences and social segregation, *Education Review* 15(1): 68–73.

Daly, P. (1991) How large are secondary school effects in Northern Ireland?, *School Effectiveness and School Improvement* 2(4): 305–23.

Davies, N. (2001) *The School Report: Why Britain's Schools are Failing?*, London: Vintage.

Davies, W. and Herbert, D. (1993) *Communities Within Cities: An Urban Social Geography*, London: Belhaven Press.

Dean (1999) Poor students shut out of grammar schools, *Times Educational Supplement* 28/5/99, 1.

Dennis, R. and Clout, H. (1980) *A Social Geography of England and Wales*, Oxford: Pergamon Press.

DES (1990) *Statistics of Education: Schools 1989*, London: Department of Education and Science.

—— (1991) *Statistics of Education: Schools 1990*, London: Department of Education and Science.

—— (1992) *Statistics of Education: Schools 1991*, London: Department of Education and Science.

DfE (1993) *Statistics of Education: Schools 1992*, London: Department for Education.

—— (1994) *Statistics of Education: Schools 1993*, London: Department for Education.

—— (1995) *Statistics of Education: Schools in England 1994*, London: HMSO.

DfEE (1996) *Statistics of Education: Schools in England 1995*, London: HMSO.

—— (1997a) *Statistics of Education: Schools in England 1996*, London: HMSO.

—— (1997b) *Statistics of Education: Examination Results 1995/1996 – England*, London: Stationery Office.

—— (1997c) *Statistics of Education. Public Examinations GCSE and GCE in England 1997*, London: HMSO.

—— (1998a) *Statistics of Education: Schools in England 1997*, London: HMSO.

—— (1998b) *Statistics of Education: Schools in England 1998*, London: HMSO.

—— (1998c) *Statistics of Education: Examination Results 1996/1997 – England*, London: Stationery Office.

—— (1999a) *School Admissions: Code of Practice*, Nottingham: Department for Education and Employment.

—— (1999b) *Statistics of Education: Examination Results 1997/1998 – England*, London: Stationery Office.

—— (2000) *Statistics of Education: Examination Results 1998/1999 – England*, London: Stationery Office.

—— (2001a) *Statistics of Education: Examination Results 1999/2000 – England*, London: Stationery Office.

—— (2001b) *Schools: Building on Success*, Norwich: HMSO.

DfES (2001a) *Parents' Experiences of the Process of Choosing a Secondary School*, DfES Research Brief 278.

—— (2001b) *Statistics of Education: Schools in England*, London: Stationery Office.

—— (2001c) *Statistics of Education: Public Examinations in England 2000*, London: Stationery Office.

—— (2001d) *Education and Training Statistics for the United Kingdom*, London: Stationery Office.

—— (2002) *Education and Skills: Investment for Reform*, London: Department for Education and Skills.

Dore, C. and Flowerdew, R. (1981) Allocation procedures and the social composition of secondary schools, *Manchester Geographer*, New Series, 2(1): 47–55.

Duncan, O. and Duncan, B. (1955a) A methodological analysis of segregation indexes, *American Sociological Review* 20: 210–17.

—— (1955b) Residential distribution and occupational stratification, *American Journal of Sociology* , 60(5): 493–503.

Duru-Bellat, M. and Kieffer, A. (2000) Inequalities in educational opportunities in France: edcuational expansion, democratization or shifting barriers?, *Journal of Education Policy* 15(3): 333–52.

Echols, F., McPherson, A. and Willms, J. (1990) Parental choice in Scotland, *Journal of Educational Policy* 5(3): 207–22.

Education Authorities Directory and Annual (1998) *The Education Authorities Directory and Annual*, Redhill: The School Government Publishing Company.

Edwards, A., Fitz, J. and Whitty, G. (1989) *The State and Private Education: An Evaluation of the Assisted Places Scheme*, London: Falmer Press.

Edwards, A. and Tomlinson, S (2002) *Selection Isn't Working. Diversity, Standards and Inequality in Education*, London: Catalyst.

Elmore, R. and Fuller, B. (1996) 'Empirical research on educational choice: what are the implications for policy-makers?', in B. Fuller and R. Elmore (eds) *Who Chooses? Who Loses?* New York: Teachers College Press.

Erickson, D. (1989). 'A libertarian perspective on schooling', in W. Boyd J. Cibulka (eds), *Private Schools and Public Policy*, London: Falmer Press.

Eurostat (1998) *Social Portrait of Europe September 1998*, Brussels: Statistical Office of the European Communities.

Fielding, A. (1998) 'Why use arbitrary point scores? Ordered categories in models of educational progress', presentation to Royal Statistical Society Conference, October 1998.

Finkelstein, N. and Grubb, N. (2000) Making sense of education and training markets: lessons from England, *American Educational Research Journal* 37(3): 601–31.

Fisk, E. and Ladd, H. (2000) *When Schools Compete: A Cautionary Tale*, Washington DC: Brookings Institution Press.

Fitz , J. and Lee, J. (1996) The fields of inspection, unpublished paper, presented at the British Educational Association Annual Conference, Lancaster, September.

Fitz, J. and Beers, B. (2002) Educational management organisations and the privatisation of education in the US and the UK, *Comparative Education* 38(2): May , 137–54.

Fitz, J., Gorard, S., Taylor, C. and White, P. (2002b) School admissions after the School Standards and Framework Act: bringing the LEAs back in? *Oxford Review of Education* 28(2): 373–93.

Fitz, J., Halpin, D. and Power, S. (1993) *Education in the Market Place: Grant-Maintained Schools*, London, Kogan Page.

Fitz, J., Taylor, C. and Gorard, S. (2002a) Local education authorities and the regulation of educational markets: four case studies, *Research Papers in Education* 17(2): 125–46.

Flatley, J., Williams, J., Coldron, J., Connolly, H., Higgins, V., Logie, A., Smith, N and Stephenson, K. (2001) *Parent's Experiences of the Process of Choosing a*

Secondary School, Research Report RR278, London: Department for Education and Skills.

Fleiss, J. (1973) *Statistical Methods for Rates and Proportions*, New York: John Wiley and Sons.

Flude, M. and Hammer, M. (eds) (1990) *The Education Reform Act, 1988: Its Origins and Implications*, London: Falmer.

Forrest, K. (1996) Catchment 22, *Education*, March, 8.

Foxman, D. (1997) *Educational League Tables: For Promotion or Relegation?*, London: Association of Teachers and Lecturers.

Friedman, M. and Friedman, R. (1980) *Free to Choose*, Harmondsworth: Penguin.

Fuller, B., Elmore, R. and Orfield, G. (1996) Policy-making in the dark, in B. Fuller and R. Elmore (eds) *Who Chooses? Who loses?* New York: Teachers College Press.

Geller, C., Sjoquist, D. and Walker, M. (2001) The effect of private school competition on public school performance, National Center for the Study of Privatization in Education. Occasional Paper 15, Columbia: Teachers College.

Gewirtz, S., Ball, S. and Bowe, R. (1995) *Markets, Choice and Equity in Education*, Buckingham: Open University Press.

Gibson, A. and Asthana, S. (1999) Schools, markets and equity: access to secondary education in England and Wales, presentation at AERA Annual Conference, Montreal.

—— (2000) What's in a number? Commentary on Gorard and Fitz's 'Investigating the determinants of segregation between schools' *Research Papers in Education* 15(2): 133–54.

Gillborn, D. and Youdell, D. (2000) *Rationing Education: Policy, Practice, Reform and Equality*, Buckingham: Open University Press.

Gipps, C. (1993) Policy-making and the use and misuse of evidence, in C. Chitty and B. Simon (eds) *Education Answers Back*, London: Lawrence and Wishart, 31–44.

Glatter, R., Woods, P. and Bagley, C. (1997) Diversity, differentiation and hierarchy. School choice and parental preferences, in R. Glatter, P. Woods and C. Bagley (eds) *Choice and Diversity in Schooling. Perspectives and Prospects*, London: Routledge.

Glennerster, H. (1991) Quasi-markets for education, *The Economic Journal* 101(408): 1268–76.

Goldhaber, D. (2000) School choice: do we know enough? *Educational Researcher* 29(8): 21–2.

Goldhaber, D. and Eide, E. (2002) What do we know (and need to know) about the impact of school choice reforms on disadvantaged students? *Harvard Educational Review* 72(2): 157–76.

Goldhaber, D., Brewer, D. and Anderson, D. (1999) A three-way error component analysis of educational productivity, *Education Economics* 7(3): 199–208.

Goldring, E. and Hausman, C. (1999) Reasons for parental choice of schools, *Journal of Education Policy* 14(5): 469–90.

Gorard, S. (1996) Fee-paying schools in Britain: a peculiarly English phenomenon, *Educational Review* 48(1): 89–93.

—— (1997a) A choice of methods: the methodology of choice, *Research in Education* 57: 45–56.

—— (1997b) *School Choice in an Established Market*, Aldershot: Ashgate.

—— (1997c) Paying for a little England: School choice and the Welsh language, *Welsh Journal of Education* 6(1): 19–32.

—— (1997d) Market forces, choice and diversity in education: the early impact, *Sociological Research Online* 2(3): 12 pp.

—— (1998a) Schooled to fail? Revisiting the Welsh school-effect, *Journal of Education Policy* 13(1): 115–24.

—— (1998b) Four errors . . . and a conspiracy? The effectiveness of schools in Wales, *Oxford Review of Education* 24(4): 459–72.

—— (1998c) Social movement in undeveloped markets: An apparent contradiction in education policy studies, *Educational Review* 50(3): 249–58.

—— (1998d) The role of nostalgia in school choice, *School Leadership and Management* 18(3): 511–24.

—— (1999a) 'Well. That about wraps it up for school choice research': a state of the art review, *School Leadership and Management* 19(18): 25–47.

—— (1999b) Keeping a sense of proportion: the 'politician's error' in analysing school outcomes, *British Journal of Educational Studies* 47(3): 235–46.

—— (2000a) *Education and Social Justice*, Cardiff: University of Wales Press.

—— (2000b) One of us cannot be wrong: the paradox of achievement gaps, *British Journal of Sociology of Education* 21(3): 391–400.

—— (2000c) Questioning the crisis account: a review of evidence for increasing polarisation in schools, *Educational Research* 42(3): 309–21.

—— (2000d) Here we go again: a reply to 'What's in a number?' by Gibson and Asthana, *Research Papers in Education* 15(2): 155–62.

—— (2001a) *Quantitative Methods in Educational Research: The Role of Numbers Made Easy*, London: Continuum.

—— (2001b) International comparisons of school effectiveness: a second component of the 'crisis account'? *Comparative Education* 37(3): 279–96.

—— (2002a) Can we overcome the methodological schism?: combining qualitative and quantitative methods, *Research Papers in Education* 17(4): 345–61.

—— (2002b) Political control: A way forward for educational research? *British Journal of Educational Studies* 50(3): 378–89.

—— (2002c) The missing impact of marketisation re-visited, *Research Papers in Education* 17(4): 412–14.

—— (2003a) *Quantitative Methods in Social Science: The Role of Numbers Made Easy*, London: Continuum.

—— (2003b) What is multi-level modelling for? *British Journal of Educational Studies* 51(1): 46–63.

Gorard, S. and Fitz, J. (1998a) Under starters orders: The established market, the Cardiff study and the Smithfield project, *International Studies in Sociology of Education* 8(3): 299–314.

—— (1998b) The more things change . . . the missing impact of marketisation, *British Journal of Sociology of Education* 19(3): 365–76.

—— (2000) Investigating the determinants of segregation between schools, *Research Papers in Education* 15(2): 115–32.

Gorard, S. and Rees, G. (2002) *Creating a Learning Society*, Bristol: Policy Press.

Gorard, S. and Taylor, C. (2001) Specialist schools in England: track record and future prospect, *School Leadership and Management* 21(4): 365–81.

—— (2002a) What is segregation? A comparison of measures in terms of strong and weak compositional invariance, *Sociology* 36(4): 875–95.

—— (2002b) Market forces and standards in education: a preliminary consideration, *British Journal of Sociology of Education* 23(1): 5–18.

Gorard, S., Fitz, J. and Taylor, C. (2001a) School choice impacts: what do we know?, *Educational Researcher* 30(7): 18–23.

Gorard, S., Rees, G. and Salisbury, J. (2001b) The differential attainment of boys and girls at school: investigating the patterns and their determinants, *British Educational Research Journal* 27(2): 125–39.

Gorard, S., Taylor, C. and Fitz, J. (2002a) Does school choice lead to 'spirals of decline'? *Journal of Education Policy* 17(3): 367–84.

—— (2002b) Markets in public policy: The case of the UK Education Reform Act 1988, *International Studies in the Sociology of Education* 12(1): 23–41.

Gordon, D. (1999) Inequalities in income, wealth, and standard of living in Britain, in C. Pantazis and D. Gordon (eds) *Tackling Inequalities*, Bristol: Policy Press.

Gray, J. (1992) *The Moral Foundations of Market Institutions*, London: Institute of Economic Affairs.

Gray, J. and Wilcox, B. (1995) *'Good School, Bad School' Evaluating Performance and Encouraging Improvement* , Buckingham: Open University Press.

Greene, J. (2000) Choosing integration, presentation to School Choice and Racial Diversity Conference, National Center for the Study of Privatization in Education Occasional Paper 12, Columbia: Teachers College.

Hackett, G. and Kelly, A. (2000) Heads question literacy gains, *Times Educational Supplement* 14/07/2000.

Hackett, G. (2000) Children still class bound, *Times Educational Supplement* 21/4/00, 11.

Halsey, A., Heath, A. and Ridge, J. (1980) *Origins and destinations*, Oxford: Oxford University Press.

Hamilton, D. (1998) The idols of the market place, in R. Slee, G. Weiner and S. Tomlinson (eds.) *School Effectiveness for Whom?* London: Falmer.

Hardman, J. and Levacic, R. (1997) The impact of competition on secondary schools, in R. Glatter, P. Woods and C. Bagley (eds) *Choice and Diversity in Schooling*, Routledge: London.

Hargreaves, D. (1996a) Diversity and choice in school education: a modified libertarian approach, *Oxford Review of Education* 22(2): 131–47.

—— (1996b) A reply to Walford, *Oxford Review of Education* 22(2): 155–7.

Hatcher, R. (1998) Class differentiation in education: rational choices?, *British Journal of Sociology of Education* 19: 1.

Haviland, J. (1988) *Take Care Mr Baker*, London: Fourth Estate.

Heath, A. (2000) The political arithmetic tradition in the sociology of education, *Oxford Review of Education* 26(3&4): 313–31.

Henry, J. (2001) Professor calls for end to 'bogus' tests, *Times Educational Supplement* 30/11/01, 3.

Herbert, D. (2000) School choice in the local environment: headteachers as gate-keepers on an uneven playing field, *School Leadership and Management* 20(1): 79–98.

Herbert, D. and Thomas, C. (1990) *Cities in Space: City as Place*, London: David Fulton.

Hertfordshire (2000) *Moving On: Secondary Schools Admissions in 2000*, Hertford: Hertfordshire County Council.

Hess, F. (2000) Hints of the pick-axe: The impact of competition on public schooling in Milwaukee, presentation at AERA, New Orleans, April.

Higham, J., Sharp, P. and Priestly, M. (2000) Developing diversity through specialisation in secondary education: Comparing approaches in New Zealand and England, *Compare* 30(2): 145–62.

Hirsch, D. (1997) What can Britain learn from abroad?, in: R. Glatter, P. Woods and C. Bagley (eds) *Choice and Diversity in Schooling. Perspectives and Prospects*, London: Routledge.

Hirschman, A. (1970) *Exit, Voice, and Loyalty: Responses to Decline in Firms, Organizations, and States*, Cambridge: Harvard University Press.

HMSO (1958) *Secondary Education For All: A New Drive*, London: HMSO.

Holme, J. (2002) Buying homes, buying schools: school choice and the social construction of school quality, *Harvard Educational Review* 72(2): 177–91.

Hook, S. (1999) Failing schools and dying cities, *Times Educational Supplement* 7/5/99, 5.

Howson, J. (1999) Numbers of special schools still falling, *Times Educational Supplement* 29/10/99, 20.

—— (2000) Solid state, *Times Educational Supplement* 14/7/00, 24.

Hutton, W. (2001) Education is not enough to scale class barriers, *Times Educational Supplement* 11/5/01, 21.

James, D. and Taeuber, K. (1985) Measures of segregation, in N. Tuma (ed) *Sociological Methodology*, San Fransisco: Jossey-Bass.

Jencks, C., Smith, M., Ackland, H., Bane, M., Cohen, D., Gintis, H., Heyns, B. and Nicholson, S. (1972) *Inequality: Assessment of the Effect of Family and Schooling in America*, New York: Basic Books.

Jesson, D. (2001) *Educational Outcomes and Value-Added Analysis of Specialist Schools for the Year 2000*, Technology Colleges Trust: London.

—— (2002) Response to the article by Schagen and Goldstein, *Research Intelligence* 80: 16–17.

Jeynes, W. (2000) Assessing school choice: a balanced perspective, *Cambridge Journal of Education* 30(2): 223–41.

Jones, G. (1996) *Wales 2010 Three Years On*, Cardiff: Institute of Welsh Affairs.

Jowett, S. (1995) *Allocating Secondary School Places*, Slough: NFER.

Kacapyr, E. (1996) Are you middle-class?, *American Demographics* www.demographics.com.

Kalter, F. (2000) *Measuring Segregation and Controlling for Independent Variables*, Mannheimer Centre for European Social Science, Working Paper 19.

Kelly, A. (2002) Academies are no panacea, *Times Educational Supplement* 5/7/02, 10 .

Kelsall, R. and Kelsall, H. (1974) *Stratification*, London: Longman.

Kerckhoff, A., Fogelman, K. and Manlove. J. (1997) Staying ahead: the middle class and school reform in England and Wales, *Sociology of Education* 70(1): 19–35.

Kitchen, A. (1999) The changing profile of entrants to mathematics at A level and to mathematical subjects in higher education, *British Educational Research Journal* 25(1): 57–74.

Kitchen, R. and Tate, N. (2000) *Conducting Research into Human Geography*, Essex: Pearson Education.

Kluge, G. (1998) *Wealth and People: Inequality Measures, Entropy and Inequality Measures*, http:\\www.ourworld.compuserve.com (as at 21/10/99).

Knox, P. (1995) *Urban Social Geography*, Essex: Longman.

Kreft, I. (1993) Using multi-level analysis to assess school effectiveness: a study of Dutch secondary schools, *Sociology of Education* 66(2): 104–29.

Lauder, H. (1999) Misconceiving the market: A note on research into the impact of educational markets in England and Wales, presentation to Kings College Market Forces Seminar (mimeo), reprinted in Gorard (2000) Appendix A.

Lauder, H., Hughes, D., Watson, S., Waslander, S., Thrupp, M., Strathdee, R., Dupuis, A., McGlinn, J. and Hamlin, J. (1999) *Trading Places: Why Markets in Education Don't Work*, Buckingham: Open University Press.

Le Grand, J. and Bartlett, W. (1993) *Quasi-Markets and Social Policy*, Basingstoke: Macmillan.

Lee V., Croninger R. and Smith J. (1994) Parental choice of schools and social stratification in education: the paradox of Detroit, *Educational Evaluation and Policy Analysis* 16(4): 434–57.

Leech, D. and Campos, E. (2000) *Is Comprehensive Education Really Free? A Study of the Effects of Secondary School Admissions Policies on House Prices*, University of Warwick Economic Research Paper 581.

Levacic, R. (2001) *An Analysis of Competition and Its Impact on Secondary School Examination Performance in England, Occasional Paper 34*, National Center for the Study of Privatization in Education, Columbia: Teachers College.

Levacic, R. and Hardman, J. (1998) Competing for resources: the impact of social disadvantage and other factors on English secondary schools' financial performance, *Oxford Review of Education* 24(3): 303–28.

—— (1999) The performance of grant-maintained schools in England: an experiment in autonomy, *Journal of Education Policy* 14(2): 185–212.

Levin, B. and Riffel, J. (1997), School system responses to external change: implications for school choice, in R. Glatter, P. Woods and C. Bagley (eds) *Choice and Diversity in Schooling. Perspectives and Prospects*, London: Routledge.

Levin, H. (1992) Market approaches to education: vouchers and school choice, *Economics of Education Review* 11(4): 279–85.

Lieberson, S, (1981) An asymmetrical approach to segregation, in C. Peach, V. Robinson and S. Smith (eds), *Ethnic Segregation in Cities*, London: Croom Helm.

Lieberson, S. and Carter, D. (1982) Temporal changes and urban differences in residential segregation: a reconsideration *American Journal of Sociology* 88: 296–310.

Luck, A. (2000) Parents cheat in school appeals, *The Sunday Times* 3/8/02, 5.

MacGregor, K. (1999) Market forces dictating, *Times Higher Educational Supplement* 16/4/99, 9.

MacKay, T. (1999) Education and the disadvantaged: is there any justice?, *The Psychologist* 12(7): 344–9.

MacKenzie, D. (1999) The science wars and the past's quiet voices, *Social Studies of Science* 29(2): 199–213.

MacLeod, D. (2001) Perils of the school run, *Guardian* 3/8/01, 7.

Maclure, S. (2000) *The Inspectors' Calling: HMI and the Shaping of Educational Policy 1945–1992,* London, Hodder and Stoughton.

Mansell, W. (2000) Missing students skews exam data, *Times Educational Supplement* 23/6/00, 3.

—— (2002a) So many types of comprehensive, *Times Educational Supplement* 19/7/02, 6.

—— (2002b) No relief in sight for worst-funded, *Times Educational Supplement* 12/7/02, 12.

Mansell, W. and Henry, J. (2000) Blunkett's hard line is softened, *Times Educational Supplement* 10/3/00, 10.

Mansell, W., Slater, J. and Ward, H. (2002) Record cash deal tied to new targets, *Times Educational Supplement* 19/7/02, 1.

Marcus, J. (2002) US breaks up large secondaries, *Times Educational Supplement* 5/7/02, 10.

Marshall, G., Swift, A. and Roberts, S. (1997) *Against the Odds? Social Class and Social Justice in Industrial Societies*, Oxford: Clarendon Press.

Massey, D. and Denton, N. (1988) The dimensions of residential segregation, *Social Forces* 67: 373–93.

Mayet, G. (1997) Admissions to schools: a study of local education authorities, in R. Glatter, P. Woods and C. Bagley (eds) *Choice and Diversity in Schooling*, London: Routledge.

Maynard, A. (1975) *Experiments with Choice in Education*, London: Institute of Economic Affairs.

McCallum, I. and Demie, F. (2001) Social class, ethnicity and educational performance, *Educational Research* 43(2): 147–59.

McGill, P. (2000) Unfair grades for 11-plus students, *Times Educational Supplement* 14/4/00, 7.

McGuinn, P. and Hess, F. (2000) Business as usual: the minimal competitive effects of the Cleveland Voucher Program, presentation at AERA, New Orleans, April.

Mickelson, R. (2001) Subverting Swann: first- and second-generation segregation in Charlotte-Mecklenburg schools, *American Educational Research Journal* 38(2): 215–52.

Midgley, S. (1999) Heads who can't bear Pandas, *Times Educational Supplement* 28/05/1999.

Miron, G. and Nelson, C. (2002) *What's Public About Charter Schools? Lessons Learned About Choice and Accountability*, Thousand Oaks, CA: Corwin Press.

Moir, H. and Selby Smith, J. (1979) Industrial segregation in the Australian labour market, *Journal of Industrial Relations* 21: 281–92.

Murphy, R., Brown, P. and Partington, J. (1990) *An Evaluation of the Effectiveness of City Technology Colleges' Selection Procedures*, Nottingham: School of Education.

Myers, K. (2000) United we stand to gain, *Times Educational Supplement* 4/8/00, 11.

Narodowski, M. and Nores, M. (2002) Socio-economic segregation with (without) competitive education policies, *Comparative Education* 38(4): 429–51.

National Commission on Education (1993) *Learning to Succeed*, London: Heinemann.

Newsam, P. (1998) Freedom to be themselves, *Times Educational Supplement* 8/5/98, 15.

NFER (1969) *Trends in Allocation Procedures*, London: National Foundation for Educational Research.

Noah, H. and Eckstein, M. (1992) 'Comparing secondary school leaving examinations', in M. Eckstein and H. Noah (eds) *Examinations: Comparative and International Studies*, Oxford: Pergamon Press.

Noden, P. (2000) Rediscovering the impact of marketisation: dimensions of social segregation in England's secondary schools, 1994–1999, *British Journal of Sociology of Education* 21(3): 371–90.

Noden, P. (2002) Education markets and social polarization: back to square one? *Research Papers in Education* 17(4): 409–12.

Noden, P. and West, A. (2001) What's so special about specialist schools?, paper presented to the Parental Choice and market forces seminar, King's College London.

Nuttall, D. (1979) The myth of comparability, *Journal of the National Association of Inspectors and Advisers* 11: 16–18.

Nuttall, D., Goldstein, H., Presser, R. and Rasbash, H. (1988) Differential school effectiveness, *International Journal of Educational Research* 13(7): 769–76.

OECD (1980) *Women and Employment*, Paris: Organisation for Economic Cooperation and Development.

—— (1985) *The Integration of Women in the Economy*, Paris: Organisation for Economic Cooperation and Development.

—— (1995) *Schools under Scrutiny*, Paris: Organisation for Cooperation and Development.

OFSTED (1999) Inspection of Brent Local Education Authority, London: OFSTED.

—— (2000) Inspection of Hertfordshire Local Education Authority, London: OFSTED.

O'Malley, B. (1998) Measuring a moving target, *Times Educational Supplement* 18/9/98, 22.

Openshaw, S. (1984) *The Modifiable Areal Unit Problem, Concepts and Techniques in Modern Geography 38*, Norwich: GeoBooks.

Pacione, M. (1997) The geography of educational disadvantage in Glasgow, *Applied Geography* 17(3): 169–92.

Parsons, E. (1998) Parental choice and the social mix of secondary schools, presentation at BERA Annual Conference, Belfast.

Parsons, E., Chalkley, B. and Jones, A. (2000) School catchments and student movements: a case study in parental choice, *Educational Studies* 26(1): 33–48.

Passmore, B. and Barnard, N. (2001) Race report attacks segregated schooling, *Times Educational Supplement* 14/12/01, 3.

Paterson, L. (2001) Education and inequality in Britain, presentation to British Association for the Advancement of Science, Glasgow 4/9/01.

Peach, C. (1975) *Urban Social Segregation*, New York: Longman.

Performance and Innovation Unit (2001) *Social Mobility: A Discussion Paper April 2001*, London: Performance and Innovation Unit.

Phillips, S. (2002) Landmark ruling paves the way for vouchers, *Times Educational Supplement* 5/7/02, 18.

Pinch, S. (1985) *Cities and Services: The Geography of Collective Consumption*, London: Routledge and Kegan Paul.

Plewis, I. (1999) Educational inequalities and education action zones, in C. Pantazis and D. Gordon (eds) *Tackling Inequalities*, Bristol: Policy Press.

Pohlmann, V. (1956) Relationship between ability, socio-economic status and choice of secondary school, *Journal of Educational Sociology* 29(9): 392–7.

Pollard, S. (1995) *Schools, Selection and the Left*, London: Social Market Foundation.

Pollock, L. (2000) SOC it to them, *Times Educational Supplement* 30/6/00, 26.

Powers, J. and Cookson, P. (1999) The politics of school choice research: fact fiction and statistics, *Educational Policy* 13(1): 104–22.

Prais, S. (2001) Grammar schools' achievements and the DfEE's measures of value-added: an attempt at clarification, *Journal of Experimental Psychology* 27(1): 69–73.

PriceWaterhouseCoopers (2001) *DfEE RR242 Building Performance: An Empirical Assessment of the Relationship Between Schools Capital Investment and Student Performance*, London: DfEE.

QCA (2001) *Five-Year Review of Standards Reports: Summary*, Qualifications and Curriculum Authority: www.qca.uk.

Reay, D. (1998) Engendering social reproduction: mothers in the educational marketplace, *British Journal of Sociology of Education* 19(2): 195–209.

Reay, D. and Ball, S. (1997) 'Spoilt for choice': The working-classes and educational markets, *Oxford Review of Education* 23(1): 89–101.

Reay, D. and Lucey, H. (2000) Children, school choice and social differences, *Educational Studies* 26(1): 83–100.

Research Fortnight (2000) A citation measure that fits all sizes, *Research Fortnight* 6(8): 18–19.

Reynolds, D. (1990) School effectiveness and school improvement: a review of the British literature, in B. Moon, J. Isaac and J. Powney (eds) *Judging Standards and Effectiveness in Education*, London: Hodder and Stoughton.

Reynolds, D. and Farrell, S. (1996) *Worlds Apart? A Review of International Surveys of Educational Achievement Involving England*, London: HMSO.

Reynolds, F. (1986) *The Problem Housing Estate*, Aldershot: Gower.

Riley, K. (1996) *From Intensive Care to Recovery, Conference Proceedings*, London: London Borough of Haringey, November.

Robson, B. (1969) *Urban Analysis: A Study of City Structure with Special Reference to Sunderland*, London: Cambridge University Press.

Rothstein, R. (2002) *Out of Balance: Our Understanding of How Schools Affect Society and How Society Affects Schools*, Chicago: The Spencer Foundation.

Rutter, M. and Madge, N. (1976) *Cycles of Disadvantage: A Review of Research*, London: Heinemann.

Sammons, P., Mortimore, P. and Thomas, S. (1996) Do schools perform consistently across outcomes and areas?, in J. Gray, D. Reynolds, C. Fitz-Gibbon and D. Jesson (eds) *Merging Traditions: the Future of Research on School Effectiveness and School Improvement*, London: Cassell.

Schagen, I. and Goldstein, H. (2002) Do specialist schools add value: some methodological problems, *Research Intelligence* 80: 12–15.

Schagen, I. and Morrison, J. (1998) *QUASE Quantitative Analysis for Self-Evaluation: Overview Report 1997: Analysis of GCSE Cohorts 1994 to 1996*, Slough: NfER.

Schagen, S., Davies, D., Rudd, P. and Schagen, I. (2002) *The Impact of Specialist and Faith Schools on Performance*, Slough: NfER.

Schoon, N. (2001) Making the best of the worst, *Times Educational Supplement* 5/10/01, 15.

Shaw, M. (2002) Private Leeds firm tries to win over hostile schools, *Times Educational Supplement* 12/7/02, 14.

Shipman, M. (1997) *The Limitations of Social Research*, Harlow: Longman.

Slater, J. (2000) Time for change, say councillors, *Times Educational Supplement* 14/7/00, 3.

Smith, E. and Gorard, S. (2002) International equity indicators in education: defending comprehensive schools III, *Forum* 44(3): 121–2.

Smith, T. and Noble, M. (1995) *Education Divides*, London: Child Poverty Action Group.

Smithers, R. (2001) Church plan for 20 new schools, *Guardian* 15/6/01.

Spring J. (1982) Dare educators build a new school system?, in M. Manley-Casimir (ed.) *Family Choice in Schooling*, Toronto: Lexington.

Stillman, A. (1990) Legislating for choice, in M. Flude and M. Hammer (eds) *The Education Reform Act 1988: Its Origins and Implications*, Lewes: Falmer.

Stoll, L. and Fink, L. (1996) *Changing Our Schools: Linking School Effectiveness and School Improvement*, Buckingham: Open University Press.

Stringfield, S. (2002) Science making a difference: let's be realistic! *School Effectiveness and School Improvement* 13, 1, 15–29.

Sutcliffe, J. (2000) Home front in war on poverty, *Times Educational Supplement* 10/3/00, 24.

—— (2001) The market has lost its appeal, *Times Educational Supplement* 14/9/01, 28–9.

Suter, L. (2000) Is student achievement immutable? *Review of Educational Research* 70(4): 529–45.

Taeuber, K. and James, D. (1982) Racial segregation among public and private schools, *Sociology of Education* 55(2/3): 133–43.

Taeuber, K., Wilson, F., James, D. and Taeuber, A. (1981) A demographic perspective in school desegregation in the USA, in C. Peach, V. Robinson and S. Smith (eds) *Ethnic Segregation In Cities*, London: Croom Helm.

Taylor, C. (2001) Hierarchies and 'local' markets: the geography of the 'lived' market place in secondary education provision, *Journal of Education Policy* 16(3): 197–214.

—— (2002) *Geography of the 'New' Education Market: School Choice in England and Wales*, Aldershot: Ashgate.

Taylor, C. and Gorard, S. (2001) The role of residence in school segregation: placing the impact of parental choice in perspective, *Environment and Planning A* 30(10): 1829–52.

Taylor, C., Gorard, S. and Fitz, J. (2000) A re-examination of segregation indices in terms of compositional invariance, *Social Research Update* 30: 1–4.

—— (2002) Market frustration: admission appeals in the UK education market, *Educational Management and Administration* 30(3): 243–60.

—— (2003) The modifiable areal unit problem: Segregation between school and levels of analysis, *International Journal of Social Research Methods* 16(1): 41–60.

TES (1999) Raising standards faster, *Times Educational Supplement* 12/11/99, 7.

—— (2001) Faith gives exam edge, *Times Educational Supplement* 21/12/01, 19.

—— (2002) Light beneath the rhetoric, *Times Educational Supplement* 28/6/02, 20.

Thornton, K. (2001) Specialists spark 'two-tier' fears, *Times Educational Supplement* 8/6/01, 34.

Thrupp, M. (1999) *Schools Making a Difference: Let's Be Realistic! School Mix, School Effectiveness and the Social Limits of Reform,* Buckingham: Open University Press.

—— (2001) School quasi-markets in England and Wales: Best understood as a class strategy? *Paper presented to the BERA Annual Conference,* Leeds, 13–15 August, 2001.

Tobler, W. (1991) Frame independent spatial analysis, in M. Goodchild and S. Gopal (eds), *Accuracy of Spatial Databases,* London: Taylor and Francis.

Tomlinson, S. (1997a) Sociological perspectives on falling rolls, *International Studies in Sociology of Education* 7(1): 81–98.

—— (1997b) Diversity, choice and ethnicity: the effects of educational markets on ethnic minorities, *Oxford Review of Education* 23(1): 63–76.

Tooley, J. (1994) In defence of markets in education, in D. Bridges and T. McLaughlin (eds) *Education and the Market Place,* London: Falmer.

Tooley, J. (1997) On school choice and social class: a rejoinder to Ball, Bowe and Gewirtz. *British Journal of Sociology of Education* 18(2): 217–30.

Tymms, P. and Fitz-Gibbon, C. (2001) Standards, achievement and educational performance: a cause for celebration?, in R. Phillips and J. Furlong (eds) *Education, Reform and the State: Twenty-five Years of Politics, Policy and Practice,* London: RoutledgeFalmer.

Tzannatos, Z. (1990) Employment segregation: can we measure it and what does the measure mean? *British Journal of Industrial Relations* 28: 105–11.

Walford, G. (1996a) Diversity and choice in school education: an alternative view, *Oxford Review of Education* 22(2): 143–54.

—— (1996b) A rejoinder to Hargreaves, *Oxford Review of Education* 22(2): 159–60.

—— (2000) From city technology colleges to sponsored grant-maintained schools, *Oxford Review of Education* 26(2): 145–58.

Waslander, S and Thrupp, M. (1995) Choice, competition, and segregation: An empirical analysis of a New Zealand secondary school market, *Journal of Education Policy* 10(1): 1–26.

Weiner, G. (2002) Auditing failure: moral competence and school effectiveness, *British Educational Research Journal* 28(6): 789–804.

Weiss, C. (1996) Foreword, in B. Fuller and R. Elmore (eds) *Who Chooses? Who Loses?,* New York: Teachers College Press.

Wells, A. (1995) African-American students' view of school choice, in B. Fuller, R. Elmore and G. Orfield (eds) *School Choice: The Cultural Logic of Families, the Political Rationality of Schools,* New York: Teachers College Press.

West, A. and Ingram, D. (2001) Making school admissions fairer?: 'Quasi-regulation' under New Labour, *Educational Management and Administration* 29(4): 459.

West, A. and Pennell, H. (1997a) Changing admissions policies and practices in inner London, in R. Glatter, P. Woods and C. Bagley (eds) *Choice and Diversity on Schooling: Perspectives and Prospects,* London: Routledge.

—— (1997b) Educational reform and school choice in England and Wales, *Education Economics* 5(3): 285–305.

—— (2000) Publishing school examination results in England: incentives and consequences, *Educational Studies* 26(4): 423–36.

—— (2002) How new is New Labour? The quasi-market and English schools 1997 to 2001, *British Journal of Educational Studies* 50(2): 206–24.

West, A., Noden, P., Kleinman, M. and Whitehead, C. (2000) *Examining the Impact of the Specialist Schools Programme*, DfEE Research Brief 196.

West, A., Pennell, H. and Noden, P. (1998) School admissions: increasing equity, accountability and transparency, *British Journal of Educational Studies* 46(2): 188–200.

White, P., Gorard, S., Fitz, J. and Taylor, C. (2001) Regional and local differences in admission arrangements for schools, *Oxford Review of Education* 27(3): 317–37.

Whitty, G., Power, S. and Halpin, D. (1998) *Devolution and Choice in Education*, Buckingham: Open University Press.

Wilby, P. (2001) Comprehensives do work: ask the Finns, *Times Educational Supplement* 14/12/01, 19.

Willms, D. (1992) *Monitoring School Performance: A Guide for Educators*, Washington, DC: Falmer Press.

—— (1996). School choice and community segregation: findings from Scotland, in A. Kerckhoff (ed.) *Generating Social Stratification: Towards a New Research Agenda*, Oxford: Westview Press.

Willms, D. and Echols, F. (1992). Alert and inert clients: the Scottish experience of parental choice of schools, *Economics of Education Review* 11(4): 339–50.

Willms, D. and Paterson, L. (1995) A multilevel model for community segregation, *Journal of Mathematical Sociology* 20(1): 23–40.

Wilson, A. (1959) Residential segregation of social classes and aspirations of high school boys, *American Sociological Review* 24: 836–45.

Witte, J. (1990) Introduction, in W. Clune and J. Witte (eds) *Choice and Control in American Education, Volume 1: The Theory of Choice and Control in Education*, London: Falmer Press.

—— (1998) The Milwaukee voucher experiment, *Educational Evaluation and Policy Analysis* 20(4): 229–51.

Wong, D. (1997) Spatial dependency of segregation indices, *The Canadian Geographer* 4: 128–36.

Wong, D., Lasus, H. and Falk, R. (1999) Exploring the variability of segregation index D with scale and zonal systems: an analysis of thirty US cities, *Environment and Planning A* 31: 507–22.

Woods, P., Bagley, C. and Glatter, R. (1997) *The Public Market in England: School Responsiveness in a Competitive Climate*. Occasional Research Paper 1, School of Education: Open University.

Worpole, K. (1999) Driving forces, *The Guardian* 8/6/99, 17.

Wright, J. (1937) Some measures of distribution, *Annals of the Association of American Geographers* 27: 177–211.

Wrigley, N. (1995) Revisiting the modifiable areal unit problem and the ecological fallacy, in A. Cliff, P. Gould, A. Hoare and N. Thrift (eds) *Diffusing Geography: Essays for Peter Haggett*, Oxford: Blackwell, Oxford, 49–71.

Yang, M. and Woodhouse, G. (2000) Progress from GCSE to A and AS level: institutional and gender differences, and trends over time, presentation at BERA, September 2000, Cardiff.

Yang, M. and Woodhouse, G. (2001). Progress from GCSE to A and AS level: institutional and gender differences, and trends over time. *British Journal of Educational Research* 27(3): 245–67.

Zirkel, P. (1999) Grade inflation: a leadership opportunity for schools of education?, *Teachers College Record* 101(2): 247–60.

Index